D1118915

DATE DUE

MUTUAL ACCUSATION:

SEVENTEENTH-CENTURY

BODY AND SOUL DIALOGUES

IN THEIR LITERARY AND

THEOLOGICAL CONTEXT

The Soul leaves the Body. (From *Complaynte of the Soule* 1526)

Rosalie Osmond

MUTUAL ACCUSATION
Seventeenth-Century
Body and Soul Dialogues
in Their Literary and
Theological Context

UNIVERSITY OF TORONTO PRESS
Toronto Buffalo London

© University of Toronto Press 1990
Toronto Buffalo London
Printed in Canada

ISBN 0-8020-5843-4

Printed on acid-free paper

Canadian Cataloguing in Publication Data

Osmond, Rosalie 1942-
Mutual accusation

Includes bibliographical references.
ISBN 0-8020-5843-4

1. Body and soul in literature.
2. English literature – Early modern, 1500-1700 –
History and criticism.
3. Man (Christian theology).
I. Title.

PR431.O84 1990   820.9'382   C90-093729-7

The frontispiece and the illustration on page 196 are reproduced
with the permission of the British Library; the illustrations on
pages 108–12 are reproduced by permission of the Syndics of
Cambridge University Library.

Publication of this book is made possible by a grant from the
Canadian Federation for the Humanities, using funds provided
by the Social Sciences and Humanities Research Council of
Canada.

TO THE MEMORY OF MY MOTHER

1907–1959

'Ihr aber seid nicht fleischlich,
sondern geistlich.'

Contents

Preface

The work that lies behind this book has been spread over a quarter of a century. My first debt, however, remains quite clear in my mind. When I left Bryn Mawr College in 1964 to begin my doctoral work at Cambridge on the relationship between body and soul in the works of John Donne, Professor K. Laurence Stapleton said that she hoped, if this work were ever published as a book, I would say that the idea was first suggested in a Bryn Mawr seminar. The effect was not merely to remind me of my debt to Bryn Mawr, but to give me the (then) audacious idea that I might produce something that would become a book.

At Cambridge the original topic underwent a substantial metamorphosis when I came upon the body and soul dialogues of William Crashaw and James Howell bound up with the medieval manuscript of the *Visio Philiberti*. From this time on the dialogues were the central focus of my work, but I became increasingly aware of the way in which an understanding of them illuminated much of the other literature of the period. During three years at Cambridge my chief debt is to my wise and kind supervisor, the late Professor J.A.W. Bennett, but I also owe much to many others, particularly to Professor Dennis Nineham, who assisted with the theological aspects of the work, Professor Muriel Bradbrook of Girton College, and Dr Richard Axton of Christ's College, who helped me with the Old French of 'Un samedi par nuit.'

After some years of teaching at York and Mount Allison universities, I received a Killam Research Fellowship at Dalhousie University in 1977. This gave me the opportunity to do substantial further work on the subject, especially the drama, body and soul ballads, and other related literature in the sixteenth century. At this time Professor Malcolm Ross read an initial version of the manuscript and established an interest in the work which has continued to the present. I am also grateful to St Andrew's United Church in Halifax, which provided me with space and quiet to work away from my young family after the Killam fellowship expired. During the process of final writing and revision a number of people have been kind enough to read and comment upon all or part of the manuscript. These include two very old friends, Dr Christie Lerch, and Dr Mary Chan of the University of New South Wales, who gave positive help and encouragement, Dr Eric Lewis and Alan Lacey of King's College, London, Lynne Broughton, and Nicholas Denyer of Trinity College, Cambridge, who gave specific help with Chapter 1, and Professor Norman Goodman of the State University of New York.

I am most grateful to the Canadian Federation for the Humanities for the financial support to enable publication of this book, and for the many helpful suggestions of their readers. Also, during the tedious process of preparing the book for publication, my thanks go to Prudence Tracy, editor at University of Toronto Press, and Jean Wilson, my copy-editor, whose painstaking attention to detail has compensated in some measure, I believe, for my own lack of it.

It is customary at this point to conclude by thanking one's spouse for assistance in typing the manuscript. I am pleased to say Oliver did *not* do that for me, but in all else he has shared this book as no one else could have done. I met him in the same week as I began work on the thesis that was its predecessor. Throughout our married life he has read and criticized it in its numerous versions, checked references, proofread it, helped with the Greek, and, most important of all, convinced me that I *must* finish and publish it. I trust our relationship will survive without it! As for my children, they can only look with a combination of awe and amusement at something that actually predates themselves in my life.

Chapter 5 uses material from my article, 'Body and Soul Dialogues in the Seventeenth Century,' published in *English Literary Renaissance* (III 4) in 1974. I am grateful to the editor, Professor Arthur Kinney, for permission to reproduce this material, though in a substantially revised form.

London, England
July 1989

Introduction

The relationship between body and soul in the seventeenth century is crucial to an understanding of the content and, frequently, the form of the literature of that period. This relationship within man is a specific extension of the dualistic philosophy that has dominated much of Western thought from the time of Plato to the present century. While early philosophers (the Milesians, Heraclitus, and the Eleatics) attempted to explain the world in terms of a single principle and their successors (Empedocles, Anaxagoras, and Democritus) in terms of a pluralistic one, with the advent of Plato both monism and pluralism gave way to the dualism that has prevailed for two thousand years. This dualism in Plato was not merely an ontological one, but was specifically applied to a mind/body dualism within man himself.

Dualism, unlike monism, is a system that allows for dynamic and dramatic possibilities. It can explain change and imperfection in the natural world, as the two distinct elements of matter and spirit or matter and form strive to accommodate themselves to one another. In the little world of man, the two elements of body and soul generate conflict as well. Essential to one another and yet incompatible, they provide both an explanation and a metaphor for the internal, psychological struggle that man feels going on within himself.

The body and soul dialogues themselves, both the medieval originals and their seventeenth-century counterparts, are at the very heart of this tradition of conflict, and portray it in its most abstract and fundamental form. They bring together psychological concerns about the nature of man and theological concerns about responsibility for sin. They provide the conceptual centre from which the multiple metaphors and analogies in the rest of the literature radiate. Complex and subtle, they do not equate a simple dualism with moral good and evil. Rather, their arguments depend ultimately on the definition of body and soul and the point of division between the two. It is because of this possibility of genuine debate between them that their disputes can serve, for example, as models for marital arguments in poetry and drama.

This book begins with an overview of the beliefs concerning body and soul as they were modified and passed on from the time of Plato to the seventeenth century. Within the seventeenth century these views, as they manifest themselves in the works of both scientific writers and theologians, are explained in some detail, since they are the necessary background for an understanding of both the dialogues and the literature in general.

The central section of the work focuses on the medieval dialogues and their seventeenth-century counterparts. Their reappearance after more than a century has puzzled some critics. However, the general ideas on body and soul prevalent in the period, as presented in the first section, reinforced by the specific echoes of both the content and form of the debates in other literature of the sixteenth and early seventeenth centuries, combine to make their reappearance unsurprising if not inevitable. The subsequent deterioration of both the form and content of the dialogues after the mid-century is also examined.

The final section of the book brings the insights of the first two parts to bear on seventeenth-century literature outside the debates themselves. There is no claim that looking at the works from this point of view excludes other interpretations. The intention is not to provide a complete 'reading' of the poems and plays but to illuminate one fundamental and little understood aspect of them. The emphasis is a threefold one. The history of ideas background in general and the debates in particular help to illuminate much of the content of the literature dealing with body and soul. Beyond that, the fundamental pattern of the body/soul relationship, through the extensive use of analogy, informs other dualistic relationships as well – that between king and kingdom, husband and wife, the human and the divine, Christ and the church. As the elements within man himself may be at peace or in conflict, so they provide analogies for both harmonious and acrimonious relationships in these other realms. These habits of thought can be seen extending their influence beyond the confines of specific metaphors and similes to embrace the whole action of certain dramatic works. It is here that one sees best the dynamic implications of the body/soul dualism worked out in its various guises. Conflict, essential to dramatic development, has a metaphysical foundation on which to base its human manifestations.

From the mid-seventeenth century, all this begins to change. There is a conscious effort first to bridge the gap between body and soul in mechanistic and scientific terms, and then to deny their fundamental opposition in theological terms as well. On one level, this tendency has continued to the present day. Dualism based on both philosophical tradition and felt experience gradually gives way to a rational monism. Mind is an extension of body; apparently spiritual phenomena are traced to mechanistic causes. Nevertheless, on another level dualism has not completely disappeared. It simply masquerades in new guises, dressed up as psychological indecision or physiological incompatibility. Insofar as the body and soul dialogues express man's self-perception, they are not totally irrelevant to literature today. We have just found new settings and different metaphors.

Part One

Body and Soul
in Philosophy
and Theology

CHAPTER ONE

Classical and Christian Views of Body and Soul

The common assumption that man consists of two distinct entities, a body and soul, has far-reaching implications that are at once philosophical, scientific, and theological. For the philosopher, the distinction between body and soul in the individual has been a distinction between two separate realms of existence, that of Being and becoming or, alternatively, that of Forms and particulars (Plato) or form and matter (Aristotle). For the scientist, it has been a distinction between an animating principle and a thing animated, and the how and why of interaction have been of prime interest. For the Christian theologian, it has been a distinction between a God-given spiritual element and the earthly receptacle of that element, and the moral responsibility of each for thought and action has been of great importance.

Until at least the seventeenth century, the three disciplines were not separated as they are today, but were often the concern of the same person. Not infrequently, therefore, the demands of one discipline, such as theology, played a large part in determining a writer's attitude to other branches of knowledge. Theories that are ostensibly purely philosophical may have important moral implications, and scientific explanations of such things as the propagation of body and soul may be influenced by attitudes towards original sin. The web of interacting forces is a complex one, as man strives to find theories that satisfy both his mundane curiosity and his spiritual beliefs and aspirations.

Although their theories have metaphysical implications for later writers, the pre-Socratics are chiefly primitive astronomers and scientists, interested in how the universe came to be and sustains itself. The Milesians – Thales, Anaximander, and Anaximenes – are materialists and monists. Heraclitus, in contrast, posits a universe that is a battleground of contrary forces ruled by a *Logos* (Justice) that attempts to impose order on them. But Heraclitus avoids value judgments; opposites are necessary to explain change and renewal. 'Out of all things can be made a unity, and out of a unity all things.'[1]

It is Pythagoras (571–497 BC) and his followers who, influenced by Orphic philosophy, conceive of a 'moral' universe with an eternal, unchanging principle of Truth (understood mathematically), and human beings composed of a 'divine' soul and recalcitrant body that must be 'pacified.'[2] Here we have the basis of the body/soul dichotomy. Not only do we have man explained as a dual creature, but the values assigned to the two parts of this duality extend in a multiplicity of other directions. In the cosmos, form, order, and light are good; indefiniteness, darkness, and disorder are evil. Sexual intercourse is suspect and should only be entered into for the purpose of procreation. The influence of these ideas on later philosophy (Plato, Plotinus, even Aristotle, and through them to Christian writers) can scarcely be exaggerated.

A formidable group of materialist philosophers – some monists (Parmenides), others pluralists (Anaxagaras, and the Atomists led by Democritus) – succeed Heraclitus and Pythagoras, but in no case do their theories assign a moral value to man or the universe. In this they remain close to the early Milesians.

Socrates reasserts a world in which moral concerns are paramount not just for their application in this life, but for eternity. The soul is an intellectual and moral personality, not merely 'psyche,' a life-breath, and it is immortal. This, however, does not lead to a Pythagorean body/soul dualism. Evil is the pursuit of an imagined good and is due to ignorance, not a contrary evil principle located in the body or, indeed, anywhere else.

The dualism that Socrates avoids becomes an essential element of the philosophy of Plato. For Plato the whole universe is divided into two distinct realms, the 'real' world of intelligible Forms, and the world of appearances, of change and flux. The former is the perfectly realized realm of Being; the latter is the state of 'becoming.'[3] Each individual partakes of the real world of Being through the form which is common to the species, but embodies it imperfectly in his own individual matter. The soul is most frequently seen as allied to the world of Forms, to 'reality,' while the body remains firmly in the world of appearances. Thus the distinction between 'Being' and 'becoming,' reality and appearance on the cosmological scale becomes the distinction between soul and body in the individual.[4] Looked at in this way, Plato (undoubtedly influenced by Pythagoras) implies that certain differences in value and moral quality are attached to soul and body. The soul is immaterial (spiritual) and immortal; the body is material and perishable, an unworthy and temporary dwelling for the soul, a prison. Since the soul is the real man, death is not to be feared as a dissolution of the person but is rather to be welcomed as a release from that which prevents him from fulfilling himself completely.[5]

Why then, if the soul is perfect and complete in itself, does it join itself to a body at all? The answer is that the extreme division between body and soul outlined above is not consistently Plato's position. The soul that appears to be a simple entity in the *Phaedo* is not at all simple in the *Republic*, the *Phaedrus*, or the *Timaeus*. In the *Timaeus* there are three faculties of the soul, each assigned to a specific part of the body – an assignation that survives into the seventeenth century. The rational element is located in the head, the spirited element in the heart, and the appetitive in the stomach. The neck, which separates the rational faculty from the rest, Plato compares to an isthmus isolating it from contamination.[6]

The same three faculties appear in the *Phaedrus* in a myth that, by making them analogous to two horses and a charioteer, seeks to explain the soul's career in union with the body. According to most interpreters, the charioteer is the rational faculty of the soul, the white horse and natural ally of reason is the spirited element or will, and the dark horse is the appetitive element. When the dark horse falls, it brings down with it the white horse and the charioteer.[7] Thus an element within the soul itself is initially responsible for its earthly career in union with the body.

Both dialogues attempt to distinguish or isolate the rational part of the soul from the other elements. In the *Phaedrus*, where only the charioteer is conceived as a human figure and the other two elements are horses, the very imagery reinforces this separation, while in the *Timaeus* the location of the rational faculty in the head works to the same end. It seems probable that when Plato speaks of soul as a simple entity, opposed to body, it is this aspect of the soul with its properties of immateriality, incorruptibility, and immortality to which he is referring. This alone is truly man.

Yet the divergent views of soul cannot all be explained so readily.[8] In the *Timaeus*, for example, the soul is said to be created, and of the three parts described above, only the rational is immortal; in the *Phaedo* it is essentially whole and eternal. Further, in the *Phaedrus*, the *Timaeus*, and the *Republic*, the appetitive faculty is part of the soul, and hence desires logically come from it. But in the *Phaedo* they are described as phenomena of the body that can struggle against the soul.[9] This uncertainty provides the intellectual essence of the body and soul debates. Who tempts? Who executes?

In more general terms, Plato is clear that the imperfections we perceive, both on the individual and cosmic scale, come from the material, not the craftsman. It is the function of soul to impose form on recalcitrant matter, and in this role – a role that becomes much more important in the thought of Plotinus – it may take on the aspect of an intermediary between the Forms and the sensible world. However, as Plato's complex ideas came to be selected by Christian philosophers, it was the dualistic elements that opposed a weak and fallible body to a soul with God-like affinities that predominated.

Aristotle's point of departure is very different from that of Plato. While Plato, like his master Socrates, is primarily concerned with the nature of an abstract truth and how to live a 'good' life, Aristotle is primarily concerned to explain man and the universe in what we might call a 'scientific' way. While Plato claims we can have no clear knowledge of anything that comes through the senses, that the intellect alone can apprehend truth, Aristotle believes the senses are our chief source of knowledge. Consequently he is highly critical of the Platonic world of forms which was, he argued, separated from the world of things of which alone we have any knowledge. His response was not to deny the existence of the form altogether but to place it within the individual, which then becomes true substance.[10] The universal abstracted by the mind remains real, but real as embodied in the substance, not in a transcendental world. Indeed, form cannot exist apart from matter which, without it, is simply changeableness and possibility; it is form that provides the stable, permanent element.

This general theory finds specific application in Aristotle's view of body and soul. There is a much closer relationship between the two than in Plato, and the highly moral overtones give way to a greater emphasis on the functional aspects of their union. The body is not the tomb of the soul. On the contrary, it is good for the soul to be united to the body since only through the body can it function.[11] The two are not completely distinct entities belonging to separate realms of being. They are related to one another as form is to matter or as end to means, fulfilment to potentiality. The soul is the first actuality of an organic body.[12] This means that, in the case of a human body, neither body nor soul can be conceived of existing independently, since its potentiality cannot be separated from actuality. 'The soul is like sight and the capacity of a tool; the body like the thing in potency. But as an eye is a pupil together with the power of sight, so is there a living thing where there are both body and soul. Therefore, it is evident enough that the soul is inseparable from the body.'[13]

This intimate relationship between body and soul prevents such a clear-cut, moral distinction between them as there is in Plato. The soul is not imprisoned in the body, a victim of its passions, but originates within the body, passed on by generation through the semen.[14] Plato's tripartite division of the soul is simplified to become a twofold division, the rational and irrational soul, though the latter is itself further divided into the vegetative and sensitive faculties. These lower faculties are present in plant and animal life, so that nutrition, growth, and sense are all attributed to 'soul,' thus stressing the continuity rather than the differences between processes in plants, animals, and man.[15]

Beyond this 'soul' or 'psyche,' however, is *nous*, the intellect. The lower part of *nous*, the 'passive intellect' is, like the rest of soul, tied to the body and perishes with it; it is the 'matter' of thought and becomes all things.[16] But the active *nous* is divine, immortal, and separable from body.[17] This separable or active reason is not a substance, but an activity. Its immortality, however, does not involve the individual immortality of the Christian soul. It does not even hold the moral connotations of Plato's soul. Yet Aristotle's sketchy account of *nous* was partly instrumental in reinforcing the passage of Platonic dualism into Christian thought. Indeed, a confusion between 'mind' and 'soul' makes it possible for later Christian philosophers, influenced by Aristotle, to speak of the soul as naturally dependent on the body and yet retaining its qualities of immateriality and immortality.

After Aristotle, Greek philosophy is dominated by the successors of Plato at the Academy, the Cynics and Stoics. Of these, the latter, whose most prominent member is Zeno, preach a renewed materialism. In complete contrast to Plato, they contend that only bodies are real. Matter and form are both bodies; even God and the soul are fiery, subtle bodies. Soul is called 'pneuma,' but this must not be confused with Aristotle's 'pneuma,' which merely acts as an instrument of the soul. Sense perception takes place when the object perceived makes an impression on the soul, like a seal on wax.[18]

While this materialistic stance may appear to be farther removed from any affinity with later Christian thought than either Plato or Aristotle, Stoicism, as it came to be combined with Platonism, has had a profound and lasting effect on Christianity. St Paul uses 'pneuma' (no longer a material substance but, modified by later Platonic thought, the creative in-breathing of God) for spirit, the Stoic belief that man's end is to live in conformity with the Ruling Principle, and that this involves not merely suppressing but eradicating desires, has its effect on Christian asceticism.

The heirs of Plato, for the most part, combine his philosophy with that of either Stoicism or Aristotelianism or, in some cases, a revived Pythagoreanism. Through the influence of the latter, the Supreme Principle (Plato's 'One' or 'Good') becomes even more remote, and under it a Demiurge or World Soul controls the lesser gods, stars, and demons which, in turn, rule and order the visible world. At the same time, the Supreme Principle unites Aristotle's Unmoved Mover and Plato's Good, and makes the Forms thoughts of God. Within man himself, the dualism of body and soul in Plato is complicated by the addition of *psyche* and *nous*, which are added to it. *Psyche* is purer than body, but less pure than *nous*, since it is subject to passions. Its intermediate position is similar to that of Aristotle's 'soul' but with stronger moral overtones. Thus on both the cosmological and individual levels, the way is prepared for the combination of monism and dualism found in the works of Plotinus and his followers.

With regard to ethics, however, the Pythagorean influence means that the Platonic identification of soul with good and matter with evil is intensified. Plutarch, Atticus, and Numenius believe in the existence of an 'evil soul' that is immanent in matter and has the material universe under its domination. Even Albinus, the least pessimistic, believes evil is the result of embodiment. For all, the object of life is to purify oneself and to prepare for disembodiment.

Plotinus' thought retains the moral values assigned to soul and body, spirit and matter, but the divided universe of Plato becomes a series of shaded gradations. There is one single Principle from which all else is derived. This Transcendent First Principle, unlike the Supreme Mind of the Middle Platonists, is beyond hierarchy. Plotinus does not call it God, but Porphyry, his disciple, does. From this One comes first the Intellectual Principle or Divine Mind, which is not a unity but a manifold,[19] and after it, in descending order on the scale of being, come the All-Soul, the souls of individuals, body, and finally matter. With the exception of the One, which is the source of Divine Mind and the World of Forms (All-Soul) but itself is neither, each gradation of being forms a bridge between that immediately higher in the scale and that directly lower. Thus the idea of the soul as a mean between the two orders of existence, the corporeal and the incorporeal, which is present in the

Timaeus (35a–37c), takes on much greater prominence. It is the link between the intellectual and material world, the only reality inhabiting both. The body, similarly, provides a link between the soul and inanimate, physical objects. 'The Neo-Platonists retain the terms of classical dualism, but only within the framework of an overarching monism.'[20]

There are, however, certain difficulties and inconsistencies in Plotinus' view of the soul as a mean. In much of his work he sees it as a 'double,' the higher part continually illumined by intellect, and with only an 'irradiation' from this entering the lower world, joining body and becoming capable of sin and suffering. Such an account does not explain man's need for purification, which is key to Plotinus' thought. In 'Against the Gnostics,' however, he describes a triple soul, of which the middle part is the 'we' that reasons and is situated between two powers, a worse and a better, sense perception and intellect.[21] This explains not only the desire for purification but man as the battleground of good and evil, the very essence of the body and soul dialogues. It also makes it explicit that the different gradations of being are on a descending scale of moral values. Yet the soul remains a unity within its hierarchical distinctions.

Plotinus, like Plato before him, struggles with the contradiction between the idea of embodiment as a fall and at the same time as a fulfilment of the soul's natural function of caring for body. On the negative side, he believes that it is the soul's association with the physical world that causes it to be a prey to passion.[22] Once the soul has been joined to the body, the composite thus formed is in its very nature unstable and fated to cause trouble and unhappiness, as he explains in a key passage that reverberates still in seventeenth-century metaphysical poetry:

> Pleasure and pain and the like must not be attributed to the Soul alone, but to the modified body and to something intermediary between soul and body and made up of both. A unity is independent; thus body alone, a lifeless thing, can suffer no hurt – in its dissolution there is no damage to the body, but merely to its unity – and soul in similar isolation cannot even suffer dissolution, and by its very nature is immune from evil.
>
> But when two distinct things become one in an artificial unity, there is a probable source of pain to them in the mere fact that they were inapt to partnership. This does not of course, refer to two bodies; that is a question of one nature, and I am speaking of two natures.

When one distinct nature seeks to associate itself with another, a different, order of being ... then the essential duality becomes also a unity but a unity standing midway between what the lower was and what it cannot absorb, and therefore a troubled unity ...[23]

Nevertheless, soul is necessary to body, and desires to remain in this lower realm so that it may bring order to it, that it may give of itself in accordance with the outgoing principle which is the very basis of the universe. 'To this power we cannot impute any halt, any limit of jealous grudging; it must move for ever outward until the universe stands accomplished to the ultimate possibility.'[24] However, the desire to descend is present only because the soul is the kind of being that *wants* to descend, and this desire is itself a kind of imperfection.[25] Yet there remains a strongly optimistic strain in Plotinus' writing. The soul that descends can also ascend; the only soul that is truly imprisoned in the body is the one that surrenders to it.

Matter, not body, is the locus of evil,[26] though even this is not a positive evil but pure negation[27] until inhabited by a soul of some kind. Thus it shares some of the characteristics of Aristotle's matter – as potentiality – but, in a Platonic way, remains more negative and resistant to the ordering of soul.

The legacy of Plotinus, insofar as it affects this study, was to retain and propagate the essential values of Platonic dualism while incorporating them into a fundamentally monistic system, which seeks to unite everything through a series of gradations into one 'chain of being.'[28] Both strains of thought are still to be found existing side by side in the works of the Cambridge Platonists. It was the Platonic, however, that was to have the greatest immediate effect on Christianity.

The body-soul dualism that came into early Christian thought was essentially Greek and not Hebraic in origin. To the Hebrews man was an animated body, not an incarnated soul.[29] The soul was not the essential nature of man, nor was the body a mere recipient of form, a tool. Neither was the New Testament contrast between 'flesh' and 'spirit' intended to hold the Platonic connotations read into it by later commentators who identified the two with body and soul respectively. When St Paul speaks of the flesh as opposed to the spirit, he is referring to man in his 'otherness' and separation from God as opposed to man in a right relationship with God.[30] He is not describing a war between passion and reason or a struggle in which body is the sinful element in man, fighting against his soul or spirit. Even the distinction between 'flesh' and 'body' as formless matter and matter endowed with form is not biblical but Neoplatonic in origin.

The Hellenization of Hebrew thought begins with Philo, the first-century Alexandrian Jew. Into certain Stoic ideas (the *pneuma* is the creative in-breathing by God of part of the Divine substance into man, which becomes the soul) he incorporates a fairly extreme form of body/soul dualism. He accepts the *Phaedrus* myth of the fall of the soul; the 'coats of skin' in Genesis are bodies; the soul dwells in the body as in a tomb and is a 'pilgrim and sojourner on earth' like Abraham.

By the time of the early Church Fathers this antithesis between soul and body and the specific image of the soul imprisoned in the body appear in Christian writings. In the second-century *Epistle to Diognetus* the soul in the body is compared to the Christian in the world. 'The flesh hates the soul, and fights against it, though suffering no wrong, because it is prevented by the soul from indulging in its pleasures; so too the world, though suffering no wrong, hates the Christians because they set themselves against its pleasures ... The soul is enclosed within the body, and itself holds the body together; so too Christians are held fast in the world as in a prison, and yet it is they who hold the world together.'[31] This is stronger and less qualified than anything in Plato or Plotinus. Perhaps the persecution of the early Christians led them to find the elements of conflict in Platonic and Neoplatonic thought particularly congenial.

Certain aspects of Christianity, particularly the doctrines of the Incarnation and Resurrection, modified this negative view of body. Athenagoras's treatise *De Resurrectione*, for example, affirms the necessity of both body and soul, each of which has a role proper to its own nature. The immortality of the soul involves the Resurrection of the body.[32] Opposition to Gnosticism had the same modifying effect on the early Church Fathers. Irenaeus, writing against the Gnostics, says that it is body *and* soul that go to make up a complete man. The body receives life from the soul and is used by it in much the same way as an artist uses an instrument (an Aristotelian comparison); however, the instrument in this case is not simply passive but itself living and united to the artist. The perfect man is the union of soul, which has received the spirit of God, to the flesh, which has been made in the image of God.[33]

Irenaeus goes so far as to suppose that all souls and spirits have an ethereal body. The soul takes the shape of the body, to which it adapts itself like water to a vase. It then keeps the imprint of this body and remembers it even after death.[34] But it is Tertullian who expounds the doctrine of the corporeal nature of the soul in greatest detail. He takes over the arguments of the Stoics, who believed that the soul was material, and refutes the objections of the Platonists, for whom the immateriality of the soul was a fundamental principle. He argues that since 'that substance which by its departure causes the living being to die is a corporeal one,' and since it is 'by the departure of the spirit, which is generated with the body, that the living being dies; therefore the spirit which is generated with the body is the soul: it follows, then, that the soul is a corporeal substance.'[35] Tertullian obviously has a very vivid, if somewhat literal, imagination. He not only believes that the soul has a shape, but he also explains how this shape has been formed at the time of creation. The breath of God, which made man a 'living soul,' solidified on condensing to form the interior man, that is, the soul.[36] And in this same image, coupled with his earlier assertion that 'that substance which by its departure causes the living being to die is a corporeal one,' we find an early ancestor of those medieval deathbed scenes in which a small, child-like form is drawn from the mouth of the body by angels and devils.

In contrast to Tertullian's materialism, Origen emphasizes the immateriality of the soul. Influenced by Plato and the Middle Platonists,[37] he sees its entrance into the physical world as a descent. The soul pre-exists, and its embodiment is a punishment for some sin in its pre-mundane state.[38] Origen insists that soul (or 'spirit' as he insists on calling the soul when free of an earthly body) is always possessed of *some* body, an aetherial vehicle, but this must not be confused with Tertullian's belief that the soul itself is corporeal. Origen constantly asserts the immateriality of the soul, while Tertullian makes it so dependent on body that it is difficult to see how he can still assert its spirituality.[39]

Origen's perception of the soul's descent into the body as a 'fall' in both the philosophical and theological sense also leads one to realize just how intimately the ostensibly philosophical beliefs of these Church Fathers are linked to theological problems. The connection between the body-soul relationship and beliefs concerning original sin is particularly intimate. The way in which the soul comes into being, whether by creation, pre-existence, or traducianism (propagation via the parents) is of prime importance for such questions as the individual role of the body and soul in sin and the transmission of original guilt.

While both Origen and Tertullian believed that the Fall had deprived man of original righteousness (which was not a superadded quality, as some of their contemporaries held,[40] but man's natural state) and consequently had plunged man into a state of utter depravity, their explanations of original sin and its transmission differed greatly. Origen's belief in the pre-existence of souls opened the way for his assertion that embodiment is itself a punishment for the sins of spirits in their pre-mundane state. Following Philo, he claims the 'coats of skin' which were given to Adam and Eve were bodies. Now bodily appetites form the raw material of sinful impulses, although in themselves they are morally neutral.[41] Tertullian's far more materialistic view of the soul makes it possible for him to explain original sin in terms of physical transmission from Adam. Since the soul itself is material, it is present in the paternal germ. At conception a fragment of the father's soul forms itself into a new soul bearing all the hereditary characteristics of its progenitor.[42] Thus the sins of the fathers are visited on the children in the most complete and literal fashion.

Each of the two positions taken by the early Church Fathers involves theological difficulties. If the soul is in its essence completely separate from body, immortal and immaterial, then how does one explain its descent into the body and its moral defectability? Even if it is the 'body' that is responsible, how can this body sway a purely rational being? Furthermore, this view is usually accompanied by a denial of the worth of the body difficult to reconcile with the Incarnation and Resurrection. If, on the other hand, the soul is itself material and intimately connected with body, how can it be akin to God, and how can it survive the death of the body? Origen's explanation of original sin saves the immateriality of the soul, but the theory of pre-mundane sin is a flimsy device to avoid making God responsible for incarcerating a 'pure' soul in a prison-like body, and it fails totally to explain the transmission of original sin. Tertullian's theory explains the transmission of original sin satisfactorily, but only at the expense of making the soul dangerously material in substance and origin. The theological arguments behind the body and soul dialogues are all present here in embryo, and the problems posed are still alive to trouble seventeenth-century theologians.

The greatest influence on the thinking and writing of Renaissance British divines was that of Augustine. They turned to him as an authority for a version of Platonic and Neoplatonic dualism between body and soul that was fully integrated with Christianity. Like Plato and Plotinus, he deprecates the objects of sense and exalts eternal and spiritual realities. Plato's doctrine of anamnesis is superceded by Augustine's teaching that the Forms are eternal truths in God, and the source of truth in our minds. And just as this activity of contemplation is superior to knowledge that comes through the senses, so soul is superior to body. This soul is not the form of the body in the way Aristotle claimed, but rather as the Platonists defined it – a separate and spiritual substance ruling and using a body. Unlike the Platonists, however, Augustine believed it to be immortal by the grace of God alone, not by virtue of its own nature.[43]

While in some ways Augustine's system is more simply dualistic than Plato's, in other respects, influenced by Neoplatonism, he emphasizes the dichotomy between body and soul rather less than Plato. Plato's attribution of the miseries that beset the soul in this life to its union with the body are not compatible with the Church's teaching that God created the body, or with the central facts of the faith – the Incarnation and Resurrection of Christ. Thus Augustine questions how, if our creation is the work of God and our body as well as our soul made in the image of God, the body can be an instrument of punishment to us.[44]

Augustine's own early experience also led him to reject the extremes of the Platonic position. For some years he was a Manichee and held, as the Gnostics had done earlier, that matter is evil. Consequently, when he broke from this sect, he was careful to refute all their teachings. It is not body itself that is evil and a burden on the soul, he reasons, but the corruptibility of body. This corruptibility and mortality is a direct consequence of the sin of Adam. Only after the Fall did the flesh and spirit war against one another.[45] But for the first sin man, both body and soul, would have been immortal. And after the Resurrection the glorified but still physical body, united to the perfected soul, will return man to his original perfection. Although the corruptibility of the body in this life is the outward sign of man's present condition, this body or flesh is not itself the cause of the Fall, as the Platonists held. The first sin came from the soul, not the body. 'For this corruption, that is so burdensome to the soul, is the punishment of the first sin, not the cause. The corruptible flesh made not the soul to sin, but the sinning soul made the flesh corruptible.'[46] This follows necessarily from the fact that Augustine makes the will and passions all faculties of the soul.

When Augustine is not arguing against the Manichees, however, he sometimes implies that since the Fall the body does have impulses of its own that are not under the control of the will. These are opposed to man's higher principles and are in themselves evil.

Although therefore there be many lusts, yet when we read the word 'lust' alone, without mention of the object, we commonly take it for the unclean motion of the generative parts. For this holds sway in the whole body, moving the whole man, without and within, with such a mixture of mental emotion and carnal appetite that hence is the highest bodily pleasure of all produced: so that ... it overwhelms almost all the light and power of cogitation ... The motion will be sometimes importunate against the will ...[47]

Here lust is a movement or emotion of the body which strives against the mind. Reading such passages, it is easy to see how Augustine became associated with the very dualism between body and soul which, in a large number of his writings, he strove to deny. His ambivalent position is perpetuated in the works of later theologians and writers, and it is this deep-rooted uncertainty about the roles and functions of body and soul in sin that makes the debates between them possible.

Augustine's position concerning the propagation of the soul is determined largely by theological considerations. His insistence on the spiritual nature of the soul makes it difficult for him to hold to physical traducianism as Tertullian did. But he asserts the principle of seminal identity and the association of original sin with the act of procreation, both of which can only be explained if the child's soul comes in some way from the parents. Augustine's most satisfactory solution to this problem seems to have been a kind of spiritual traducianism. The soul of the child comes from the soul of the parent. In this way the spirituality of the soul is not endangered, and the transmission of original sin is explained.

Augustine maintains body and soul as the two components of man without espousing a dualism as radical as that of the Manichees. He asserts the immateriality and superiority of soul without denying completely the worth of the body. He avoids the pitfalls of both the spirituality of Origen and the materiality of Tertullian. For the Christians of the fifth century, his position fulfilled the important requirements of following, for the most part, the basic assumptions of Platonism and making them compatible with the Christian faith. Not until Thomas Aquinas was his doctrine seriously questioned and modified.

As Augustine had taken Plato as his point of departure, so Aquinas took Aristotle. Soul in itself is not man, as Plato held, but soul united to body as form is to matter. This union is natural and necessary for the soul. It is not a punishment; on the contrary, it is for the soul's good, and only through it can the soul fulfil its own greatest potential. For its part, body is wholly dependent on soul and cannot exist alone. Neither body nor soul was created prior to the other, but both were made together on the sixth day.[48] This philosophical union of body and soul is reinforced by his theological concept of nature and grace, according to which man has a natural desire for the supreme good, and the direction of this desire to the supreme good, the vision of God, is completed by the work of grace.[49]

The interdependence of soul and body is linked to the way in which Aquinas conceives of the different powers of the soul. He distinguishes three faculties in the soul – the sensitive, the appetitive, and the rational. This is similar to the division made by Plato, but while Plato believed all three powers to be attributes of the soul alone, Aquinas insists that only the intelligence belongs exclusively to the soul.[50] Thus the soul cannot be the man unless one attributes to it powers that Aquinas will grant only to the composite. The body alone is similarly limited and can neither feel nor desire; it is the soul acting *through* the body that does these things. Consequently, these powers that belong to the composite soul and body do not remain after their dissolution.[51] The soul remains essentially immaterial, immortal, a thing subsistent in its own right. It can and does exist separated from all body. But Aquinas refuses to regard this as a state more perfect and natural to it than that of union with the body.

Emotions, passions, and hence the impulse to action, whether good or evil, are also the responsibility of the composite. The second faculty of the soul, the appetitive, is divided into two parts, the intellectual and the sensitive appetite. The intellectual appetite, which is synonymous with will, does not belong to the composite, and is therefore not moved by different notions of a particular good. But the sensitive appetite, commonly referred to simply as 'appetite,' is part of the realm of things belonging to both body and soul, and it is here that good and evil passions, which are the impulse to action, arise. Before the Fall only good passions existed in the appetite, and these were always under the control of reason, but now this is not the case. Imagination and sense influence the appetite and may move it contrary to reason.[52] Thus, while reason and will must in the end consent before passion becomes act,[53] they may be misled by appetite. And the close link between this 'appetite' and the body means that the latter is implicated in sin, even though ultimate responsibility rests with reason and the will.[54] In this way Aquinas avoids the double pitfalls of reducing the role of body to that of a mere agent as Augustine does in some passages and of making it a separate principle with impulses contrary to those of the higher powers as Augustine also tends to do at times.

This unified view of man, never universal,[55] did not survive the Reformation, which brought with it a dramatic return to Augustinian ways of thought. The Reformation climate also encouraged thinkers to regard problems such as the body-soul relationship in an exclusively theological light rather than from a philosophical *and* theological point of view. Luther pours scorn on those who would 'turn the whole of theology into philosophy and into specious prattle.'[56] This attitude meant that Luther himself never wrote a systematic account of his views on man's composition, leaving them to be inferred from biblical commentaries and discussion of other theological matters.

His commentary on Genesis shows that he accepts the common definition of man as a composite of two contrary elements, body and soul, one of which is physical and mortal, akin to the animals, the other immaterial and immortal. He adopts the Augustinian division of the soul into three faculties of memory, mind, and will, but in keeping with his general rejection of multiple meanings is sceptical of allegorical interpretations that see in these three faculties an image of the Trinity in man.[57] Just as he rejects a philosophical gloss on theology in general, so he rejects Aquinas' synthesis of the Aristotelian doctrine of the soul and Christian belief, which he considers unsatisfactory from both the classical and Christian points of view. 'If Aristotle heard this he would burst into laughter and conclude that although this is not an unlovely yarn, it is nevertheless a most absurd one – that, so far as the first origin is concerned, man had been a clod but was formed by divine wisdom and so created that he was fit for immortality.'[58]

Luther is interested neither in this kind of synthesis nor in the mechanics of the interaction between body and soul but rather in the theological implications of their relationship before and after the Fall. He insists that the body in itself is not a punishment for original sin. Man would have had a body, flesh and bones, even if he had never sinned. But it would not have been the same body we have now. 'Before sin Adam had the clearest eyes, the most delicate and delightful odor, and a body very well suited and obedient for procreation. But how our limbs today lack that vigor!'[59] Similarly, the soul and all its faculties have been depraved. Not even Augustine took a more extreme view of the contrast between man before and after the Fall. Original righteousness was not a quality added to man as a gift, but was an integral part of his nature.[60] It is the whole man, body and soul, that exists in this state of original righteousness; similarly, it is the whole man that falls into complete depravity. This depravity does not consist simply in those sins which are most easily attributed to the body:

> When the sophists speak of original sin, they are speaking only of wretched and hideous lust or concupiscence. But original sin really means that human nature has completely fallen; that the intellect has become darkened, so that we no longer know God and His will and no longer perceive the works of God; furthermore, that the will is extraordinarily depraved, so that we do not trust the mercy of God and do not fear God but are unconcerned, disregard the Word and will of God, and follow the desire and impulses of the flesh.[61]

Precisely what the word 'flesh' means in the above passage is a key question. 'Flesh' and 'spirit' are often used in Luther's writings not as equivalents of 'body' and 'soul' but, in keeping with St Paul's original intention, as terms to indicate the two ways of life which the whole man can choose to follow. This is evident in one of his commentaries on Galatians 5.17 ('For the flesh lusteth against the Spirit, and the Spirit against the flesh: and these are contrary the one to the other ...'): 'The faithful therefore receive great consolation by this doctrine of Paul, in that they know themselves to have partly the flesh, and partly the spirit, but yet so notwithstanding that the spirit ruleth and the flesh is subdued, that righteousness reigneth and sin serveth.'[62] But another passage on the same scripture verse indicates that this state of sin, or of 'the flesh' understood figuratively, is connected with the state of being in the flesh literally, that is, in the body. Here Luther is speaking of the consolation he might have offered to himself when he was a monk: 'Martin, thou shalt not utterly be without sin, for thou hast yet flesh: thou shalt therefore feel the battle thereof, according to that saying of Paul: "The flesh resisteth the spirit".'[63] It seems that the body is a separate principle that can move to evil, can overcome will and reason in a way more direct than Aquinas would allow. 'Now, after sin, we all know how great passion is in the flesh, which is not only passionate in its desire but also in its disgust after it has acquired what it wanted. Thus in both instances we see neither reason nor will impaired, but passion greater than that of cattle.'[64] From this it seems a short step to 'Th'expense of spirit in a waste of shame' – Shakespeare's great sonnet of self-loathing.

As in the writings of Augustine, the passages in Luther that indicate it is the whole man who is righteous or depraved are counterbalanced by others that lend themselves to a dualistic interpretation of man. This may be in part because Luther sees body and soul imaginatively as concrete entities composing man in a way unmodified by abstract philosophical concepts such as those of matter and form – something quite unusual in theologians since the days of the early church.

On the rational level, Calvin is quite as insistent as Luther that it is the whole man who is in a state of righteousness or depravity. He uses the word 'concupiscence' to describe the completely depraved state of man since the Fall, making it clear that the term does not refer merely to fleshly lust but to the whole man.[65] He denies the existence of two souls in man, the sensitive and the rational, seeing this as a false explanation of the strife which everyone feels within himself. This strife can well exist entirely within the reason alone, for reason may be 'at cross-purposes with itself, just like armies at war.'[66]

Nevertheless, there are passages in his writing which reflect his early training in Platonism. In these we find such things as the doctrine of innate ideas[67] and the conviction that the body is the prison of the soul, not its natural habitation. The latter, particularly, encourages those who wish to read into his works a radical opposition between body and soul, though the bulk of his writings will not support this interpretation.

This brief historical survey shows a variety of forces, many of them incompatible, that shaped beliefs concerning body and soul and their relationship to one another. There was a fundamental conflict between Platonism, which saw body and soul as opposed entities, and Aristotelianism, which saw them as differing in function but mutually necessary and complementary. The task of making each of these systems compatible with Christianity produced further tensions. The dualism of Platonism, when equated with the forces of good and evil, could be used to explain the moral struggle a man felt within himself. But the negation of the body that went with this position could scarcely be reconciled with the Incarnation and the Resurrection. Also, paradoxically, this system of thought which disparages the body at the same time reduces it to the role of matter and hence makes it logically incapable of sin – a fact that the authors of medieval body and soul dialogues did not fail to exploit. The Aristotelian position fully recognizes the value of the body but makes it less easy to maintain the separateness and uniqueness of the soul, its immateriality and immortality. This in turn makes it more difficult to differentiate between the responsibility of body and soul for sin.

Finally, there is a conflict between the philosophical and the imaginative apprehension of body and soul. On the one hand, writers tend to see their relationship as an abstract concept – form and matter, thinker and thought. On the other, there is the human tendency to visualize them directly as concrete components of man – a second human figure sitting inside the physical body, a child-like being, 'green as a chive,' talking to a skeleton. This tendency to conceive of the soul in an imaginative way, which is found particularly in the works of Luther, is even more prevalent in popular writing and art. With this conflict between the philosophical and imaginative conception of body and soul goes a corresponding inconsistency in the moral realm. Considered philosophically, their relationship is such that one could not sin without the other; responsibility has to be shared. Considered imaginatively, they are two separate beings between whom conflict is possible.

In addition to these conflicting influences on Christian thought one can see ambiguities inherent in the writings of both philosophers and theologians that contributed to the uncertainty of later writers. The confusion concerning the dividing line between body and soul in Plato's various dialogues is one such instance. Others arise from the statements of Augustine, Luther, and Calvin about the relative responsibility of body and soul for sin. Logically they believe that sin must spring primarily from the will, a faculty of the soul, and involve the whole man. But the body, synonymous with the 'sinning flesh,' often becomes the personification of temptation and the forces of evil. This, I have suggested, is directly linked with the imaginative concept of body and soul as warring entities – a concept which, coupled with the confusion over the dividing line between body and soul, provides the basis of the body and soul dialogues and underlies the treatment of body and soul in much Renaissance and seventeenth-century literature.

CHAPTER TWO

Renaissance
Views of
Body and Soul

Man continued to be defined as the union of body and soul throughout the sixteenth and much of the seventeenth centuries. Cranmer enshrined it in the Anglican liturgy – 'ourselves, our souls and bodies' – a definition so commonplace as to be scarcely a definition at all. Most writers continued to think of body and soul in fairly traditional terms. Indeed, in a period of such great intellectual activity, it is surprising to discover just how many of the books, pamphlets, and tracts on the subject are either direct translations of works of the early Church Fathers or of foreign writers whose works are themselves derivative. An even larger number, while not direct translations, acknowledge a large debt to ancient and foreign sources. It seems that in these matters the regard for authority lasted much longer than it did in many other areas. There were, of course, exceptions, and in the early seventeenth century such influential figures as Francis Bacon and Descartes prepared the way for a more wholly philosophical and scientific approach to the subject. Yet the older approaches to the issue were not quickly abandoned, and often one finds a curious fusion of the two in works such as those of Sir Thomas Browne.

Blended with these literal philosophical/theological views of body and soul and almost inextricable from them are the moral and figurative associations they held. Often under the guise of 'flesh' and 'spirit' they war against one another, locked in a struggle without any possible resolution on this earth. And, as in the medieval period, it is often difficult to determine precisely to what extent the literal body and soul are believed to be engaged in this figurative struggle. Here the imprecise use of language is also a factor to be reckoned with, as writers use the terms 'body' and 'flesh,' 'soul' and 'spirit' carelessly, sometimes interchangeably.

Attributes of Body and Soul

There are two fundamentally different views of body prevalent in the Renaissance. One is Aristotelian and sees the body as the instrument of the soul; the other is Platonic and sees it as the soul's prison. In the first case, body is either a positive good or at least morally neutral, unfit rather than evil.[1] In the second case, there is no limit to the abuse that can be heaped on a villainous body from which it must be every man's desire to escape. The body is a 'dounghylle, and a sacke of stykynge myste';[2] it is 'a ruinous tabernacle of ... corruptible flesh';[3] it is the sepulchre of the soul. The ancient image of the body as the prison of the soul occurs in the works of such prominent divines as Donne, Adams, Baxter, Taylor, and Whichcote, to name only a few. Adams specifically mentions Plato as his source: 'Our graves shall as surely be Coffins to our bodies, as our bodies have beene Coffins to our soules ... *Soma, quasi sema*, as *Plato* affirmes.'[4]

It would be beautifully simple if one could divide writers into Aristotelians or Platonists who, accordingly, espoused one or other view of the body, but this is not possible. The reliance on authority noted above often led to an uncritical acceptance of snippets from different writers with contradictory opinions. Thus in the same treatise in which Guillemand, citing Plato as his source, calls the body the sepulchre of the soul he also, quoting Seneca, describes it as the instrument of the soul.[5]

This diverse and uncritical borrowing of ideas is not the only or even the prime factor at work for it merely perpetuates the inherently contradictory theological views of body prevalent in accepted Christian doctrine. Identified with the flesh that fights against the spirit (Gal 5:17), it becomes the implacable enemy of all that is good. Created by God, it is of infinite value; sanctified by Christ's incarnation, it is 'the temple of the Holy Ghost' (1 Cor 6:19).[6] Renaissance divines could not resist adding their own long series of footnotes to these incompatible positions. And, as for their ancient and medieval predecessors, the whole problem is bound up with the question of original sin and the role of the body and soul in sin – matters that must be considered later.

There is no such basic discrepancy in attitudes towards the soul, but as an entity in itself its nature and functions are far more complex. There was a widespread, if somewhat academic, interest in the nature and operations of the soul as the many surviving tracts, treatises, and even poems on the subject testify. One can discern in them a gradual development away from the exclusive dependence on ancient authorities to a more pragmatic approach.

The defining characteristic of the rational or divine soul is its immortality. While there is firm biblical support for this, its identification with the *nous* of the Aristotelian tripartite soul means that this belief in its immortality is reinforced by the famous but rather ambiguous passage from *De Anima*: 'Only separated, however, is it [mind] what it really is. And this alone is immortal and perpetual.'[7] By the late sixteenth and early seventeenth centuries the large number of tracts dealing with the subject show that this immortality was felt to be threatened. At the beginning of the seventeenth century these tracts are directed chiefly against the Anabaptists, and even as late as 1655 Edmund Porter mentions them specifically in *God Incarnate*.[8] Most authors writing this late in the century, however, recognized in Hobbes a far more formidable foe than the Anabaptists.[9]

When one turns from the exclusively rational and divine soul to the complex creation that was usually understood by that name, one still finds that, in the early part of the period at least, it is the received ideas that dominate men's thinking, although there are some interesting adaptations of these to make them relate to new theological and psychological realities. Aristotle's tripartite division of the soul into vegetative, sensitive, and rational 'souls' is commonly accepted. None of these remains as a separate soul within the individual in this life; the higher always includes the lower.[10] However, the Platonic division of the soul into sensitive, appetitive, and rational faculties, reinforced by Aquinas, also had wide currency, with the result that the two theories may be combined. Thus some writers add the divine soul as a fourth, although most see the rational and divine souls as synonymous. Other fusions (or confusions) of Platonic and Aristotelian theories result in the appetitive faculty being added between the Aristotelian sensitive and intellectual souls[11] or, alternatively, the appetite becoming a faculty of the sensitive soul or the rational soul – or of both![12] In the latter case, the appetitive faculty of the intellectual soul is synonymous with will. It is more common, however, to ascribe the appetite exclusively to the sensitive soul and to give will an independent status as a faculty of the rational soul, along with understanding and memory.[13]

Either theory, that of the two 'appetites' or that of a 'will' in the rational soul and an 'appetite' in the sensitive soul, can explain conflict within the individual and hence sin. For the appetite of the sensitive soul and that of the rational soul (or the will) do not seek the same objects. As Hooker puts it, 'The object of Appetite is whatsoever sensible good may be wished for; the object of Will is that good which Reason doth lead us to seek.'[14] This makes it appear that will and reason are inevitably in accord, and that any conflict that arises must therefore exist between these two and the sensitive appetite. But such is not really the case. The will has the freedom to take or refuse any particular object presented to it. Good may have difficulty or unpleasantness annexed to it, or evil an apparent good. And as long as reason does not present a good to the will with absolute certainty, 'still there is place left for the Will to take or leave.'[15]

This explanation of error and sin in human action is typical of both Hooker's temperamental moderation and his dependency on Aristotle. Other writers, of a more Augustinian cast of mind, see the will itself as positively perverse and depraved since the Fall. It is not compelled to follow the understanding, even if the object presented to it by reason is clearly a good. Donne, for example, denies that 'the last act of the Understanding is the Will.'[16] Will is ultimately free to override reason. Indeed, the Calvinists held that since the Fall the will is constrained to follow not good, but evil.[17] What appears to be a curious attempt to harmonize the Aristotelian position (that if the will is clearly presented with a good it must adhere to it) and the Puritan/Anglican view that the will is essentially corrupt is found in the following passage by Joseph Hall:

> The will is no lesse cunning; which though it make faire pretences of a generall inclination to good, yet ... in particulars, hangs towards a pleasing euill; Yea though the Vnderstanding haue sufficiently informed it of the worthinesse of good, and the turpitude of euill, yet being ouercome with the false delectablenesse of sinne, it yeelds to a misse-assent; Reason being (as Aquinas speakes) either swallowed vp by some passion, or held downe by some vicious habit: It is true, still the Will followes the Reason, neither can doe otherwise; but therefore, if Reason misled be contrary to Reason, and a schisme arise in the soule, it must follow that the Will must needs be contrary to Will and Reason ...[18]

Hall begins by seeing the will as perverse, prone to choose evil, and then resorts to a verbal quibble (Reason is contrary to Reason, Will to Will), to save the Aristotelian view. But the dominant impression in this passage, as elsewhere in theological treatises, is of a will that, while it should choose in accordance with reason, has the freedom to choose evil – and very often does.

This conflict between faculties of the soul must be seen in the context of the emphasis on the need for proper subordination among these faculties. Ideally the appetite and senses should serve to inform reason and will. Reason then dictates a choice, which will translates into action. But again, since the Fall, the ideal order has been upset: 'For since the Fall, the sweet Harmony and Subordination of Sense to Reason, and of Reason to God is broken; and the highest Faculties of the Soule become themselves Sensuall and Carnall. And the Restraint when the Will is desirous to obey the Dictates of Reason, or of Grace; and Lust by her tyranny overbeares the Soule, and leads it captive to the Law of Sinne, so that a man cannot do the things which he would.'[19]

Thus the freedom of the will to choose is not an absolute one. Like everything else, from the state to the individual, the faculties of the soul exist within the framework of a predetermined order. Their deviance from this order is a mark of their corruption and sinfulness. The latter part of this passage, with its echoes of Romans 7:19 ('For the good that I would I do not: but the evil which I would not, that I do') and verse 23 ('But I see another law in my members, warring against the law of my mind, and bringing me into captivity to the law of sin which is in my members'), conjures up all those traditional biblical associations of body and soul, flesh and spirit, thus moving the scene of conflict away from the soul in isolation to soul and body as they interact.

Body and Soul in Relationship to One Another

The union of body and soul in this life, which is the distinctive mark of a man, places him firmly on the scale of being as a bridge between the purely spiritual and the material. Whether this union is good or evil, it sets him apart from all the rest of creation and is terminated only by death, which is defined by its dissolution, just as life is defined by its existence. 'Bodily death is nothing else but the separation of the soule from the bodie, as bodily life is the conjunction of bodie and soule.'[20]

The precise way in which they are united in this life is open to speculation. On the physical level, they are believed to be joined by the animal spirits. This was a view that could blend science, fancy, and theology in a most curious way: 'For thy Spirit it is called *vinculum* and *vehiculum*, a bond and a Chariot, It it [sic] a bond to vnite a diuine and heauenly soule, to an earthly elementary body; both these extreames meet friendly by this *Tertium*, a firmamentall Spirit. It is called a Chariot, because it carrieth the soules faculties to all organs and parts of the body, and that with wonderfull speede.'[21] Attempts at a truly scientific explanation come only later in the period with Descartes and the Cambridge Platonists. Donne is quite happy with the suggestion that, on the metaphysical plane, they are united by the understanding, the faculty that proceeds to its conclusions by ratiocination, involving both body and soul, rather by intuition and faith, which involve the soul alone.[22]

When thinking in philosophical terms, writers are often content to express the relationship between body and soul in one of the old Aristotelian analogies – the body is to the soul as a tool is to an artificer; the body is to the soul as matter is to form. Although these concepts are functional rather than moral in origin, they could and did take on moral overtones. The first, which sees the body as the soul's instrument, is sometimes combined with the Platonic notion of man as a soul merely *using* a body, and as such it can be used to denigrate the body.[23] The matter/form analogy, on the other hand, implies that body is part of a compound and prepares the way for an acknowledgment of the mutual need one has for the other. The soul desires body as form desires matter, and this desire is used as an argument for the reunion of body and soul after death. The soul will come to its body again just as 'a Form naturally desires the Matter to which it relates, and without the Matter it is but imperfect ...'[24] Finally, there is still the common Platonic analogy that sees the body as the prison of the soul. Explicitly moral rather than functional in intent, it nevertheless has functional implications for such things as theories of knowledge. The 'prison body' clouds the soul's ability to know, insofar as this ability is intuitive; the soul as 'form' needs the body to acquire knowledge, which must come through the senses.[25]

There are many minor variations on these two contrary views of the body/soul relationship that prevailed throughout the period, but fundamentally one sees body and soul united for their composite good, while the other sees their union as mutually destructive. (That it is *mutually* destructive is shown by the number of passages that argue that the soul is detrimental to the body as well. 'Man hath a soule that kils his body, like vnto a sword that cuts his scabberd ...')[26] These apparently contradictory views are not as irreconcilable as they first seem to be. The nature of their relationship is linked not only to classical sources but also to their mutual behaviour. Thus the relationship between a good body and soul is harmonious and supportive, while that between an evil soul and body is acrimonious. Models of the happy relationship are found in man before the Fall and after the Resurrection, when a perfected body will be joined to a purified soul. This final union is man's greatest glory, setting him above even the angels.[27] But this ideal relationship between body and soul is not normally possible in this life: 'I must have this body with me to heaven, or else salvation it self is not perfect; And yet I cannot have this body thither, except as S. Paul did his, *I beat down this body*, attenuate this body by mortification; *Wretched man that I am, who shall deliver me from this body of death?'*[28]

The emphasis on subduing the body in this passage points to the only way body and soul can live together in harmony on this earth – body must be subordinate to soul. The soul, the God-given element of man, is naturally superior to body, the earthly element. This is implicit in the form/matter analogy and explicit when this is combined with another: the soul is the 'forme of that body, the King of that Kingdome.'[29] The soul is not made for the body, but the body for the soul, says Adams, quoting Chrysostom.[30] A corollary of this is the belief that the soul should rule the body, just as the higher faculties of the soul, the understanding and reason, should control the lower, the will, passions, and appetite. This was the essence of the harmonious relationship between body and soul before the Fall, and its absence is the mark of fallen man. Within the Christian framework of Renaissance England, the basic incompatibility that a classical philosopher such as Plotinus took to be the inevitable condition of the union of two dissimilar substances is seen specifically as a result of original sin. Once the soul rebelled against God, the body rebelled against the soul.[31]

Original Sin

Since it is original sin that has overthrown the proper subordination that maintains harmony between body and soul and among the various faculties of the soul, doctrines concerning it have a direct bearing on the body/soul relationship. Here there is a marked disagreement between those of different religious beliefs. Puritans, such as Baxter and Sibbes, take a much more serious view of the Fall and of man's consequent depravity than does a moderate Anglican such as Jeremy Taylor. While these differences are similar to those noted among the Church Fathers in the first chapter, their antiquity does nothing to diminish the vehemence with which they are pursued in the seventeenth century. Baxter and Sibbes (and they are representative of Puritan opinion in this), both insist that original righteousness was an intrinsic part of man's nature and that its loss entails the total depravity of all of man's faculties.[32] Taylor contends that original righteousness was a superadded quality in man and that the Fall merely reduced him to his natural state.[33] Hence our faculties are not completely depraved; the Fall has left us 'powers & capacities to serve and glorifie God; Gods service was made much harder, but not impossible ... Our *Will* was abused, but yet not destroyed; our Understanding was cosened, but yet still capable of the best instructions.'[34] Baxter is as violently opposed to this lenient view of original sin as Luther might have been, and attacks Taylor directly: 'I find Dr *Taylor* and others that deny Original sin, do build on this supposition, that Infants are deprived of this Righteousness as some superadded thing, and yet be *in puris naturalibus* without sin. But there is no such state, nor ever was, as a state of *pure nature* in a rational creature, without *holiness* or *sin* ...'[35] It was this extreme Puritan view of the Fall that led to a heightened interest in the role and responsibility of body and soul in sin in the early seventeenth century.

As perplexing as the effects of original sin (and logically prior to them) is the problem of how we come to be involved in this state of sin. Donne, like Augustine, insists that we were, in some way, participant in the original act. 'All our wils were in *Adam*, and we sinned wilfully, when he did so, and so Original sin is a voluntary sin.'[36] Half a century later, Baxter still insists on our individual participation in Adam's sin and explains the manner of it in more detail. 'As we did not *personally exist* in *Adam*, so did *we not will* that act in *Adam*: But yet when *we received a will from* Adam, it was *quadeam natura*, and *guilty* of what *his will* was guilty, though not by the guilt of actual commission, yet of *derivation* and *participation*: And thus it is *reputatively voluntary.*'[37]

This passage also shows the common belief that original sin comes to us from Adam and through our immediate parents by propagation. Hooker, Adams, Donne, Perkins, and Baxter all agree on this point, but differ widely in their understanding of precisely what this 'propagation' entails. While Hooker's explanation in no way singles out the members of the body which perform the act of generation for particular blame, Donne's appears to do just that. Original sin is 'the effect of those disobedient Members, which derive sinne, upon us, in the sinfull generation of our parents ...'[38] This would seem at first glance to imply that it is the body, not the soul, that is the guilty party in the transmission of original sin, and some writers, such as Adams, are very specific about this: '*Adam* was called *the sonne of God* ... But all his posterity the *sonnes of men*: Wee receiving from him both flesh, and the corruption of flesh, yea and of the soule too; though the substance thereof be inspired of *God*, not traduced from *man*: for the purest *soule* becomes stain'd and corrupt, when it once toucheth the body.'[39] But Donne, despite his grim view of the process of generation, takes a more complex position. He argues that while once united to the soul in the parent the body is the *agent* of corruption, and thus sin comes from 'the effect of those disobedient Members,' the body alone is passive matter and guilty of nothing. Neither is soul alone guilty, 'yet in the first minute, that this body and soule meet, and are united, we become in that instant, guilty of *Adams* sinne, committed *six thousand years* before.'[40] He does not suggest, as does Perkins, that this is because God withdraws his image from the soul. It is rather as if Adam's sin has made the two component parts of man, body and soul, basically incompatible so that now their very union is the means of propagating the original evil, and each in this life harms the other. Thus Plotinus' purely philosophical view is given theological credence.[41]

All these explanations of the inheritance of sin are based on the soul's transmission by infusion. Created by God, it must be pure when placed into the body; hence the alternatives that the body is the corrupting agent, or that God deserts the soul at the moment of infusion, or that there is a basic incompatibility between the two. The opposing theory of traducianism was by no means dead, however, and the motives that lead a seventeenth-century theologian to opt for one or the other are often little different from those that impelled Origen and Tertullian. Infusion defends the separate nature of the soul, its immortality and incorporality. Over against this, traducianism asserts the wholeness of man and makes it easier to explain the transmission of original sin. Unfortunately, these two benefits of traducianism are themselves basically incompatible and are rarely found co-existing in the same author. Those, usually Calvinist by temperament, who are very anxious to find an explanation for original sin, are not similarly motivated to demonstrate the wholeness of man. They associate the body and materiality in general with negative qualities and are therefore anxious to have a clear line of division between it and the soul in origin as well as in nature. These requirements infusion, not traducianism, fulfils. Hence William Perkins prefers to struggle with the difficulties of explaining the transmission of original sin to a pure soul rather than opt for traducianism. But Baxter, giving priority to the need to explain our sinful nature, makes the opposite choice and counters the charge of wedding the soul too closely to the body and making it too 'material' by saying that 'material' means not Aristotle's prime matter but simply 'substantial,' and everyone must agree that in this sense the soul is 'material.'[42]

The protracted nature of the infusion/traducianism conflict is, perhaps, an indication of what should have been apparent to everyone involved in it: neither option provides a completely satisfactory solution to the problem of original sin if by original sin is meant complete depravity. Jeremy Taylor gives a different perspective through his different assumptions about the nature of original sin itself. Since original righteousness is a quality superadded to man's nature, and Adam's sin has not left man completely depraved but 'in our meer nature such as it was, and such as it is,'[43] there is no inherent evil in man that must be explained by the physical propagation of the soul or by God's abandonment of the soul when it is infused into the body. Adam's sin 'infected us with death, and this infection we derive in our birth, that is, we are born mortal. *Adams* sin was imputed to us unto a natural death; in him we are sinners, as in him we die. But this sin is not real and inherent, but imputed onely to such a degree.'[44] This is probably as close as the seventeenth century could come to a philosophically satisfactory solution to the problem, but its basic premise, which minimized the importance of original sin, was unacceptable to many.

Roles of Body and Soul in Actual Sin

While dualism was of little help to Christian theology in explaining original sin, it did play an important part in the understanding of actual sin throughout our lives. It is in these actual sins, to which we have consented,[45] that we feel the contrary impulses within us that provide the psychological basis of the body and soul debates.

The fact that consent, an act of the will, is necessary for sin, would seem to exonerate the body. But it is not so simple. The clear division of faculties between soul and body outlined at the beginning of this chapter is a theoretical division only. There is still as much confusion about the attribution of faculties to body and soul and how those faculties interact as in the writings of medieval and reformation theologians. The will is the *immediate* cause of sin, but the total act involves a complex of impulses and faculties.

According to the theoretical division appetite, will, and reason are all located in the soul (either the sensitive or rational), but it is very common to find the faculties of the sensitive soul identified, either explicitly or implicitly, with the body. This confusion that has its origin in Plato is a typical one between the faculty itself and the organ through which that faculty works. Thus Richard Sibbes refers to the soul as giving us

'sight, taste, speech, motion,' but in the same work two pages earlier
we find him attributing these senses to the body.[46] And while Hooker
claims that 'appetite is the Will's solicitor, and the Will is Appetite's
controller,'[47] Jeremy Taylor translates this into a struggle between body
and soul. In his case this is because he refuses to divide the appetitive
faculty into sensitive appetite and will. Rather he views them both as
two aspects of a single will, and the effect of this is to make material
objects act directly on the will rather than on it via the sensitive appetite.

> It is an useless and a groundless proposition in Philosophy, to make
> the Passions to be distinct faculties, and seated in a differing region;
> for ... when the Object is immateriall, or the motives such, the act of
> the Will is so meerly intellectuall, that it is then spirituall, and the
> acts are proper and Symbolicall; but if the Object is materiall or
> corporall, the acts of the Will are adhaesion and aversation, and these
> it receives by the needs and inclinations of the body; now because
> many of the bodies needs are naturally necessary, and the rest are
> made so by being thought needs, and by being so naturally pleasant,
> and that this is the bodies day, and it rules here in its own place and
> time, therefore it is that the will is so great a scene of passion and we
> so great servants of our bodies.[48]

Here the will has become a battleground where the senses and reason
fight for supremacy. While will is still the determining factor in sin, the
struggle is really between the senses and reason, and this conflict, in
turn, is equated with that between body and soul.

Most theologians did not go this far in identifying the senses with the
body, claiming instead that while the faculty of sense can only be
exercised *through* the body it is, properly speaking, an attribute of the
soul. The body is matter, an instrument to be used by it. But this, as
John Downame points out, goes to the opposite extreme from Taylor's
position and appears to relieve the body of all responsibility for sin: 'Yea
so far is it off that our bodies should be chiefely corrupted, and the
principall authors of sinne, that if we speake properly the soule onely
sinneth, and the corruption of the soule alone is sinfull, and as for the
corruption of the bodie it is rather the punishment of sinne then sinne
it selfe.'[49]

More usual than either of these extreme positions that blame *either*
body or soul for sin is that which differentiates their roles but shares
the burden of guilt. The classic expression of this differentiated role but

shared responsibility, the ancient Hebrew parable of the blind man and the lame, is repeated in a sermon by Adams: 'It is questioned, whether in transgressing, the body or the soule be more culpable? I am sure, either is guiltie. It is all one: a man that wants Eyes, carries a man that wants Feete ... The Bodie without the Soule wants Eyes: the Soule without the Body wants Feete; but either supplyes the other to purloine Gods glory: Discusse, whether more, that list; I am certaine, both the blind and the lame are guiltie.'[50]

If it is only when body and soul collaborate that sin is possible, man is, by definition, just such a being in which they do and must collaborate. Thus man's position as a being in a 'middle state,' which has been described as being one of his chief glories, is also the very thing that makes him vulnerable to sin. Donne marvels that man is 'waited on' by those very creatures that, because of their simple nature, are more pure and 'further from corruption' than he. 'He [God] might have preserved him [man] by makinge him an angell in a confirmed estate, and he might have preserved him, by makinge him a beast without a reasonable soule, for then he cold not have sinned, and he had byn the better for it.'[51]

The union of body and soul not only makes sin possible; it makes the punishment for it more prolonged and horrible. The damned soul will be in a worse condition than the worm, because the latter, being only flesh, will die and not live eternally in torment. The damned soul will be in an even worse condition than the devil himself, because the devil, being solely spirit, will not have a body to be tormented.[52] Indeed, one of the reasons for the resurrection of the body is to enable the wicked to be tormented more effectively! 'The bodies of the wicked are the instruments of sinne, and the bodies of the righteous are the weapons of righteousnesse; and therefore their bodies must rise againe, that both in bodie and soule they may receive a reward, according to that which they have wrought in them.'[53]

The latter part of this passage emphasizes that to the Christian soul and body are not natural enemies as Plotinus suggests. Even in this life the soul loves and cares for its body and longs for its ultimate reunion with it, though the loss of original righteousness has made the relationship on earth a difficult one, and for the blessed in the Resurrection the reunion of body and soul will be a joyful event. But for the bodies and souls of the damned, their reunion will be a bitter one filled with mutual recriminations for their past wickedness: 'But O the miserable Condition of the Wicked in that Day! Death now breaks their Bodies and Souls into an irreconcileable Enmity, and how sad will their Conjunction be! The Soul will accuse the Body to have been Sins Sollicitor, continually tempting to Sensualities: and the Body will upbraid more than ever it allured the Soul, for its wicked Compliance: Then the Sinner shall be an entire Sacrifice burning, but never consumed.'[54]

These recriminations between a damned body and soul at the last day show that the acknowledgment of shared responsibility for sin does not remove all possibility of debate between the condemned partners. Even once mutual guilt is established, there can still be a subsidiary argument about whether this guilt is shared equally or whether one or other of the culprits is chiefly to blame. A writer like Lancelot Andrewes, who places sense firmly in the soul and therefore sees the body as merely exhibiting the fruits of sin, would naturally make the soul chiefly responsible.[55] The fact that will, the agent ultimately responsible for action, belongs to the soul is further grounds for placing the heavier share of blame on the soul. But the body, even when regarded primarily as an instrument, is almost never seen as a completely passive one. On the contrary, it may actively tempt the soul and so itself initiate sinful action.[56] And, if it rebels against the soul, who is chiefly responsible – the body that initiates the insurrection, or the weak soul that fails to control it? There cannot be any final answer to this argument about relative guilt, given the confusion built into the premises. For this very reason it is able to provide the basis of the seventeenth-century body and soul dialogues as it did the medieval ones.

These discussions of the role and responsibility of body and soul in sin bring together most of the aspects of each discussed in this chapter. The attribution of sense to body, and the insistence that even the instrument that enacts evil is implicated in the deed, all combine to establish the guilt of the body. Only if the definition of body as passive matter is narrowly adhered to can it be exonerated. As for the soul, the attribution to it of the will and often of the faculties of sense as well implicates it fully. The lack of proper subordination, an important cause of sin, can be blamed either on a rebel body or on a weak soul that ought to impose its will more forcibly. Because of the uncertainty as to where the dividing line between body and soul should be drawn and the confusion inherent in the subordination issue, the whole problem of responsibility for sin is open to dispute. An excellent case can be made for blaming either the soul or the body – and an even better one for condemning them mutually and equally.

Body and Soul, Flesh and Spirit:
Literal and Figurative Uses

One additional element that coloured the perception of body and soul in the English Renaissance is the association of the literal body and soul with the figurative flesh and spirit. The latter are used chiefly to indicate man's evil and good impulses respectively. Galatians 5:17 is the main source of this concept of two warring protagonists within man, but its application is much wider than this single passage might indicate.

The battle between the flesh and the spirit could be read into many texts other than those which specifically mentioned it and provided sermon writers with a dramatic framework for their message. A case in point is Henry Smith's application of it to a most unlikely text from Ecclesiastes 11:9 ('Rejoice, O young man, in thy youth ... but know thou, that for all these things God will bring thee into judgment'):

> Methinks I see the dialogue between the flesh and the spirit: the worst speaketh first, and the flesh saith, Soul, take thine ease, eat, drink, and go brave, lie soft ... But the soul cometh in ... and saith, I pray thee remember judgment, thou must give account for all these things; for unless you repent, you shall surely perish. No, saith the flesh, talk not of such grave matters, but tell me of fine matters, of soft beds and pleasant things ...[57]

Almost certainly, Henry Smith is here thinking of the parable of the rich fool (Luke 12:16–21) as well as the Ecclesiastes text, but even in the former there is no precedent for such a dialogue between flesh and spirit. The dialogue in that parable is between the man, his soul, and God. Smith's casting of the whole into a form with such strong overtones of the Galatians passage shows its popularity and versatility, both of which can be substantiated by examples from many other sermon writers.[58]

A very exhaustive treatment of the subject is to be found in William Perkins' treatise 'Of the combat of the Flesh and Spirit.' Perkins is careful to define his terms to show that by 'flesh' and 'spirit' he, like Luther, means contrary impulses within man that are not to be identified with actual parts of his anatomy. The flesh and spirit have 'divers significations,' which he lists and discards one by one until the sense in which he uses the terms in the treatise is established beyond any doubt: the spirit signifies 'a created quality of holiness' and the flesh 'the naturale corruption or inclination of the mind, will, and affections to that which is against the lawe ...'[59] Both of these are qualities within the soul.

Perkins' precision is not typical, however, and in many writers the identification of flesh with body is common. One of the chief sources of this identification is not the Galatians passage but Romans 7:23, where the 'law of sin' is definitely in the 'members.' Since, as we have seen, it is in and through the body that our evil nature is most clearly manifest, this identification is a natural one. Even John Downame, who is always careful to avoid calling the flesh body, understands that it may often be so called 'because this corruption dwelleth in the bodie, and exerciseth it selfe in it by it, as by it[s] instrument in the committing and perpetrating of all the workes of darkness ...'[60]

Less frequently, the lack of distinction between flesh and body means that flesh can take on the morally neutral connotations of body or may even be used to denote the literal body.[61] Such is the confusion that Richard Sibbes can write, 'His [St Paul's] desire of death was to be freed from the *body of sin*, more than to be taken out of the flesh,'[62] thus completely reversing the usage so carefully illustrated by Perkins.

The terms 'spirit' and 'soul' also have multiple meanings. It is evident that in a passage coupling 'flesh' and 'spirit,' where 'flesh' stands for man's sinful nature, 'spirit' will stand for his regenerate nature. But spirit is also used to designate part of a triad composing man and consisting of body, soul, and spirit. Within this triad there are at least two possible arrangements. In the first, body is the inanimate physical shell of man, soul is the sensible part, and spirit is the rational element. In Aristotelian terms, 'soul' corresponds to the sensitive soul, 'spirit' to *nous* or mind.[63] The other arrangement of the triad makes 'spirit' (here usually, but not always, found in the plural) the vehicle in the blood that unites body and soul. There are three kinds of 'spirits' in this sense – animal, vital, and natural. Each is located in a different part of the body according to the Platonic location of the three faculties of the soul. The animal spirits are seated in the brain, the vital in the heart, and the natural in the liver. Using 'spirit' in this way, Thomas Adams explains the Pauline triad thus: 'For to make up one man, there is an elementary body, a divine soule, and a firmamentall spirit.'[64] Yet another distinction between soul and spirit defines soul as embodied spirit. Hence after death when our soul is freed from the body it becomes spirit. This explains Baxter's otherwise curious statement that 'all created Spirits are Souls in all probability, and actuate some Matter or other.'[65]

These academic distinctions, essential to an understanding of some writers, were misunderstood or ignored by others. Thus the terms 'body' and 'soul,' 'flesh' and 'spirit' can be used literally or figuratively – even interchangeably! 'If the *soule* be coming, he [the devil] is sure the *body* will follow. If he cannot reach the *spirit*, then have at the *flesh*.'[66] The negative and positive connotations of flesh and spirit continue to be associated with the two real components making up man, the body and the soul, but rational analysis sinks defeated in the face of the general confusion of thought and terminology. In the poetry of the period, however, we shall see how this is put to positive use. There confusion gives way to deliberate ambiguity to produce wit, irony, and sometimes genuine insight.

Philosophical and Scientific Writers

Contemporary in time, but often very far removed in assumptions and approach from these theological writers were those who were beginning to look at body and soul from what we would regard as a more scientific point of view. Their direct influence on literature was certainly less important early in the century than that of the theologians, but as their ideas moved gradually from the area of erudite speculation to general acceptance they came to have a widespread effect. And in some cases – notably those of Sir Thomas Browne and Henry More – literary writer and thinker were the same person in different roles.

Sir Francis Bacon was first among this new breed of scientific and philosophical writers. His attitude to the relationship between body and soul is grounded in his theory of knowledge in general, which affirms that the basis of all human knowledge is sense experience. Sense is not infallible; it can fail either by giving no information or by giving false information;[67] but reason, the obvious alternative to sense, is even less satisfactory. Its weakness is that it is subjective, affected by desire and emotion. One observes that this influence which, to a theologian, would be seen as a cause of sin is, in Bacon, seen as a cause of unreliability. 'The human understanding is no dry light, but receives an infusion from the will and affections; whence proceed sciences which may be called "sciences as one would." For what a man had rather were true he more readily believes.'[68] This unreliability of the understanding means that the senses must not be rejected, but rather assisted by instruments and experiments. Among classical philosophers, he is far more at home with the materialistic theories of Democritus than with

Aristotle who, he charges, 'made his natural philosophy a mere bond servant to his logic.'[69]

We have here a complete change of emphasis from that of the theological writers. Bacon is much more interested in *how* the soul operates within the body than in its metaphysical relationship with the body. Or, to return to the terminology we have been using, he is more interested in the irrational or sensitive soul than in the rational, distinctively human soul. Yet even within this confined area, Bacon's achievements are distinctly limited. While he deplores the lack of inquiry into the precise way in which the spirit acts upon matter and claims that since the soul is now known to be a corporeal and material substance, not merely a function,[70] this inquiry is possible, Bacon does not himself undertake it with any vigour. He fails, for example, to explain precisely how motion is caused, or how sense impressions are received and recorded.

When one comes to his treatment of the rational soul, the root cause of these limitations is apparent. The rational soul cannot be investigated by means of scientific experimentation, and for this reason even the confined area of purely material things that can be is unsatisfactorily dealt with. Knowledge, in the end, 'must be bounded by religion, or else it will be subject to deceit and delusion.' As for the rational soul itself, just as its creation was immediately inspired by God, so 'true knowledge of the nature and state of the soul, must come by the same inspiration that gave the substance.'[71]

With these convictions as his starting point, it is not surprising that Bacon adds little to any investigation of the rational soul. He contrasts its simple nature with that of the body, which is a compound, and reiterates the commonplace six faculties (understanding, reason, imagination, memory, appetite, and will), which he divides according to which of the two chief branches of human endeavour they relate to, logic or ethics. The imagination performs a double office in both provinces, 'the judicial and the ministerial.'[72]

The superior role Bacon assigns to imagination is the only original feature of his analysis. For most philosophers, particularly the Platonic, imagination must be strictly controlled by reason and understanding. But for Bacon it becomes something similar to 'faith' – a means by which we rise above the sort of 'reality' that reason manifests to a higher 'reality' that comes by revelation. 'The divine grace uses the motions of the imagination as an instrument of illumination, just as it uses the motions of the will as an instrument of virtue; which is the reason why religion ever sought access to the mind by similitudes, types, parables, visions, dreams.'[73] This last passage seems to relate more closely to the province of literature than of science, to Bacon the writer than to Bacon the emerging scientist. Bacon marks the beginning of a new era in English thought, but his own contribution to it is restricted by the retention of old presuppositions. Experiment and detailed explanation are limited to the irrational part of the soul. References to the rational soul are always somewhat inhibited by the conviction that it is wrong to inquire too curiously into a mystery. The result is that while the sensitive soul is related to the body in an intelligible way, there is no attempt to do the same with the rational soul, which includes all the higher powers and operations of the mind.

Descartes was unquestionably bolder and more consistent than Bacon. His definition of 'soul' restricts it to the rational, human soul, and he does try to give an explanation in physical terms of the relationship between this rational soul and the body, both of which together compose man. Unlike Bacon, he begins with the mind, not the senses, which he claims can know nothing adequately, not even bodies.[74] The 'notion of thought' precedes that of all corporeal things and is the most certain ...'[75] It is the mind or soul that is the essential 'I.'[76] The exaltation of thought and corresponding denigration of the senses means that, in effect, the two are quite distinct. Since, for Descartes, the senses are unambiguously attached to the body, what this really means is that there is a radical separation between soul and body. The body is divisible; the mind (soul) is indivisible. The essence of the body is extension; the essence of the mind is thought.

Yet Descartes recognizes that man does not feel himself to be composed of two unrelated halves but of one whole. Body and soul are conjoined, and by the sensations of pain, hunger, and thirst man discovers that he is not only lodged in his body as a pilot in a vessel but is so closely united with it that the two seem to compose one integral being. Everyday experience can only be explained through the interaction of soul and body, and Descartes makes two successive attempts to explain this interaction in his works.

The earlier of the two accounts (*Rules for the Direction of the Mind* [1628]) is a simple one and suggests that the external senses receive a stimulus just as wax receives an impression from a seal. This figure is then conveyed instantly to the 'common sense,' which also functions as a seal and impresses the fancy or imagination. (The latter is here a genuine part of the body, able to retain these impressions.) The retention of the image also explains memory. The whole process can work in reverse as well; fancy moves the motor force or nerves which derive their origin from the brain in which the fancy is located. However, all this only explains the process by which we receive sense impressions; the power by which we actually know is something other, 'purely spiritual, and not less distinct from every part of the body than blood from bone, or hand from eye.'[77] Thus there is no resolution of the dualism inherent in his system of thought.

It is in *The Passions of the Soul* (1649) that Descartes gives the more mature and better-known account of the interaction between body and soul, one that attempts to explain feeling and knowing in a broader sense. The soul is united to all parts of the body conjointly because it is indivisible and of a nature that has no relation to extension. But there is one part of the brain, the pineal gland, in which the soul exercises its functions more particularly than in other parts. The slightest movements which take place in it 'may alter very greatly the course of these spirits; and reciprocally ... the smallest changes which occur in the course of the spirits may do much to change the movements of this gland.'[78] 'These spirits' are the animal spirits, material bodies that assist in carrying impressions from the senses to the brain.[79] In this treatise, unlike the earlier one in which sense impressions were transmitted instantly and without the passage of any real entity, Descartes says that the soul, from its seat in the pineal gland, radiates forth through the remainder of the body by means of animal spirits, nerves, and blood. The gland is so suspended between the cavities that contain spirits that it can either be moved by objects or, moved by the soul, it can thrust the spirits towards the pores of the brain 'which conduct them by the nerves into the muscles, by which means it causes them to move the limbs.'[80] Thus Descartes explains both actions and perceptions arising from the soul as well as those arising from the body and external world.

The division of actions and perceptions between those that originate in the soul and those that originate in the body is key to this book, for it leads Descartes away from problems dealing strictly with the 'how' of interaction to moral considerations of responsibility for action. Clearly, actions that originate within the soul must be within its power. Those passions that originate in the body, however, 'can only indirectly be altered by the soul, excepting when it is itself their cause.'[81] They are frequently a stimulus to action, and hence a conflict may arise between what they incite the soul to do and what the soul's own nature dictates. Since Descartes, in contrast to Bacon, insists that there is only one soul and that the animal spirits and other faculties by which the body takes in sense impressions are themselves part of the body, the moral conflict man feels within himself is between the body and the soul:

And it is only in the repugnance which exists between the movements which the body by its animal spirits, and the soul by its will, tend to excite in the gland at the same time, that all the strife which we are in the habit of conceiving to exist between the inferior part of the soul, which we call the sensuous, and the superior which is rational, or as we may say, between the natural appetites and the will, consists. For there is within us but one soul, and this soul has not in itself any diversity of parts; the same part that is subject to sense impressions is rational, and all the soul's appetites are acts of will. The error which has been committed in making it play the part of various personages, usually in opposition to one another, only proceeds from the fact that we have not properly distinguished its functions from those of the body, to which alone we must attribute every thing which can be observed in us that is opposed to our reason.[82]

Certain passions of the body do attempt to affect the will and to make it desire that which it alone would avoid. Then the will tries to overcome the influence of the animal spirits. But though they can change their course for a moment, the spirits immediately revert to the same course 'because the disposition which has before held its place in the nerves, heart, and blood has not changed.'[83] Thus the soul feels itself impelled at almost the same moment to desire and not desire the same thing. The physical part of the strife is localized in the pineal gland, which is thrust to one side by the soul and to the other by the animal spirits. Through this struggle a person can discover the strength or weakness of his soul, 'for those in whom by nature the will can most easily conquer the passions and arrest the movements of the body which accompany them, without doubt possess the strongest souls.'[84] Ultimately it is the soul that should determine the course of action taken; Descartes does not question the freedom of the will. The whole presents a curious and original attempt to explain a moral conflict in physiological terms.

Descartes is the first thinker to define the soul as an immaterial thinking substance and then to attempt to explain in scientific terms how it is related to the physical, extended substance of body. He attempts to keep body and soul distinguished from one another on the moral plane and at the same time to integrate them as parts of a single human organism. He states that the essence of man is the soul (mind), but insists that the body is more than simply the instrument of this soul.[85] His explanation of interaction remains, nevertheless, an artificial one which, instead of bringing body and soul together, really separates them radically. This is particularly true on the moral plane, where his system of thought leaves man as a dual being, at war within himself.

Sir Kenelm Digby, unlike Descartes, is not a particularly original thinker. He is important primarily because he reflects and synthesizes many of the important preoccupations of the age and, in turn, influenced many of his contemporaries, in particular James Howell, author of the most ambitious seventeenth-century body and soul dialogue.[86]

Digby was strongly influenced by Descartes and cites his explanation of sense impressions with approval,[87] but the tension one finds in his work between the demands of a logical, scientific explanation of man and accepted Christian beliefs concerning the nature of the soul reminds one of Bacon. This tension is reflected in both the structure and the content of his work, which is divided neatly into two treatises, one on body and the other on soul. The treatise on bodies attempts to be completely scientific; reflection and abstract thought can lead to gross errors. Its explanations, as a result, turn out to be rather crudely mechanical. While Digby accepts, in general, Descartes' theory of the animal spirits, he insists that some tiny, solid material bodies come from the objects themselves and lodge in the vacant cells of the brain until stirred from them by chance or the will of the person.[88] At other times, and in contrast to his mechanistic stance, a curiously anthropomorphic note creeps into his writing. For example, he explains our occasional failure to receive and note sense impressions by saying that the spirits are the porters of all nerves to the brain, and if they are busy with something else a particular impression may not be received at all or with the same force as it would if the spirits were unoccupied.[89]

Digby does not seek to deny the existence of anything beyond the world of sense experience. On the contrary, when the reader turns to Digby's treatise on the soul, he realizes that the object of explaining the body as a completely mechanical thing, explicable in terms of quantity and motion, is to prove from this the existence of a substance that cannot be so explained – the soul, which is an immortal or spiritual substance. This treatise is quite different in method. It is based on logic, not sense experience, and the premises of the argument are not verifiable by experiment. In this context, the body is chiefly a hindrance to the soul. Our actions proceed from two principles, the understanding and sense, which are identified with soul and body and, by implication, with the behaviour of angels and beasts respectively. (Thus, as for Descartes, the moral conflict within man is between body and soul, not between various faculties of the soul.) Digby reasserts the principle of proper subordination; reason ought always to control sense and passion. His explanation of why this is not always so is remarkably similar to and just as mechanical as that of Descartes. Reason can cause no act without the assistance of the spirits in the brain, from which it follows that it may be swayed by the turbulence of those spirits sent up to the brain from the desired object, 'for whatever beateth on the fansie occasioneth her to worke ...'[90]

All this, of course, applies to Reason (Soul) only in its limited state on this earth. Out of the body it is free and limitless; its sojourn here is merely a period of probation in which it perfects or damns itself forever. What it has been on earth it remains in the highest degree for eternity: 'There can be no change made in her, after the first instant of her parting from her body; but, what happiness or misery betideth her in that instant, continueth with her for all eternity.'[91]

Digby's treatises on body and soul, which begin as a scientific investigation of their natures, end on an almost mystical note. The overall impression is of yet another scientific/philosophical writer who has ended by separating rather than uniting body and soul, their attributes and modes of operation. Digby is not only unsuccessful in reconciling body and soul on the moral and scientific planes; like Bacon, he does not even attempt to investigate them by similar methods.

Thomas Hobbes gave an emphatic answer to this unsatisfactory dualism, but it came in a form the period was unable to accept. Hobbes' alternative to the dualism of Descartes and Digby was to deny the existence of two realms of Being, one material and the other immaterial. Man could be explained solely as a physical organism without reference to an incorporeal element. There was no 'spirit' in Descartes' sense of the word; there were no clear and distinct ideas other than those gathered from the senses. Hobbes, unlike Descartes, refused to acknowledge the primacy of abstract thought. For him all thought must be 'imaginable,' that is, grounded in sense impressions. In his 'Objections' to Descartes' *Meditations*, he attacks Descartes' proof that knowledge of thought precedes knowledge of the material body. Since knowledge of the proposition 'I exist' depends on knowledge of 'I think' and 'the knowledge of it upon the fact that we cannot separate thought from a matter that thinks, the proper inference seems to be that that which thinks is material rather than immaterial.'[92] Activity cannot be thought of apart from its subject, and perception and behaviour are explained in purely mechanical terms. Even concepts come, in the first instance, from the senses. Thought is coherent because of the coherence of the images first produced by the sense objects.[93] Understanding is merely a more sophisticated form of conception caused by speech, and even reasoning is a mechanical process. 'When a man *reasoneth*, he does nothing else but conceive a sum total, from *addition* of parcels; or conceive a remainder, from *subtraction* of one sum from another ...'[94] The emotions also arise from the activity of the senses. Appetite is the beginning of animal motion towards something that pleases; aversion is motion away from something that displeases.[95] Hobbes attacks the scholastic definition of will, that it is a *rational appetite*, on the grounds that if it were there could be no voluntary act against reason.[96] In Hobbes' sense, even animals that deliberate can will. This, of course, removes the moral element from the process altogether.

Hobbes' system has the beauty of consistency, but most seventeenth-century thinkers believed it was heretical as well. While he does not openly deny the truth of revealed religion, much of his philosophy appears to imply such a denial. He does not believe that either God or the soul is incorporeal, chiefly on the grounds that an incorporeal spirit is 'unimaginable' and therefore impossible.[97] Commenting on part of 1 Corinthians 15:44 ('It is raised a spiritual body'), he says that these are 'bodily spirits; which is not difficult to understand. For air and many other things are bodies, though not flesh and bone, or any other gross body to be discerned by the eye.'[98] If denying the incorporeal nature of the soul makes him an atheist, then so is Tertullian one. He reminds his detractors that the Eastern Church always believed that angels and soul were corporeal and were only called incorporeal because their bodies were different from ours.

Hobbes not only denies that spirits are incorporeal but also that they are distinct from the body. He attributes the belief in a separate soul to the 'demonology of the Greeks'[99] – a view that has some plausibility. His own position is much more Hebraic. There is no separate soul, ready to do battle with the carnal body; rather, soul is the life of the body. He does not deny the Christian belief in immortality; both body and soul will rise at the last day, and those of the faithful will then receive immortality as a special gift of God. But neither is immortal by virtue of its nature – that is, by creation.

Most seventeenth-century Christian thinkers did not feel that these concessions of Hobbes' were sufficient to keep him within the bounds of orthodoxy. To deny the essential immortality and incorporality of the soul was to deny the faith as they understood it. The materialistic explanation of man and the universe might work on one level, but they were unprepared to admit that it could explain what they regarded as spiritual phenomena as well. While Hobbes effected a reconciliation of the two realms of matter and spirit, it was only by reducing one to the other, and this his contemporaries were unwilling to accept as valid. Nor did they understand or accept his claim that an immaterial substance was 'unimaginable' and that man could only conceive of things that were 'imaginable' – that is, able to be presented to the mind pictorially. Yet this, as we have seen, did not stop them from alternating between two quite different ways of looking at body and soul themselves. On the one hand, they clung to their abstract 'unimaginable' definitions; on the other, they thought and spoke of body and soul as concrete, 'imaginable' entities. Hobbes at least saw the incongruity of this.

Sir Thomas Browne, who manifests in his work the tension between the scientific approach of Bacon, Descartes, and Digby and the dogmatic attitude of revealed religion found in the theological writers, appropriately concludes this brief survey of scientific and philosophical writers. Although he was a medical doctor, Browne's interest in the soul and its relationship to the body is primarily moral rather than scientific. While he relies on observation to some extent – for example, to substantiate the immateriality of the soul[100] – he does not limit himself to this sort of proof and counts the antiquity of the Greeks' belief in the immateriality and immortality of the soul as of equal weight with it: 'Before *Plato* could speak, the soul had wings in *Homer*, which fell not, but flew out of the body into the mansions of the dead.'[101]

The whole cast of Browne's mind is very different from that of Hobbes. Even when he confesses to having held at one time a view similar to that of the latter, 'that the soules of men perished with their bodies, but should yet bee raised againe at the last day,' both his reason for the belief and the language in which it is expressed are totally unlike Hobbes' cold rationality: 'Surely it is but the merits of our unworthy natures, if wee sleepe in darknesse, until the last alarum.'[102] And when he speaks of the power of imagination, he means something quite other than what Hobbes meant. Hobbes believed that only the 'imaginable' (picturable) was rational and, hence, that the rational must also be 'imaginable.' Browne's discussion of 'imagination' begins where Bacon's left off. It is something akin to faith, and should be assisted by reason, but rationality is not a criterion of it; imagination can go where reason cannot follow. He delights in the unprovable, the paradoxical; his interest in archeological findings has as its end metaphysical speculation on mortality.

His beliefs concerning the soul are quite orthodox. He accepts its division into vegetative, sensitive, and rational or divine but, like Bacon, treats the divine in a manner wholly different from the first two. This soul knows intuitively, without the mediation of sense or reason. Yet when he is speaking of 'soul' in a more inclusive sense, containing the faculties of sense, reason, and passion (will), then body, since sense is dependent on it, is necessary for the acquisition of knowledge.

Like Bacon (and unlike Descartes and Digby), Browne places the moral conflict within man not between body and soul but between the faculties of the soul itself. 'As Reason is a rebell unto Faith, so Passion unto Reason.'[103] His explanation of the first sin of Adam and Eve gives an explicit example of the roles he assigns to the faculties of the soul in sin. Adam and Eve were deceived both by the conduct of their senses and by temptations from the object working upon those senses. The real sin was one of improper insubordination and originated chiefly in the soul by means of the lower faculties gaining control over reason. 'They were deceived through the Conduct of their Senses, and by Temptations from the object it self; whereby although their intellectuals had not failed in the Theory of truth, yet did the inservient and brutal Faculties controll the suggestion of Reason: Pleasure and Profit already overswaying the instructions of Honesty, and Sensuality perturbing the reasonable commands of Vertue.'[104]

He suggests that the whole may be an allegory of the seduction of the higher part of the soul (Adam) by the inferior and feminine faculties (Eve). He then applies this to the present condition of mankind, deceived by sense and dominated by appetite: 'Their understanding is so feeble in the discernment of falsities, and averting the Errors of reason, that it submitteth unto the fallacies of sense, and is unable to rectifie the Error of its sensations.'[105] It is significant that Browne does not attempt to explain in scientific terms *how* this conflict within man takes place as do Descartes and Digby. His treatment of the subject is an excellent example of the way in which allegory could still exist side by side with science as late as the mid-seventeenth century.

The Cambridge Platonists

A retreat to allegory was not a permanent answer to the dualism of most of the scientists and philosophers of the period, nor to the monism of that atheistic rationalist, Hobbes. In the second half of the seventeenth century, a group of Christian thinkers who became known as the Cambridge Platonists, convinced of the necessity to couple reason with revealed Christian truths,[106] set out to answer both the intellectually unsatisfactory dualism of Descartes and the material monism of Hobbes.

In its origins, the Platonist school at Cambridge did not represent a radical break with the existing religious tradition but was closely connected with the Puritan community in the university. Benjamin Whichcote was a student and later a Fellow of Emmanuel College, a centre of Puritan influence. In 1644, when Samuel Collins was ejected from his position as Provost of King's, Whichcote was chosen to fill the post because he was acceptable to the Puritans. Unlike most Puritans, however, Whichcote believed in the use of reason as an aid to faith. This emphasis on the use of reason was not an isolated, superficial difference from his fellows, but was part of his optimistic view of human nature as a whole. The use of reason was possible because man was not totally depraved as the Calvinists insisted. 'The spirit of a man is the Candle of the Lord,' he asserted repeatedly. Our natural faculties are God-given and so are able to help us in reaching God.[107]

While Whichcote disagrees completely with the Puritan position in this respect, in matters dealing directly with body and soul one finds little that is new in his work. The fundamental dichotomy between the two still exists as does the ambivalent attitude toward body which is, at different times, the prison of the soul or the temple of the Holy Ghost.

It is in the works of John Smith that Whichcote's exaltation of human reason begins to bear fruit in a questioning of some conventional assumptions about body and soul and in a movement away from dualism itself. Smith is interested in the mechanics of interaction between body and soul, a subject that did not concern Whichcote at all, and it is when he speaks about this that he tends to minimize the division between them, thus supporting the argument that the new scientific approach was one of the factors that made extreme dualism untenable.

As a Platonist, Smith's tendency is to perpetuate the gulf between body and soul. The existence and immortality of the soul is carefully proven. In man, goodness is associated with the soul and evil with the body. Indeed, men are classified into four types according to the proportion of 'soul' and 'body' (here obviously used in a figurative sense) they possess.[108] But when he begins to consider the way in which the soul is united to the body, how it can share its needs and desires, there is a different note. The soul shares the passions and infirmities of the body since it could not provide for it if it had no way of feeling its needs.[109] While some of his ideas come from ancient authority (he quotes Proclus and Heraclitus), there is also a reference to the theory of 'a late sagacious philosopher' (presumably Descartes) who says that the interaction between soul and body originates in 'that part of the Brain from whence all those Nerves that conduct the Animal Spirits up and down the Body take their first Original.'[110] In the context of this discussion of interaction, he admits there is nothing wrong with the communication between body and soul; each is necessary to the other.

Nevertheless, it would be too simple to conclude that Platonism reinforced the dichotomy between body and soul in a writer such as Smith, while the new science had the reverse effect. Platonism, as adopted by these thinkers, was largely Neoplatonism, and Neoplatonism, as we have seen, contains monistic as well as dualistic elements. The different gradations of men that Smith describes, with their varying proportions of body and soul, are a good example of this. There is not an inseparable gulf between spirit and matter, but a descending scale of being.

In the works of Henry More and Ralph Cudworth, the opposed tendencies of Neoplatonism – the assertion of the reality and superiority of spirit on the one hand, and the union of matter and spirit as part of one continuum on the other – coincide with the refutation of Hobbes and Descartes respectively. Against Hobbes they had to assert the immateriality and immortality of the soul; against Descartes they had to assert that reality is a unity, that matter and spirit, body and soul, are not merely united in an artificial and purely mechanical way but that they are wholly interdependent. Both exist on a scale of being in which one merges into the other.[111] These needs are to some extent incompatible, but just as Plotinus attempted to satisfy the demands of transcendence and immanence within one philosophical system, so do More and Cudworth.

When he is writing against Hobbes, Henry More uses arguments for the existence of spirit that are rather similar to those of Descartes. They spring, for the most part, from the individual's own consciousness of reality, the innate ideas to be found within his own mind. We have within us the idea of a perfect being, God. Since the idea of a perfect being contains 'the Idea of necessary existence,' therefore He must exist. Such a perfect being cannot be a body. 'These things cannot be attributed to matter,' he concludes.[112] Neither is the soul merely a modification of the body. The animal spirits and the brain alone are not capable of memory and reason. In 'The Immortality of the Soul' he brings forward other, more empirical arguments as well. Matter cannot account for motion because it is not self-movable, nor can it explain sensation. Hobbes may insist that sensation is caused by the impress of matter upon matter, but this does not explain satisfactorily what we feel. 'The distinct Impression of any considerable extent of variegated *Matter* cannot be received by a mere point of *Matter*.'[113] Such reasoning clearly points to the existence of some kind of spirit.

If More's stand against Hobbes is to be convincing, however, this spirit must be distinctly different from matter. He defines it as 'an Immaterial substance intrinsically endued with Life and the faculty of Motion'; it is penetrable and indiscerpible.[114] Body, on the contrary, is unable to move itself, is impenetrable and discerpible.

These differences may seem to be as absolute as those of Descartes, but in fact they are not at all. Spirit is distinct from matter, but the absolute cleavage between the two found in Descartes' work does not exist in More's. First, he denies one of Descartes' chief distinctions between matter and spirit, that the former has extension while the latter does not, concluding that even immateriality does not, by definition, exclude extension. Nevertheless, extension itself does not necessarily imply all the properties we associate with body – divisibility and penetrability.[115] Thus he preserves the uniqueness of spirit, while still ostensibly narrowing the gap between it and matter.

Second, More counters the extremes of dualism by stating that the soul is not ideally free of all body but always united to a body of some sort.[116] This position is tenable because his concept of 'body' is not restricted to the gross earthly body. Just as spirit can have a property normally associated with body, so body may be an 'airy' body, which is the habitation of the soul after death and of angels and demons. There is even a celestial, aetherial body which righteous souls may attain after death.[117] Body and soul are united in each case by a 'vital congruity,' a principle 'of a natural adaptation of matter to soul, of some turning in the matter itself toward the soul which is to give it life, and in the soul to that part of matter which is to form its body.'[118] There is a triple vital congruity in the soul corresponding to the three types of bodies it may inhabit. Thus at death there is a smooth transition from one plane of existence to another.[119]

The result of attributing to soul the property of extension, traditionally associated only with body, and of broadening the concept of body to include an 'aetherial' body is, naturally, to lessen the distinction between the two. In this way More succeeds, within his own terms of reference at least, in assuming a position that asserts the reality and superiority of spirit against Hobbes, while minimizing the gulf between it and body or matter.

Ralph Cudworth is obsessed with the same two-sided problem, but his approach is somewhat different. Although he is even more violently opposed to Hobbes' materialistic philosophy than is More, he is acute enough to realize that in some respects Hobbes is an ally. By carrying materialism to its extreme, he has made it easy to prove the existence of a non-material substance simply by virtue of the things the material cannot explain.

Cudworth's arguments for the existence of spirit are drawn from both authority and logic. Those from authority are unconvincing to a modern reader largely because, like most of his contemporaries, he lacks an understanding of the history of ideas. Empedocles, Plato, Pythagoras, and Thales are all drawn upon indiscriminately, nor does he distinguish between Plato, Plotinus, and Plotinus as interpreted by later commentators such as Ficino. The argument from logic on which he chiefly rests his case is, happily, more coherent. Matter or body, which is nothing but 'Magnitude, Figure, Site, and Motion or Rest,' cannot produce spirit or any of the manifestations of spirit. The scale of entities which makes up the universe cannot be a scale of ascent from lower to higher but must be a way of descent from higher to lower.[120] The cause must be greater than the effect.

By reducing Hobbes' theory to absurdity, Cudworth extends the realm of the spiritual and contracts that of matter to an even greater degree than does More. Practically everything that is not dead, inert matter is 'soul.' Even animals have a soul. In thus broadening the definition of 'soul' Cudworth has made it easier to prove its existence, but the proof becomes correspondingly less significant and has little to do with 'soul' in the Christian or even moral sense. If his argument is to have any value, he must distinguish between the souls of brutes and those of humans. Although he concedes that the souls of brutes are probably not eternal as are human souls and that, while reason can assure one of the existence of an incorporeal substance, only our knowledge of God's nature can convince us of the existence of a peculiarly human soul, this distinction is not enough to satisfy most of his critics. The strict dualism of Descartes has been avoided, but the corporeal has been reduced almost to non-existence.[121]

Cudworth may have been led to his comprehensive definition of spirit by a desire to reduce Hobbes' theory to absurdity, but the avoidance of dualism was more than a happy side result. The search for a unifying principle is one of his main objectives and reveals itself on many levels of his thought. On the lowest level, that of the physical world, this desire for unity is reflected in his theory of plastic nature. This 'plastic nature' is 'an Inferiour kind of Life or Soul'[122] that spans the gap between

God and matter, cause and effect. God works through this plastic nature, but since it may not carry out perfectly the divine will, it makes possible an explanation of causation without determination. When speaking of the union of matter and spirit on a metaphysical level, however, Cudworth abandons this sort of physical explanation and resorts to analogical and symbolic thought. The god Pan, whose lower parts were rough and goatish, but whose upper parts were human, is an effective representation of this second type of union: 'Pan therefore was not the mere Corporeal World Senseless and Inanimate, but the Deity as displaying it self therein, and pervading All things.'[123] Pan is symbolic of the ideal pattern of life in which mind and body are balanced, and it was to him that Socrates prayed that the external things of life might agree with a right internal disposition of mind. He is also identified with Christ, both man and God, and functions as a symbol of the union of body and spirit both in the physical sense and on the religious and moral plane.

This union Cudworth sees unambiguously as a good. With More, he believes that there are three types of body – the gross earthly, the airy, and the aetherial – which represent degrees of moral perfection, and spirits are always united to one of these.[124] Human souls are not themselves bodies, nor are they extended (as More believed) but they are always *in* bodies. Only the Deity is in both senses incorporeal.[125] These various types of body and soul make it impossible to think of 'body' and 'soul' in the literal sense as simple entities with fixed moral qualities. When occasionally Cudworth does endow them with such qualities their use is purely figurative and unconnected with the literal body or soul.

Opposition to the philosophy of More, Cudworth and their school came chiefly from the ranks of the Puritans and concentrates, predictably, on precisely those aspects of the Cambridge Platonists' philosophy that minimize the distinction between body and soul. Although Baxter himself, by opting for traducianism, risks the charge of making soul material, he still insists that their substance is 'materia metaphysica' as opposed to 'materia physica.'[126] He accuses Henry More of making spirits material and part of the compound animal. Baxter also takes exception, as one would expect, to More's belief in the pre-existence of souls (derived from Origen) and their infusion into the body. Finally, and significantly, he objects not only to the content of More's work but also to his rational method of inquiry and accuses More of 'presuming to enquire into unrevealed things.'[127]

We see here a conflict between older patterns of thought in which theological considerations are supreme and authority a dominant force and a newer cast of mind which, while still ostensibly 'Christian,' looks to a combination of empirical evidence and rational deduction for its inspiration. The first perpetuated the ancient dualism between body and soul, the inherent confusion over the division of attributes between them, and consequently over their role in sin. It also fostered a tradition of personifying these essentially abstract things as living and imaginable entities. In the second, science and rationalism combined to create an atmosphere in which strict dualism was untenable and in which the ambiguous nature of body and soul must be rethought in clear, consistent terms. None of this happened instantly, and there were thinkers, notably Descartes, whose attempts to unite body and soul had precisely the opposite effect. New and old patterns of thought continued to exist side by side for a long time, and in some of the 'old' writers, such as Baxter, knowledge of the new only led to a conscious rejection of methods which 'presume to inquire into unrevealed things.' But the general movement of the age is away from this stance to one that sees the old insistence on authority being coupled with, and often subordinated to, the scientific and rational spirit that was to prevail in the eighteenth century.

For literature, the most significant aspect of these varied accounts of body and soul remains the intense (and to us peculiar) interest that underlay them. They were not erudite exercises; they were matters germane to salvation or damnation, and through sermons and popular tracts they filtered down to every level of society. Consequently writers not only alluded to their content quite naturally but used the presuppositions about them figuratively and metaphorically as well. In the early part of the century they reinforced an already prevalent dualistic view of the universe and functioned as an analogy for that dualism. In addition to these general effects, they provided a fertile ground for the revival of a literary genre that had largely disappeared since the fifteenth century – the body and soul dialogue.

Part Two

Body and Soul
Dialogues

CHAPTER THREE

Body and Soul Dialogues in the Middle Ages

The body and soul dialogues in the Middle Ages cannot be dismissed merely as a bizarre outgrowth of the darker side of the medieval imagination nor as the logical development of earlier theological and literary forces. It is true that an historical development from ancient sources can be traced; it is also true that the dialogues have marked affinities with other medieval literary forms such as the dance of death, with other debates, and with the vision literature in general. But the unique force and popularity of the body and soul debate argues that it satisfied certain deep-seated needs fundamental to the age.

At the peak of its development in the early fourteenth century, the debate consisted of a series of bitter recriminations, cast in the form of a vision, between the body and soul of a dead man, and focused on their relative responsibility for the sin the individual had committed during his life. The vision framework, with its ultimately repentant witness to the debate, places the genre firmly in the tradition of medieval *exempla*. The sinning auditor must amend his life if he is to avoid the terrible fate of the damned man. However, the content of the debate itself is too complex to allow it to be reduced merely to a didactic, moralistic tale. Didactic elements are certainly present in the accusations soul hurls at body, which identify it with 'flesh' and charge it with every sensual evil. But with the body's reply the simplicity of this position is exposed. The body argues that (1) it cannot be responsible for sin because it is merely passive matter and (2) that even if it has rebelled against the soul, it is the soul's own fault for not having exercised stricter control over it. (The two arguments are really mutually exclusive, since the first presupposes a passive body, which the second implicitly denies, but comprehensiveness rather than consistency was a medieval priority!) Here we move beyond a simple moral dispute to one with philosophical and psychological implications. Where is the dividing line between body and soul, and what correspondence does the internal warfare between good and evil that we experience have to the physical and psychic reality of our being? This complex mixture of the moral and the philosophical touches on some of the deepest problems affecting the medieval consciousness. Finally, and more superficially, the debate provides a setting for indulging in the popular denigration of the joys of life in the face of imminent death, as the decaying corpse is reminded by the soul of the beauty and possessions that belong to it no more.[1] There is no resolution to these debates, only an imposed conclusion in which devils seize the soul and bundle it off to hell, shouting that the body will inevitably follow at the last judgment. Thus the issue of the relative responsibility for sin is never resolved as, indeed, it could not be, given the complex theological background to the dispute that has been outlined. And so, combined with the popular motifs associated with death, the moral and philosophical issues remained tantalizingly alive throughout the numerous reincarnations of the debate.

Although the debate satisfied a unique combination of needs in the Middle Ages, and its final form is the product of those needs and that period, its origins are almost certainly as ancient as the Coptic legend dealing with the separation of the soul from the body at the time of death. The good soul is coaxed out gently, while the evil soul is removed by demons with instruments of torture. The whole obviously depends on a concrete concept of the soul as part of the living person. It is not, however, so much in the philosophical implications of the Egyptian tradition as in the presentation of concrete details such as the presence of angels or demons at the deathbed that the connection with later body and soul literature is evident. The scene of the deathbed surrounded by demons has a very lengthy history in both art and literature, which we shall see continuing with surprisingly little change into the sixteenth and seventeenth centuries. In many medieval illustrations devils wait with angels to grapple for the departing soul of the dying man,[2] and in accounts of saints' deaths the whole hierarchy of heaven often surrounds the deathbed, although the purpose of these angels, to remove the soul of the dying man, is forgotten. The angels or demons who remove souls are also confused with the spirits who come to meet it after its separation, to lead it to heaven or hell. This belief in a 'perilous path' to heaven, beset with angels or demons, is found in both Cyril of Alexandria and Origen, and can be traced directly to the religion of ancient Egypt.[3]

Speculation regarding the separation of the soul from the body is found in Chrysostom's commentaries on Matthew, and the earlier fourth-century writings of Ephraem already contain a farewell of the soul to the body at the time of death.[4] The specific form of the later address of the soul to the body, the predecessor of the body and soul dialogue, seems to have developed from two main fourth-century sources, 'The Homily of Macarius,' and the 'Visio Pauli.'[5] The original version of the 'Homily' tells how Macarius, walking in the desert with two angels, comes upon a corpse that stinks badly. The angels explain that the bad odour comes from the sins of the soul, and they then go on to explain how the soul is separated from the body and to describe the tour of the universe.[6] A much later manuscript of this legend, dating from the eleventh or twelfth century, actually incorporates addresses from both a good soul and an evil one to their respective bodies.[7] As demons come to seize the soul, it laments and accuses its body of the evil it has done. While it hears these accusations, the body itself changes in appearance and becomes physically uglier. Then, in contrast, a good soul is separated from its body; it thanks the body for having endured suffering during life, and as it does so the body is transformed and becomes beautiful.

The 'Homily,' in this later version, links the address of the soul to the body with the hour of death and the separation of the two, thus reinforcing Louise Dudley's theory about its ancient Coptic origins. But not all body and soul debates are set at the time of death; the most popular medieval ones take place well after death has occurred and are set in a vision framework. These two elements have most likely been added to the form by the 'Visio Pauli.' The 'Visio,' based on the slender evidence of 2 Corinthians 12:2, is closely related to the Macarius legend in its fundamentals. It too includes a separation scene of soul and body, witnessed in this case by Paul, and a tour of the universe. But the elements which made a distinctive contribution to the body and soul literature were the vision form itself and Paul's descent to hell and his plea for the weekly release of the souls there. It is assumed that when, in response to Paul's plea, God gives the souls of the damned a weekly respite from their torments from Saturday evening until Sunday night, they will go back to their bodies to reproach them for the evil they did when living. This becomes an important influence on the time and setting of the dialogues. Thus the two sources both contribute some of the elements to the addresses and dialogues and help to explain certain discrepancies among them.[8]

The soul's complaint to the body, with its emphasis on the consequences of an evil life and the terrors death holds for the damned, provided ideal material for sermons and homilies. Indeed, it is in just such homilies that most of the early addresses of the soul to the body, including the later version of the legend of Macarius cited above, are to be found.[9] But as early as the tenth century we also have a verse address of the soul to the body existing independently of any such context, and furthermore, this poem survives in two manuscript versions.[10] It is not cast in the form of a vision, but it does show affinities with the 'Visio Pauli' in that the time of the address is not the hour of death, but during a weekly return of the soul to the body. 'The spirit shall come / sad in spirit, / always after seven nights, / the soul to find / the body ...' (ll 17–21). The soul reproaches the body (also called 'flesh') for its misdeeds, taunts it with its love of possessions, and looks ahead to the last judgment when both will be damned forever. After the accusations of the evil soul, we have the rather self-satisfied thanks of a good soul to its body. 'But we ourselves may / there at the judgement / take pride in our deeds, / what earnings / ours were' (ll 321–5).

The 'Irish Homily,' probably two centuries later in origin,[11] is not in the form of a vision, but the setting of the whole is apparently that of the first episode of the 'Visio Pauli.' The separation of soul and body and the reference in the introduction to the climb of the soul to the seventh heaven presumably both come from the same source. In this work it is the devils that come to remove the soul from the body with instruments of torture that speak first. They taunt the soul as it tries vainly to escape from the body by the mouth, nose, eyes, and ears. Finally it comes out through the crown of the head and alights on it outside. The influence of Origen is surely present in its queries about the bright garment of air it used to possess, in contrast to the one of perturbed air it now finds enclosing it. In answer, the devils smite the soul and tell it that this is 'the garment of death and sin,' which now becomes a purely figurative thing that has been worn by Adam, Cain, Judas, and others. The demons draw the body's attention to its abysmal, newly deserted dwelling place, but only after they force it back from a brief ascent towards heaven does the soul return to reproach its body. Following this, as in the Old English address, we witness the separation of a good soul from its body.

The double separation or double address has its origins in the Macarius legend. As homiletical material it was obviously useful, but as drama the congratulatory stance of the blessed soul left something to be desired, and in later medieval body and soul literature this disappears, leaving only the episode of the damned soul and body. This change roughly coincides with and may even be partly linked to another more important one – the transformation of the address into a dialogue. In 'The Irish Homily,' the body replies to the soul, but this reply, with the exception of one element noted below, is primarily abusive rather than argumentative. In other twelfth-century body and soul literature, however, we find that the body's reply is fully developed into a detailed argument for its own innocence. The address has become a debate. The reasons for this change are unclear, and most critics take refuge in suggesting lost links between the address and dialogue form and making general statements that attribute the development to 'the literary pressures of the twelfth century.'[12]

The popularity of the dialogue as a literary form in the Middle Ages is undisputed. Classical influences came from both the few Platonic dialogues known and from fables in which animals and even inanimate objects debate. These fables themselves have strong ethical and didactic elements, and the link between the dialogue form as manifested here and in the body and soul literature can be readily discerned.[13] The debate of the stomach and limbs by Menenius Agrippa is a pattern for the medieval 'Dialogus membrorum,' which, in turn, is incorporated into the thirteenth-century Italian body and soul dialogue of Bonvesin da Riva,[14] and finds its most famous expression in Shakespeare's *Coriolanus* (I.i. 96–155). Scholastic debate and rhetoric also influenced the form of medieval body and soul literature, and one can see some of the dialogues moving away from a primarily didactic stance to incorporate elements of philosophical dispute. In addition to classical and scholastic influences, the debate is also linked to the developing medieval drama. We know that dialogues, whether originally written for that purpose or not, were performed on the stage (Robert Grosseteste, the thirteenth-century Bishop of Lincoln, has left written evidence of the performance of debates between summer and winter as dramas),[15] and in some cases it is difficult to know whether an individual debate belongs to a dramatic or dialogue genre. As well as dialogues performed as dramas, there are sections of dramas that have an obvious affinity with other pieces belonging to the dialogue genre – most notably the speech of the soul to the body in 'The Castle of Perseverance.'

None of these general observations, unfortunately, brings us any closer to a specific historical description of the development of the address of the soul into a dialogue between soul and body. All we know for certain is that in the Latin 'Nuper huiuscemodi visionem somnii,' most likely the prototype of later debates in Latin and the vernacular,[16] the change has already taken place. There is only one speech each by soul and body in this work, unlike 'Saint Bernard's Vision,'[17] 'Als I Lay in a Winteris Nyt,'[18] and other later debates in which they speak several times. Because of this, as well as the probable date of the poem, it seems reasonable to assume that it represents an early stage in the transition from address to dialogue.[19] The poem that most closely resembles it is the French 'Un samedi par nuit.'[20] Here as well there is only one speech each by body and soul; in both the debate takes place on a Saturday night, as it presumably does in the 'Address,' and the soul has the form of a child. In addition to these similarities, specific figures of speech are common to both. The greed of the body, for example, is like the unquenched thirst of a dropsical man. It seems clear that the French poet must have based his work on the twelfth-century debate, and if 'Saint Bernard's Vision,' though less closely linked, is also based on 'Nuper huiuscemodi visionem somnii,' the common source explains similarities between the 'Visio' and 'Un samedi par nuit' more satisfactorily than if one of these latter works is derived from the other.[21]

It was 'Saint Bernard's Vision' that had the greatest effect on the subsequent debate literature, and its influence is particularly strong in the various versions of the best-known English debate, 'Als I Lay in a Winteris Nyt.' By the time of the writing of this poem the vision framework has become standard, and even the one English poem that does not make use of it, 'In a thestri stude,'[22] uses another distancing device – that of having the debate between the body, which is lying on a bier in a church, and its soul overheard by the author, who is standing in the vestry. The use of this sort of framework enables the author, through the auditor, to comment on the debate, and means that neither homiletical teaching nor drama need be sacrificed to the other.

The time at which the debate takes place is much less uniform than the vision setting. Unlike the earlier 'Address,' in 'Saint Bernard's Vision' the weekly return on Saturday night is no longer specifically indicated, and the dispute has been divorced from actual separation scenes as well. Here, despite the fact that the soul is described as 'Neewly departed,' it must already have been to hell since the body asks it to describe the torments of that place. ('Si tu apud inferes anima fuisti, / dic mihe, te deprecor, ibi quid vidisti?' ll 232–3.) 'In a thestri stude,' in which the corpse is lying on a bier, obviously takes place between the time of death and burial, but in others the body is already beginning to decay ('Fro the cometh a wikked wef'), the wife of the deceased has stopped mourning, and his heirs are fighting over the estate. One can only conclude that as the arguments of the debate developed and became more sophisticated, so the original designation of the time and setting of the debate became vaguer and less important.

Interesting as are the externals of the debates, their sources, and derivations, they are less relevant to this book than their content and the assumptions about body and soul underlying it. In the early body and soul literature, it is the emphasis on death, its physical and mental torments, and the consequent vanity of earthly possessions and pleasures that is dominant. This is a ubiquitous medieval concern, and the passages in the poems can be paralleled by those in countless sermons and homilies:

> Thou wert in food luxurious
> and sated with wine;
> in splendour thou wert proud
> and I was thirsty for
> God's body ...
>
> ...
>
> Thou mayst not now take thee
> the red ornaments,
> nor gold nor silver,
> nor any of thy goods,
> nor thy bridal crown,
> nor thy dwelling,
> nor any of the goods
> which thou before didst own;
> but here shall remain
> the naked bones
> slit with thy sins.[23]

In later works, such as 'Saint Bernard's Vision,' these sentiments are formalized in *ubi sunt* and *quid valent* passages:

> Quid valent palatia, pulchria vel quid aedes?
> vix nunc tuus tumulus septem capit pedes.   (ll 21–2)

Once the address has developed into a dialogue, however, the chief interest shifts from these homiletical themes to the moral and philosophical question of the relative responsibility of body and soul for sin.

The germ of the idea thus developed is not specifically Christian. The parable in the Talmud of the blind man and the lame, with its specific application to body and soul, shows how ancient is the notion of their differing function but shared responsibility. The original of this parable (which we have encountered in abbreviated form in a seventeenth-century sermon by Thomas Adams)[24] tells the story of a prince who sets a blind man and a lame to guard the precious fruits that grow in his garden. The fruit will, presumably, be safe from its guardians since the blind man cannot see it and the lame man cannot climb up to pick it. But the lame man climbs up to the branches on the back of the blind, and both enjoy the spoils. Thus it is with the body and the soul. When accused, the soul says that the body is guilty. Scarcely had the latter left it when it flew, pure, like a bird through the air. The body, for its part, says the soul alone is guilty. Of itself it can do nothing; it was barely free of the soul when it lay motionless on the earth. But God puts the soul back into its body and says, 'See, you have recovered; now be accountable.'[25]

While the Talmud parable emphasizes mutual guilt, another ancient source, a fragment by Plutarch summarizing the views of Democritus and Theophrastus, attempts to establish relative guilt.[26] According to Democritus, the guilt is the soul's since it has not known how to direct the body, which is only its tool or instrument. But Theophrastus, on the contrary, accuses the body; it is because of its emotions of anger, fear, desire, and jealousy that the soul has suffered greatly during life.

Christianity, with its emphasis on the reunion of body and soul at the Resurrection, preferred the Talmud's resolution that emphasized mutual responsibility rather than the open-ended dispute of Plutarch's account. But the unresolved nature of Plutarch's arguments fitted well with the established medieval sense of the dichotomy between body and soul: 'þe saule and þe lycome / selde he beaþ isome.'[27] John Lydgate's translation of Guillaume de Deguileville's *Pilgrimage of the Life of Man*[28] also assumes an inherent enmity between body and soul. Deguileville holds that the body itself is contaminated by the transmission of original sin (understood in a very literal way) and of its own accord can do nothing good. Consequently, there is continual warfare between the God-given element, the soul, and the earthly element, the body:

> ffor, (as I shal to the devyse),
> Atwyxë yow (yt ys no faylle)
> Ther ys werre & strong bataylle,
> And contynuelly ther shal be.   (ll 9510–13)

Later in the poem, the contrary motions of body and soul are symbolized by two wheels revolving in opposite directions, the outer (the body) moving towards the west and the inner (the soul) towards the east (ll 12271–303). The ubiquitous image of the soul imprisoned in the body as a bird in a cage reflects the same idea. This sense of dichotomy between body and soul, coupled with the inherited uncertainties about the function and attributes of each, means that while the ultimate verdict of the debates (made concrete by the appearance of punitive devils) is one of mutual guilt, within this framework the question of relative culpability is discussed without any resolution.

The shared fate of body and soul is certainly a basic assumption of the Old English 'Address.' In its desperation, the soul anticipates the Last Day and questions, 'But what shall we two do? / Then shall we two together / afterwards suffer / such miseries / as thou preparedst here for us before' (ll 198–202). Since the body does not reply, the soul has it all its own way as far as relative guilt goes. It taunts the body about its present state, and says it would have been better off to have been created a bird or a fish or a brute animal – even a worm – than a man to receive baptism and answer for sins. This remarkable sentiment appears again in the 'Irish Homily,' but here it is spoken by the body, which insists that it would have been as free from torture and suffering as earth and trees if it had not taken the soul into union with it. Thus the soul's assertion in the Old English poem that the body would have been better off if it had been created as a lower form of being is here taken up by the body, which laments that this is not the case, and points out that it is precisely its union with the soul that has made the difference!

In the debates proper, such as 'Saint Bernard's Vision,' 'Un samedi par nuit,' and 'Als I Lay,' the arguments between body and soul are fully developed in a more sophisticated way. Of these, the 'Vision' was not only the most influential but the most scholastic in tone, with the arguments for and against stated more concisely than in later, vernacular debates. The whole is presented in two different versions, either as the vision of one Philibert (also Filbert or Fulbert), a Frenchman of good family now living as a hermit, or directly, as the vision of the author. In the silence of a winter's night, he sees a newly departed spirit standing over its body and bewailing its sins. It derides the body, reminds it of its former wealth and position, and contrasts this with its present miserable state. The soul complains that the body did not allow it a single good thing when alive. Now there is no hope of pardon; suffering is inevitable. The body is bereft not only of its physical possessions but of friends as well. His wife no longer sorrows; his heirs will certainly not lament. When the soul stops speaking, the body raises itself in its bier with groans and denies the justness of the accusations brought against it. The body may commit sinful actions, but the guilt is really the soul's. It was created good and noble, given reason and made mistress over the body. The world and the devil have made a compact and implicated the flesh. Therefore, if the soul does not repress it, it will sin. If the body has dominated the soul, it is not its own fault; the soul should have subdued it by force. Body without soul does nothing; it merely executes the soul's commands. Therefore the guilt must rest with the soul.

In its reply, the soul admits that much of what the body has said is true, but it insists that the body was intractable and by its sensual appetites resisted its influence. At length the body admits that both are guilty, but not equally. Of him to whom much is given, much is expected ('cui major gratia virtutum donatur, / ab eo vult ratio quod plus exigatur,' ll 193–4). It also repeats its previous argument, that it can do nothing without the soul:

> Dic mihi, si noveris, argumento claro,
> exeunte spiritu a carne quid sit caro?
> movetne se postea cito, sive raro?   (ll 204–6)

Then follows a passage, unrelated to the rest of the debate, in which the body vindicates God of any responsibility for sin. The Lord tried to save the soul and cannot be blamed for its damnation. After this the body asks the soul, if it has been in hell, to tell it of that place, whether there is any hope for those who enter and whether earthly riches and position can influence the powers ruling there. The soul assures the body that there is no hope; the more exalted a person's station on earth, the heavier is his guilt and punishment if he should sin. The debate is concluded by the appearance of two devils, blacker than pitch, who bind and torture the soul and drag it off to hell. The soul weeps and calls on Jesus, but to no avail. Philibert (or the author) wakes from the vision terrified and cries to God to be preserved. He renounces the world and gives himself up to the service of Christ. In a few versions a lament on the state of the world follows as well, sometimes without a break to indicate that it is not part of the debate proper.

The body, in 'Saint Bernard's Vision,' has put forward two chief lines of argument in its defence against the soul's accusations that it has been unruly, has got the upper hand of it, and has enticed it by worldly allurements to do evil. The first, while not usually stated as a philosophical principle, is based on the idea that the body is merely the instrument of the soul and simply executes the latter's commands (in Aristotelian terms) or that it is passive matter (in Platonic terms). We have seen that Christian sanction for this view can be found in the writings of Augustine, although he is not consistent on this point. In a body and soul dialogue contained in Guillaume de Deguileville's *Pylgremage of the Sowle*,[29] the body claims that the soul was active as fire while it remained passive as wood. Thus the soul is perceived as both the initiator of action and the actor, while the body is merely the passive sufferer. When this point of view is rigidly adhered to, it does indeed seem that the body has the better of the argument. But the body, presented as a sentient, concrete being, is in a weak position to sustain this argument, and when the soul accuses it of having been seduced by the world's vanities it does not deny the charge, which would be absurd if it were strictly passive matter. Thus in the same speech referred to above in which body claims it was as passive as wood, we find the following:

> Al that I have desyred was but only of naturell inclination
> to the countre which I come of, that was this wretchid erthe.

Thus 'body' as a dramatic persona perpetuates the confusion about the attributes of 'body' as the physical part of man.

Even if it concedes that it can desire and therefore tempt the soul, the body has a second line of defence based on the argument for proper subordination. Though it may have lured the soul with earthly vanities, the fault must still lie with the soul who, as the superior partner, should not have been weak enough to have been deflected from what it knew to be right. The body accepts the need for proper subordination but insists that once it has been overthrown responsibility must rest with the higher element, which ought to have imposed its authority more effectively, rather than with the lower element that has rebelled. In this second context, where sense and desire are attributes of the soul, the real issue in the debate is whether chief responsibility rests with the external actor who initiates and executes the deed (the body), or the agent that wills and consents to it (the soul). In the absence of any philosophical solution, the devils come as a dramatic one.

A close look at several surviving versions of this dialogue suggests that the struggle between the literal body and soul is reinforced by their identification with the figurative flesh and spirit. For example, in the Cambridge manuscript line 16 reads, 'Corporis cum gemitu sic plangit excessus.' The corresponding line in the text printed by Thomas Wright reads, 'Qui carnis cum gemitu sic plangit excessus.' In many of the vernacular versions as well the terms are interchangeable. The soul in vernacular versions as well the terms are interchangeable. The soul in the Vernon manuscript of 'Als I Lay in a Winteris Nyt,' addresses the body as 'fikele flesch,' yet later in the same poem uses the term 'bodi.' But while body and soul take on these associated negative and positive connotations, they are never in any danger of being identified solely with flesh and spirit; they are also real parts of man's being, as the sophistication and strength of the body's case proves.[30]

Most of the vernacular poems follow the main arguments of the 'Vision' as they have been presented, although there are differences of detail. In 'Als I Lay on a Winteris Nyt,' the language is more colloquial and the tone ruder, and there are minor variations in content as well. For example, while in 'Saint Bernard's Vision,' as in the Old English 'Address,' it is the soul that wishes it had been a beast, here (as in the 'Irish Homily') it is the body that laments it was ever made a human creature:

> I scholde have ben dumb as a schep, or as a nouwe, or as a
> suyn,
> That et and drank and lay and slep, slayn and passid al his
> pin;
> Nevere of catel he ne kep, ne wyste wat was water ne wyn;
> No leyn in helle that is so dep; nevere ne wist I of al that was
> tin.[31]

Probably the most significant addition to 'Als I Lay' is the incorporation of the classical horse and rider analogy to illustrate the need for proper subordination between body and soul:

> To teche ʒwere thouʒ me bi-tauʒt, ac ʒwan thouʒ thoʒ test of
> the qued,
> With thi teth the bridel thouʒ lauʒt, thouʒ dist al that I the
> forbed.[32]

Here the horses are not faculties of the soul as they are in the *Phaedrus* myth, but of the body. The importance of this cannot be missed; the conflict that in Plato was confined to various parts of the soul has here been transferred to that between soul and body.[33]

Despite the 'expansion' of the role of body in this particular instance, the same dialogue, in other passages, emphasizes the passivity of the body to a greater extent than the 'Vision.' In response to the soul's accusation that the body made it its thrall, the body responds that

> Ondi nevere on live nou3t, I ne rafte ne I ne stal,
> That furst of the ne kam the thou3t, abyyt that aby3e schal!
>
> (p 336)

This line is argued even more strongly in 'Un samedi par nuit,' where the body insists it is wholly the corrupt soul that was covetous, that desired costly clothes and ornaments. The body merely satisfied these desires:

> Tu le mal enginnas, e puis le me nuncias;
> Tu pensas e je l'fis, cume dolenz 3 entif.[34]

The importance of assigning responsibility for action and hence for sin is shown in other related debates, notably those between the heart and the eye, which fundamentally deal with the same question.[35] Here eye is analogous to body, the external part that desires, and heart to soul, the internal that can choose or refuse. In the well-known Latin heart and eye debate, 'Disputatio inter Cor et Oculum,'[36] Reason, who arbitrates the dispute, draws a philosophical distinction between the cause and occasion of sin, thus linking it closely with the sophisticated arguments of 'Saint Bernard's Vision,'[37] but in a much shorter Latin prose version of the debate only the mutual guilt of the two is acknowledged, and Reason assigns appropriate penance to both heart and eye. An English debate found in the Commonplace Book compiled by Johannis de Grimestone in 1372[38] is similar to the Latin prose text. As Carleton Brown concludes, 'The purpose of the poem is literary and philosophical, while that of the prose text [and the English debate are] definitely homiletical.'[39]

In addition to these dialogues between body and soul and the related heart and eye debates, there is another group of disputes that are usually linked with them – those between flesh and spirit. That they are linked is indisputable, but they should not be seen as identical, as they so often are. The body and soul dialogues proper take place between the actual components making up man, and their balanced dialectic depends on the subtle association between these literal components and the purely figurative flesh and spirit. Those dialogues that are simply between flesh and spirit may demonstrate the extent to which the body/soul dichotomy was seen as symbolic of the warring impulses within man, but they lack the depth and interest of the genuine body and soul dialogues. Here there is no ambiguity and no connection with man's physiological and psychological make-up; the conflict is between two abstract concepts. Because this struggle (in the spirit of Galatians 5:17) is their chief concern rather than sin and damnation, they usually take place during life, not at or after death.

Two Latin examples of this type of debate, both printed by Walther, are fairly typical. In the 'Altercacio Carnis et Spiritus,'[40] the spirit attacks the physical joys of life and the flesh defends them. The spirit warns of sorrow to follow if the fleeting pleasures of this life are pursued; the flesh replies that God himself created flowers and fruit, birds and animals for man to have dominion over and to enjoy. 'To reject the gift is to spurn the giver.' Spirit answers that created things are for the survival of mankind, not for indulgence. There is a Pauline note in its warning that the body must abjure love (sex) or be damned in hell. Later, when flesh insists that since God has created two sexes this sort of enjoyment must be lawful, the spirit partially relents and says that for those whom no inner vow of chastity binds, intercourse in secret may be lawful for the continuance of the race! The debate is concluded by the person of Racio, who mediates the dispute and decides, predictably, in favour of spirit:

> Spiritui subiaceat,
> motus prauos coherceat
> metu tremende iudicis,
> ut dolor cordis supplicis
> iram refrenet iudicis.

The 'Debate between Carnal and Spiritual Man'[41] is very similar in content. Carnal man wants to pluck the 'great flower of the world,' which will bring honour and praise. He concludes:

> Est nihil in uita, tibi dico, dulcius ista
> Sedulo quam mundi letis successibus uti
> Viribus et totis carnis succurrere uotis.　　　　(ll 14–16)

But the spiritual man replies:

> Est nihil in uita, tibi dico, stultius ista
> Sedulo quam mundi letis successibus uti
> Omnibus atque modis carnis succerrere uotis.　　　(ll 37–9)

The opposing points of view are set off with a neat antithesis that allows no room for doubt about the outcome. Nevertheless, these platitudinous flesh and spirit dialogues have their seventeenth-century descendants just as the body and soul dialogues do.

The medieval body and soul dialogues were bound up with the preoccupations of an age obsessed by death and viewing life primarily as a preparation for it; they had little place in the sixteenth century, when the chief energies were secular and life-directed. What any study of the literature and theology of the Renaissance makes plain, however, is that both the basic assumptions fundamental to the debate – an espousal of dualism coupled with an uncertainty about exactly what attributes belonged to soul and what to body – and the literary form of the dialogue or dispute continued without interruption throughout the sixteenth and into the seventeenth centuries. The general theological and philosophical beliefs about body and soul in the Renaissance have already been examined; it remains to show that more specific echoes of both the content and form of the medieval dialogues also persist in the period.

CHAPTER FOUR

Survivals of Body and Soul Literature in the English Renaissance

While the body and soul dialogue as a distinct literary form disappeared with the end of the Middle Ages, its content did not. It retreated, rather, to the sermons and homilies from which it first sprang, where it is to be found fragmented but still recognizable. Meanwhile, the dialogue form and the vision framework both flourished, displaying a new versatility in meeting the needs of the age.

Continuity of Content

The content of the body and soul literature did not reach the Renaissance exclusively via the Middle Ages but also, as a result of the humanist interest in translating ancient authors, more directly from the ancient sources that influenced the development of the medieval form in the first place. The philosophical views of Nemesius on body and soul, which were disseminated in the seventeenth century by the translation of George Wither,[1] were one such influence. Similarly, an anonymous translation of John Chrysostom's *Exposition upon the Epistle to the Ephesians* in 1581 shows that some of the original material that 'fed' the medieval debates was now available to a much wider audience than those who could read Greek. Here we find not only the classical horse and rider analogy applied to the relationship between body and soul[2] but also the basic content of the body and soul dialogues, a discussion of their relative responsibility for sin (with chief blame, in this case, assigned to the soul) in abbreviated form. A separation scene between body and soul is preserved by George Gascoigne in a 1576 translation of an anonymous treatise that he entitles 'The Droomme of Doomesday.' After a description of three of the pains that the wicked suffer at their death, we find the following climactic account of the fourth: 'The fourth payne is when the soule (being yet in the bodye) doeth see the wicked spirites readye to receyue it. Wherein the dread is such and so vnspeakable payne, that the myserable soule, (although it be now parted from the body,) doeth runne about as long as it may, to redeeme the tyme of hir captiuitie before shee forsake the body.'³

Translations from ancient sources were, of course, still secondary as an influence to the survivals of the medieval period. As late as 1519 we find a 'Complaynt of the Soule' printed by Wynken de Worde, containing a detailed picture of a deathbed scene in which angels and devils struggle for the soul that appears to have just emerged from the crown of the head, as it does in the 'Irish Homily' (see reproduction included in this book). In this particular case, the angel in the top right-hand corner of the illustration seems to have the soul firmly in its grasp, but the devils dancing around the bed and shouting such imprecations as 'Heu infame' and 'Spes nobis nulla' are a lively reminder of other possibilities! The content of the 'complaint' is more a general lament for a sinful and ill-spent life than it is a medieval address of the soul to the body, and consists largely of the soul's chastisement of the whole man. When the issue of the relative responsibility of body and soul for sin does arise, it is the soul that is found guilty while the body is exonerated, although it must share in the punishment.⁴

Such specific examples of entire works influenced by the dramatic and pictorial elements in medieval body and soul literature do not exist later in the sixteenth century, but related literary forms such as the 'Dance of Death' do have a continuous history⁵ and many of the donnés of the body and soul dialogues, such as the complicity of the two in sin, are commonplace illustrations in sermons and devotional tracts. We find, for example, that the incorporation of a flesh/soul conflict into a most unlikely sermon text was not unique to Henry Smith⁶ but can be found considerably prior to him in 'A Sommon to repentance' (1584): 'The flesh is stout and sturdie, the soule is faint and feble ... The flesh is affected to all kinds of iniquities, and thereby the soule is dangerously wounded with transgression so that both body and soule is become most monstrous in the eies of the Lorde our God ...'⁷ But like most works that equate body with flesh (and unlike the medieval debates or the essentially medieval 'Lamentation' quoted above) this passage betrays a certain simplicity of thought, a glib recital of supposedly self-evident truths in which everything is blamed on body/flesh. The sentiments have neither the weight of original thought nor felt experience behind them.

It is precisely this weight of felt experience that one does feel behind the many sermons, tracts, and miscellaneous writings on sin and death that began to appear in the early seventeenth century. Naturally, the extent to which this is present varies from writer to writer; there is a certain amount of pose in all widespread movements in both literature and religion, and doubtless the early seventeenth-century preoccupation with sin and death was no exception. But there is a certain amount of sincerity as well in such movements, and the transition from Byrd's 'This Sweet and Merry Month of May' to Wilbye's 'Draw on Sweet Night' reflected something deeper than a mere change in musical and literary taste. 'Practice, and endeuor, / To liue well, so to die wel, and liue euer,' exhorts John Hagthorpe in 1622.[8] We are here confronted with an attitude of mind that has more in common with the Middle Ages than with the sixteenth century and is convincingly illustrated by the sheer quantity of printed material dealing with death and sinful man's preparation for it – a quantity unparalleled in any other period.[9] This concern with mortality was not limited to those of a single religious persuasion (the 1603 'Dialogue of Dying Wel,' written first in Italian and published in Antwerp, for example, is Catholic), but the Puritan emphasis on the seriousness of the Fall and of original sin, with its consequently exaggerated view of the peril of eternal damnation, was particularly conducive to an attitude of mind that saw life merely as a preparation for a future life. The heated controversy that was waged in the seventeenth century over the means by which original sin is transmitted is just one indication of the new importance that the old issues of the origin and effects of sin took on. In the midst of this resurrection of ancient theological concerns linked to the debates we also find evidence of the revival of specific elements in them, such as the Macarius legend separation scenes, and the issue of the relative responsibility of body and soul for sin, which is fundamental to their content.

The legend of Macarius, believed to be the original source of the medieval body and soul dialogues, reappears in both J. Guillemand's 'A Combat betwixt Man and Death,' and Edmund Porter's *God Incarnate*, published as late as 1655.[10] The French treatise summarizes the separation scene in very explicit terms: 'There is a great Mistery, sith hee [Macarius], accomplished in soules going out of the bodies; for if they bee guilty of sinne, troopes of divells and bad angells flocking about them, seaze vpon those soules, as their slaves, and carry them away &c. But if they bee in good estate, the companies of good Angells carrying them to a better life, present them vnto the Lord ...'[11]

More general descriptions of separation scenes, not specifically attributed to the Macarius legend, in which devils appear to struggle for the soul, are quite common. The best-known occurs in Donne's 'Second Anniversarie,' where Satan's Sergeants crowd around the dying man, thrusting for legacies.[12] In the Catholic 'A Dialogue of Dying Wel,' after an address to the skull of a dead man in the *ubi sunt* tradition, one finds a less famous but more extended description of the same thing. The 'synful soul,' forsaken by the body she loved dearly, attempts to comfort herself but is only confronted by her sins and surrounded by devils.[13] There is a recapitulation of most of the original setting of the soul's address to the body, coupled with an acknowledgment of the soul's loathing for the body, but the address itself with its specific acccusations of sin is lacking.

Even this last element is supplied in a truly remarkable work entitled *The Soules Progresse to the Celestiall Canaan, or Heavenly Jervsalem*, by John Welles of Beccles.[14] Welles' cluster of preoccupations is revealed on the title-page, where he claims to deal with the 'divine Essence ... of God ... the creation, fall, state, death and misery of an unregenerated man, both in this life and in the world to come.' The literal nature of his imagination and theological understanding is illustrated in his description of the wicked Serpent waiting at our heel for us in our death throes because 'the heele ... is the extreme part of our body, and the last terme of our life ...' (p 46). Despite (or perhaps because of) this, his deathbed scene is unrivalled since the Middle Ages. First come the devils to fetch the soul, which then 'feeles the body begin by degrees to dye, and ready, like a ruinous house, to fall upon her head'; yet she is afraid to come forth from the body 'because of those hell-hounds which wait for her comming' (pp 111–12). At this point the soul, seeing all her pleasures gone, addresses herself to those members of the body that in the past delighted her – the eyes, the ears, the feet, the hands. None can help or give her pleasure now. The conventional motifs of *ubi sunt* and *contemptus mundi* are invoked, and the soul repents her misspent life, wishing she could begin it again. Then the soul addresses the body as a whole and reviles it, yet acknowledges a mutual responsibility that is not usually present in the medieval address: 'But, O corrupt carkasse, and stinking carion, how hath the divell deluded us? and how have wee served and deceived each other, and pulled swift damnation upon us both!' (pp 114–15). The familiar plaint that the soul is more miserable than a beast that perishes follows, and finally the soul curses its very union with the body.[15] When the soul finally comes forth, trembling, it is seized by the fiends 'who carry her with violence *terrenti simili* to the bottomlesse lake, that burneth with fire and brimstone, where shee is kept as a prisoner in torment, till the generall judgement of the last great day' (p 115). At that time the soul will greet the flesh with even greater imprecations than before, and both will be punished, 'that as they sinned together, so they may be tormented together eternally' (p 116).

The motifs of *ubi sunt* and *contemptus mundi*, the deathbed scene with the ever-present devils, the address to the members, the address to the soul, and the acknowledgment of the unhappiness of the body/soul partnership and their mutual responsibility for damnation combine to make this a most comprehensive seventeenth-century repository of medieval body and soul literature. Significantly, it appears not on its own but as part of a long treatise whose chief purpose is theological and instructive. From the whole, one discovers that Welles took a very serious view of the Fall and original sin, emphasizing the degeneracy of the will and appetite.[16] Other less spectacular survivals of the medieval dialogues show that this is not accidental; it was precisely those 'Puritan' elements in the seventeenth century that emphasized man's depravity that also found the medieval material most congenial.[17]

While there are few seventeenth-century works, apart from the dialogues proper, that contain as much of both the framework and content of the medieval literature as that by John Welles, it is not difficult to find variations on the content alone in many treatises and devotional writings. William Bates' chilling rhetoric describing the recriminations of soul and body at the last day, which is theologically more precise than anything in Welles' treatise, has already been cited.[18]

Even more specifically medieval in content is the body and soul conflict described in a sermon by William Foster. While its setting, unusually, is divorced from the immediate threats of death and hell, in most other respects it could be a paraphrase of the arguments of a medieval dialogue:

I know there is a great dispute betwixt the bodie and soule, each endeuoring to put off the enormitie of sinning to the other. The bodie pleads for itselfe; that that is but *inanimis truncus*, a dead and senslesse trunke, voyd of all action and motion, and so could not sinne, nor exercise any operation, if the soule did not actuate and enforce it. The soule, that pleads for it selfe, that that is *purus &*

simplex spiritus, a pure and simple spirit, voyd of all organs, without eyes to behold vanitie, without hands to commit folly, without feet to follow enormitie, and if the bodie did not detaine it as prisoner, it would mount aloft, to take vp residence in the place of spirits, and therefore the fault of sinning must needs rest on the bodie. But the verie truth is, that neither the bodie sinnes without the soule, nor the soule without the bodie ...[19]

Then follows, predictably, a retelling of the parable of the blind man and the lame.

Here we have manifested most of the theological characteristics of the relationship between body and soul since the Fall discussed in Chapter 2 – the differentiated role but shared culpability for sin – cast in a form very close to that of the medieval disputes. Yet there is no sense that Foster is merely resurrecting an archaic literary form and an outmoded argument. All the evidence suggests that he felt both form and argument to be wholly compatible with the theology of the age and the expectations of his audience.

In summary, it is clear that the original legends (such as that of Macarius) that fostered the medieval dialogues and the content of those dialogues came into the seventeenth century both directly from the writings of the early Church Fathers, often newly translated, and also through survivals of the medieval tradition. They happened to be particularly compatible with certain elements of religious thought in the period and took root anew in theological writings. This compatibility extended to their imaginative elements as well. The bodies and souls in these seventeenth-century treatises are not mere theological abstractions; although they lack the concrete setting of those in the debates proper, they are very much real dramatic persons, each with a voice and a distinctive line of argument. In John Welles' treatise this personification is emphasized by the attribution of sex to the soul, which is referred to as 'she' throughout. This tendency to dramatize and make concrete the conflict between essentially abstract entities is a well-known Puritan characteristic, of which *Pilgrim's Progress* is merely the most famous example. Thus the dispute between body and soul had an explicable place in the imagination and thought of the early seventeenth century. The transformations that took place in this conflict as it was once again cast in the literary form of a dialogue can, however, only be understood in the context of the development of the dialogue form itself during the sixteenth and seventeenth centuries.

The Dialogue Form in the English Renaissance

The humanist influence of such writers as Sir Thomas More in the early part of the sixteenth century led to the production of dialogues that at least attempted to discuss important issues with some degree of objectivity and sophistication. But very few writers were capable of mastering the subtlety of the form as More practised it. Discussion quickly deteriorated into polemical argument, and general questions were ignored in favour of specific issues.

The largest single category of dialogue written after 1534 deals with religious matters. These dialogues are of two main types – those designed to instruct and those written to argue a controversial point.[20] Those of instruction are primarily didactic in purpose, but those of controversy often appear to have had a literary purpose as well.

The didactic, instructive dialogues allow little room for moderation or charity. In 'A Dialogve, or Familiar Talke betwene Two Neighbours ... ,' subtitled 'A Talke Betwene Olyuer a Professour of the Gospell, and Nicholas Noseled in the Blynde Superstitions' and printed in 1554, Nicholas is, naturally, no match for Oliver, who recites all the conventional arguments for consubstantiation and concludes with this condescending remark: 'Alas it is pitie to se [sic] the plain and simple people, thus deluded and brought to suche a miserable case, that they embrace lyes, in stede of truth, and errour and superstition, in place of true godlynes, and Christian religion.'[21]

Other works, such as 'A Short Dialogve, wherein is proved, that no man can be saved without good workes,'[22] while still tending to instruction and conversion, gives a more genuine dispute to the participants and shows a better literary style. This 'Short Dialogve' takes place between a Gallant, a Scholler of Oxford, and a Church-Papist and, contrary to what one might assume from its title, is not a Catholic treatise defending works, but a Protestant exposition of the need for works to complete faith. Not only is the content thus more sophisticated than many such dialogues,[23] but the liveliness of the presentation is such that at one point the Gallant threatens to box the Scholar on the ear and take his coat to see whether he will resist or maintain a scriptural calm!

In these dialogues cited so far, the participants have been either genuine people, such as the neighbours Nicholas and Oliver, or at least well-dramatized representative types, such as the Oxford Scholar and the Gallant. This, however, is not usually the case, particularly in the seventeenth century. Very often the predetermined outcome of the debate is revealed through the very names of the disputants themselves, who never diverge from the narrow opinions of the types they portray. These characters do not emerge as individuals at all, but remain cloaked behind such tag names as 'Orthodoxus,' 'Conformist,' and 'Lucretius.' The literary pretensions of the author fail as well at this point. While the Greek names of some of the disputants (Philopones, Philalethes) betray the author's belief that he is modelling his work on classical dialogues (and in some cases the debt to Plato is made explicit),[24] nothing could be farther from the real Platonic dialogue than most of these works. There is no genuine searching for truth – merely the exposition and refutation of an opponent's position. Indeed, for these writers, the attraction of the dialogue form lay not just in its classical origins but in its facility for expounding an opponent's position (sometimes exaggerated and satirical) while still ultimately refuting it in the guise of an Orthodoxus. They could claim to have given due weight to the opposition ('Neither may any be justly greeved, that we have put downe manie more *objections* than *our adversaries* would ever have made: for therein, we have rather *furthered*, than *foundered* the free passage of their *cause* whatsoever')[25] without ever letting the argument slip out of their control.

In contrast to these dialogues that take place between types thinly disguised as individuals, there are dialogues that take place between abstractions such as Knowledge and Simplicity, Custom and Veritie, or Pride and Lowliness. These dialogues do not look primarily to classical sources for models at all, but to the medieval debates and morality plays. They are still dialogues of either instruction or contention; indeed, by dispensing with even the pretence of human disputants, the opposing sides can be more sharply defined. Despite this, in some dialogues such as 'The debate betweene *Pride and Lowlines*' attributed to Francis Thynne[26] (later reworked by Robert Greene as 'A Quip for an Upstart Courtier'), these 'abstractions' are more clearly characterized than many of the human 'types' in the dialogues discussed above. Here the literary aims, while less pretentious, are both more important and more fully realized as the writers drew on a vital tradition they understood, rather than a scholastic one they had mastered imperfectly.

'A new dialoge called the endightment agaynste mother Messe,'[27] printed in 1548, is a splendid example of this dramatic personification of abstractions and an illustration of just how close many of these dialogues are to medieval drama. Mother Mass herself, an old whore who has brought the people to her devilish trade, is accused in court by Verity and Knowledge, while Covetousness and Stiffneck plead for her.

She is an all-too-human figure, not averse to bribery to save her own neck – her accusers will get a bishopric if they let her go! Of course she is condemned, and her appropriate punishment is to be taken in a painful way and bound over to her Father the Pope. Clearly polemical in intention, its dramatic conception is in sharp contrast to the 1609 'Profitable Dialogue for a peruerted Papist,' which also deals with the Protestant interpretation of the Eucharist but takes place between two people – a 'Lay man' and 'certayne graue Diuines,' and is predictably undramatic in its presentation.[28]

While religious controversy was the most popular dialogue topic, it was by no means the only one. There are dialogues discussing witches and witchcraft,[29] dialogues about the relative merits of love and war,[30] dialogues defending women,[31] and even a dialogue between the cap and the head![32] The last two of these are of particular interest because, like the 'Endightment agaynst mother Messe,' each shows the survival of elements of the medieval dialogue well into the sixteenth century. The 'Dyalogue defensyve for Women' is, in fact, a bird dialogue taking place between a falcon and pye with the author as auditor. Its religious and moral nature is shown both by the setting, in which the author rises on a cold December morning and reads an oration against the vice of detraction before he goes out to walk in the woods where he overhears the birds, and by the conclusion in which the pye, who has argued against women, is converted as the author makes an appeal for grace. The winter season, the presence of an auditor who draws a moral, and the conversion at the end, all link this debate to medieval dialogues such as 'Saint Bernard's Vision.'

The dialogue between the cap and head is really an argument about the importance of external versus internal qualities and therefore also has a connection with medieval debates such as those between the heart and the eye. There is, however, a significant difference. It is the cap, the external element, that denigrates appearance and berates the head for forcing it to wear different ridiculous ornaments to accord with its master's whims. The cap argues that the attributes of a person are to be found in his internal qualities, not in external ornament. The result is almost as if the body were to display a moral sense superior to that of the soul and to chastize the latter for using it in unworthy ways. The form of the debate is remembered; its purpose and significance are not. The cap has no will of its own, must suffer the strange fancies of the head, yet possesses enough sense to know, in contrast to the head, that honour is obtained through virtue, not through external show. The cap wins the debate decisively, and, in a superb anticlimax, the head, to reward him, promises to let him rest as soon as he can find a new cap. This dialogue has clear affinities with medieval debates, but the content has been divorced from the speakers; the external element argues for the primacy of internal qualities. We shall find a similar divorce between speaker and content in at least one body and soul dialogue in the seventeenth century.

If these dialogues containing personified abstractions, animals, or inanimate objects have medieval origins while those between persons – even persons with improbable names such as Orthodoxus and no character apart from their names – have their origins in humanism, it is not surprising that the former do not appear in the seventeenth century with the same frequency as the latter. They do not disappear entirely – indeed, *A Poetical Rhapsody* contains examples such as 'A Dialogue betweene the Lover and His Heart,' and 'A Dialogue betweene a Lover, Death, and Love,'[33] and *The Paradise of Dainty Devices* contains a heart and eye debate[34] – but they have lost much of their original vitality, and both their thought and expression have lost rather than gained in interest compared with their medieval prototypes. Indeed, they often cease to be genuine contentions and take on aspects of the dialogue of instruction as does, for example, *The Crowne of Life*[35] by Bartholomew Robertson, where Spirit and Flesh have the roles not of combatants but of Master and Pupil or Pastor and Parishioner.

The two areas in which the dialogues of medieval origin exhibit some renewed vitality are the ballad and the dialogue song. In the unsophisticated form of the ballad, dialogues such as that between a remarried woman, a widow, and a young wife,[36] though originating in the first half of the century, flourished well beyond that time. The body and soul dialogues themselves, as we shall see in the following chapter, were adapted to the ballad form and flourished there. And in a manuscript collection of songs (many of them dialogues) believed to date from 1649 there is a dialogue between a dying man, an angel, and a devil that reproduces the conflict for the soul of the medieval deathbed scenes.[37] In this case the angel wins, and a chorus of two angels and the dying man celebrate the victory of 'blest soules' that drown in the seas of 'Everlastinge Love' in Heaven.

The discussion dialogue enjoys increased popularity as the century progresses. It continues to be used for polemical ends, particularly by the Puritans, and there are still no writers who can rival the early sixteenth-century masters of the form, such as More. Nevertheless, one can see the form changing as the century progresses, moving towards the dialogues of the eighteenth century, which are closer to their Platonic models than any written in the seventeenth century.

The seventeenth-century body and soul dialogues belong primarily to the category of those debates that have their origins in the Middle Ages. Unlike many other seventeenth-century dialogues in that category, however, they were able to draw a more immediate inspiration from the content of the sermons and religious tracts which, as we have seen, were often far more 'dramatic' than the purely literary debates. It is a curious irony that the Puritans, who were so opposed to drama on the stage, should have fostered it assiduously in other forms. Not only does it emerge in their religious writings, but dialogues of all kinds flourished during the Commonwealth – the result, it has been suggested, of lack of any other legitimate outlet for the drama.[38] In keeping with this impetus, the body and soul dialogues displayed a great versatility in adapting themselves to the interests and needs of the new age. Thus, as well as those works that are simply based on medieval models, there are those that have become philosophical in tone rather than moral, and still others have progressed in the direction of the discussion dialogue and have assimilated certain characteristics of that form.

Vision Literature in the Renaissance

The vision framework, present in many medieval body and soul dialogues, also has a continuous literary history throughout the sixteenth and early seventeenth centuries, and its purpose continues to be both literary and moral.

As a literary framework, it provides an intermediary between the tale and the reader who can, by his own conversion, give an example for the latter. Thus, at the end of 'A Dreame of the Diuell and Diues,' Theophilus, who has listened to Eumenides describe the vision that converted him, responds, 'Now you haue meruellously instructed me, thinking verely thorow your telling me this your dreame, that I shall despise this worlde the more, and offend God the lesse ...'[39]

The vision's continuous literary history is confirmed by even a casual look at collections of sixteenth-century poetry such as those in the Ashmolean manuscript, edited by Thomas Wright and ascribed by him to the reign of Mary I. Many of the 'vision' poems in this manuscript, however, are political rather than moral in intent and show a new literary use of the framework not found in the Middle Ages – that of enabling the author to express sentiments that might be unacceptable in a more direct form. The anti-establishment jibes of 'As I lay slombrynge in manner of a trans'[40] definitely fall into this category.

The moral aspect of the vision framework, manifest in those dialogues that most resemble the medieval ones, is closely linked to its setting which is, typically, very similar to that of 'Saint Bernard's Vision.' It takes place at night, preferably in winter, after the author has gone to bed, thus playing upon all the traditional associations of night and bed with age and death.

> And in that silent time, when sullen night
> Did hide heau'ns twinckling tapers from our sight,
> And on the earth with blackest lookes did lowre,
> When euery clocke chimb'd twelue, the midnight houre,
> In which imprison'd ghoasts free licence haue
> About the world to wander from their graue;
> When hungrie wolues and wakeful dogges do howle
> At euery breach of aire, when the sad owle
> On the house top beating her baleful wings,
> And shreeking out her doleful ditty, sings
> The song of death, vnto the sicke that lie
> Hopelesse of health, forewarning them to die:
> Just at that houre, I thought my chamber dore
> Did softly open ...[41]

One of the most elaborate vision settings, found in 'A Winter Nights Vision' by the same author,[42] links the winter scene to the general theme of mutability, which takes on a specific reality as the end of day is announced by the striking of a clock:

> Then clad in cloake of mistie fogges the darke night vp did
>   come,
> And with grim gristlie looke did seeme to bid me get me home.
>
>   (p 557)

The author goes to bed; the clock strikes again – and an elaborate moralization of the scene follows:

> The daylight past, as life I deeme, the night as death to come,
> The clocke that chim'd, deaths fatall knell, that call'd me to
>   my doome,

> Still silence rest from worldly cares, my bed the graue I thinke,
> In which, with heart to heau'n up-lift, at length I downe did
> sinke.   (p 558)

These common associations make it obvious why the vision was a form
particularly suitable 'for the correcting of vice, and terrifying of the
wicked.'[43]

A second moral purpose of the vision framework drew on the commonplace belief that in sleep the soul, unhampered by the body, is able
to discern things that are hidden from it at other times. In 'A Midnights
Trance,' by W.D., the author plays on this assumption, claiming that
he rouses often in the night in horror and ascribing this to 'that secret
for-knowledg & presageing Power of the Propheticke Mind ...'[44]

In the late sixteenth and early seventeenth centuries the vision form
appears with increasing frequency, which is what one would expect
given the dominant religious and didactic tone of the literature. Many
of these 'visions' have, in content, little in common with body and soul
literature,[45] but other works do show a close connection with it.

One of these is The Combat, betweene Conscience and Couetous-
nesse in the Minde of Man by Richard Barnfield.[46] The Combat has
been dismissed as 'the least distinguished of all Barnfield's verse,'[47] but
it provides an excellent example of the union of the vision framework
with a dialogue that definitely belongs 'to the genre of such poems as the
Disputation between the Body and the Soul ...'[48] If it is also described by
the same author as 'a curious throwback to medievalism,' this merely
provides additional evidence of such a quantity of 'throwbacks' that
they cease to be 'curious' at all. In this case, the evocation of all the
now-familiar elements – the setting of ominous night and the waking
of true perception during the sleep of the senses [49] – lead to a dispute
between two personified abstractions closely linked to those of the body
and soul dialogues. Conscience is demure, sad, without ornament;
Covetousness is 'clad in a Cassock, like a Vsurer,' which is made of
poor men's skins. The blending of abstract and concrete elements, so
characteristic of the medieval dialogues, is manifest here when Covetousness says:

> Alas, poore Conscience, how thou are deceav'd?
> As though of senses, thou wert quite bereaud.   (D2ᵛ)

The two disputants argue about which is the elder, and covetousness,
claiming that fear, not conscience, restrained man before the Fall, wins

the argument. Conscience then laments her expulsion from man's heart, and covetousness is left to rule. At this the author is struck with sorrow and awakens from his dream. There are many points of difference between this work and the body and soul literature – notably the lack of any real philosophical interest, and the resolution of the dispute as opposed to the open-ended nature of the body and soul dialogues – but in its form, characterization, and moral intention it shows close affinities with them.

If Richard Barnfield's 'Combat' demonstrates the continuing linkage of the vision form to the genre of the body and soul dialogues, W.D.'s 'A Midnights Trance'[50] shows it to their content. Here the vision framework introduces not a dialogue but a prolonged meditation on 'death, the nature of soules, and estate of Immortalitie.' It is all very derivative – one finds quotations from both *Hamlet* and 'The first Anniversary'; there are the usual invectives against ambition and the pursuit of worldly fame; the body is described variously as the prison of the soul and a 'mortall Bride,' waiting to be glorified; both body and soul must be reunited at the last day because, since both have sinned, both must arise to receive punishment. Yet even this eclectic and ill-digested collection of ideas concerning body and soul, collected within the vision framework, confirms the survival of the medieval link between the vision form and the meditation on mortality.

The treatment of both the content and related literary forms of body and soul literature in this chapter is necessarily representative, not exhaustive. It does demonstrate conclusively, however, that while the dialogues themselves do not exist in the sixteenth century, the assumptions that fostered them and the literary forms to which they are related do exist, and that they enjoy renewed popularity in the late sixteenth and early seventeenth centuries. The reappearance of the body and soul dialogues in the seventeenth century is not 'inexplicable'[51] at all.

CHAPTER FIVE

Seventeenth-Century Body and Soul Dialogues

The body and soul dialogues that appeared in England in the seventeenth century can be divided into three distinct categories. First, there are those dialogues that are modelled on and remain close to their medieval prototypes; these are still primarily moral and didactic in tone. Second, there are those which, while still retaining the framework of the medieval dialogues, have assimilated elements of the 'discussion' dialogue that, as we have seen, was gaining in popularity in the period. Third, there are those that have moved away from the specific medieval setting and, although still taking place between a genuine body and soul, have become philosophical rather than moral in their tone and intention.

'Medieval' Body and Soul Dialogues in the Seventeenth Century

Any discussion of seventeenth-century body and soul dialogues must begin with William Crashaw's translation of the 'Visio Philiberti' (his version of 'Saint Bernard's Vision') first published in 1613.[1] Crashaw possessed an extensive library consisting, in 1614, of over three thousand volumes and five hundred manuscript volumes, 'many never printed.'[2] Presumably the 'Visio' was among these manuscripts when it was chosen by him for translation and publication. But antiquarian interests, although he undoubtedly possessed them, do not alone account for this particular selection among his numerous manuscripts. The 'Epistle Dedicatorie' that prefaces the work dispels any such notion:

The end, and highest happinesse of a Christian man, is to honour

God in this life, and to die well: the way to die well is to liue well: and no better prouocation to good life, nor preparatiue to a good death, then a continuall and serious meditation of the mortality of this life, the certainty of our end ... the terriblenesse of the last judgement, and the account that each one must make then ...

One euidence thereof is this short and sweet Dialogue, which (as a fore-runner of others that may follow) being diuulged, and desired by many to bee englished, I am therefore induced to make it common: This being an age that needs al helps to holinesse, and inticements to devotion: And this the rather in as much, as though it was made in the mist of Popery, euen not long after the Diuell was let loose; yet is it not tainted with Popish corruption, nor scarce smels of any superstition, whereas it is stuft with godly truthes, and wholesome instructions ...

This dialogue, then, is a moral document with a message pertinent to Crashaw's contemporaries. His Puritan sympathies, which were in marked contrast to those of his more famous son, should make this perfectly explicable, given the emphasis on the vanity of life and the imminence of death found in other writers of a similar religious disposition. The revival of this dialogue, when seen in the context of both the general religious preoccupations of the age discussed in Chapter 2, and the specific echoes of the debates cited in Chapter 4, is not in the least incongruous. The first edition, published in 1613, was followed by a second in 1616 (appended to *A Manual for True Catholicks*), a third in 1622, and a fourth in 1632, thus demonstrating the work's continued popularity.

Since Crashaw's dialogue is a translation of a medieval manuscript version, it differs little from the content of the 'Vision' discussed in Chapter 3. All the fourteenth-century assumptions about the relative responsibility of body and soul for sin, their mutual judgment and damnation, as well as the vision framework and the imaginative representation of body and soul as concrete entities are resurrected without apology. It is presented directly as the vision of the author rather than at one remove as the vision of Philibert, the hermit (as in the Cambridge manuscript), and it is this form of the vision that influences later seventeenth-century versions of the debate.

The extent to which this translation was the single or even the prime motivating factor behind the reappearance of body and soul debates in the seventeenth century is difficult to determine. Only one dialogue dates from the period before 1613, and that is a 'philosophical' dialogue, distinct from those derived directly from the medieval genre. On chronological grounds, therefore, it is possible that Crashaw's translation was a seminal influence, and it certainly was the direct source of the ballad version that appeared later in the century. But in the light of the widespread currency of the content of the debates in sermons and in other treatises, it seems unnecessary to attribute the whole of the revival of body and soul literature to this one factor. Crashaw's translation almost certainly gave an added impetus to the popularity of the debate in the seventeenth century, but the factors that led him to select that particular manuscript for translation in the first place are sufficient in themselves to explain the reappearance of the form in other guises, independent of such a model. The ideas in the debate did not need to be 'resurrected' because they had never completely died.

While Crashaw's dialogue was written in English, it was still the product of a cleric and an antiquarian and could not be said to have reached or intended to reach a 'popular' audience. Around 1640, however, we find the dialogue appearing in the form of a ballad entitled 'Saint Bernards Vision.'[4] The similarities between this and Crashaw's translation are so striking that one can only conclude that the ballad is derived from the older and more scholarly work. The ballad is, in fact, a condensed version of the translation, approximately half its length, but with most of the structure and content intact. The main arguments are unchanged, and specific descriptions are often identical as well. The devils in both versions bear sharp steel forks (or pricks), breathe fire, have tusked teeth 'like crooked mattocks,' and snakes crawling about their nostrils. The body is taunted and told that its formerly high roof now meets its nose, that it has been changed so as to be fouler than a toad. In style as well, there are marked similarities. The same phrases and rhymes recur with only minor variations, though the shortened form of the ballad necessitates some omissions and adaptations.[5]

Despite its shortened length, there are some additions to the ballad, and among these the echoes of the Prayer Book that unexpectedly appear are most interesting. The first of these has its origin in Crashaw's translation of the Latin 'Nostra sociaberis dehinc aciei' as 'Thou art a Souldier / of our Campe enrol'd,' which appears to parody the baptismal service in which the infant becomes 'Christ's faithful soldier and servant' so that he may manfully 'fight under his banner against the world, the flesh, and the devil.' This is taken over verbatim by the ballad writer and appears in all succeeding versions. In addition to this, the appeal to 'preserve our Soules and Bodies,' which appears in the second last stanza of the ballad, is pure Cranmer, and the final prayer for 'the King, the Queene and Progeny, / The Clergy, Councell, and Nobility' has its approximate, though not exact, equivalents in the liturgy of the new church.

There can be no doubt that the ballad is a popularized version of the medieval 'Vision' based directly on Crashaw's translation. Sung, as directed, to the solemn tune 'Fortune My Foe,' it must have provided dubious cheer for seventeenth-century listeners! Its perennial appeal is, nevertheless, shown by the appearance of a later edition entered in the Stationer's Register in 1675, two eighteenth-century adaptations, and even a somewhat altered, but still recognizable, nineteenth-century descendant.[6] Thus it is in this popular form that the debate continues to survive long after it has disappeared from more sophisticated literature. The persistence of dance of death ballads (see n5, Chapter 4) makes this less of an anomaly, but the demonstrable popularity of this charnal house drama is still difficult for a modern reader to comprehend.

Body and soul literature that can be shown to derive directly from the medieval 'Vision' and Crashaw's translation of it is limited to these ballads, but there are other works that come from the same general tradition and are essentially akin to the medieval works. Significantly, the first of these is also by a Puritan, William Prynne. 'The Soules Complaint against the Bodies Encroachments on Her'[7] is, as its title indicates, not a proper dialogue, but an address of the soul in which the body does not speak. Its similarity both in this respect and in its general tone to twelfth- and thirteenth-century addresses of the soul cannot be taken as evidence of derivation, however, since these medieval works were unknown in the seventeenth century. In any case, Prynne's address, unlike the medieval poems, takes place during life, not after death. Consequently, the portrayal of the torments of hell is placed in the future tense, and the whole is completely divorced from the separation scene of soul and body in which the address originated. In this poem there is still time to repent and be saved. A further difference from the 'address' is that the soul appears to be speaking not exclusively to the body but rather directing complaints about the body to the whole person who, nevertheless, primarily represents 'body.' In this context, soul can refer to 'body' in the third person, while the final appeal to repent is addressed to the general 'you':

> This flesh, this body, which to mee have beene
> So traitrous, so unkinde, Mee to enthrall
> Unto their lusts, and spurre Mee into All
> That might undoe, damne, both them Mee, and you,

And wee shall in hels flames for ever rue?
If this be true: O then whiles life, time, space,
Ar left you to repent and seeke for grace;
Beewaile what's past, and henceforth learne to be
More loyall, kind, respectfull unto Mee.   (p 183)[8]

Some aspects of Prynne's work are, however, very reminiscent of the
medieval poems. One of these is the soul's strongly worded abuse of
the body coupled with its assertion that without it the body can do
nothing – a point that in the debates is important to the body's defence:

What is the body, but *a loathsome Masse*
Of dust and ashes, brittle as a glasse.   (p 181)
...
What hath the flesh or body worthy love,
Or praise, but that which from mee first doth move?
Let mee desert them, all their worth is lost,
And wither'd like a grasse nipt with winters frost.   (p 182)

Another feature that this poem shares with both medieval and other
seventeenth-century works is the identification of body with flesh. It is
this that enables the soul to view the body as passive matter, as in the
passage above, and yet fail to see that this should exonerate body. At
the same time, and in defiance of all logic, the author can endow the
body exclusively with negative attributes such as would only be applied
to 'flesh' in the figurative sense. The phrase 'the flesh or body' quoted
above proves the lack of any real distinction between them.

It is quite possible that Prynne knew and was influenced by Crashaw's
dialogue, but the differences, both in form and content, are sufficiently
great to indicate that it was probably not a source. It is more likely
simply another example of the pervasiveness of these general dualistic
ideas in the early seventeenth century.

A more banal poem on the same theme is Humphrey Mill's 'A
divine speech of the Soule to the bodie,' included in the volume *Poems
Occasioned by a Melancholy Vision.*[9] The 'melancholy vision' is an
allegorical one in which a destructive Time, followed closely by darkness, sin, death, and the devil, are all vanquished as the author muses
on Christ. The address of the soul follows in the second part of the
volume, entitled *Poems Pleasant and Profitable.* In it Soul attributes
the power of independent action to the body, which is accused of selling
itself to sin and, indeed, of selling the soul as well. There is less open

confusion here about the identity of body than in the work by Prynne, but its identification with the whole man must be in the back of the author's mind when he heads the reply of the body, *'The speech of the Soule workes effectually bringing the Sinner to the brinke of desparie.'* Most of the conventional ideas appear, but the author doesn't seem to know quite how to use them. There is a brief allusion to the *contemptus mundi* theme ('All thy delights, then quickly will be past'), and a perfunctory rehearsal of the ideal relationship between body and soul ('Wast thou not made to help and succour me? / Was I not made to teach and comfort thee?' [ll 11–12]), but this is not used to provide an introduction to the issue of proper subordination, as one might expect. Such issues are well beyond the capabilities of this versifier, as he has the soul glibly recite the conventional comparisons of the body to a prison and a dunghill. Strangely enough, these efforts work effectively to bring the body, if not the reader, to repentance ('My wisedome is true folly I descrie'). At least this saves it (and the author) from the intellectual effort of refuting the soul's charges, the usual response. The conclusion is not a comfortable one; Body's repentance is akin to despair as it contemplates the mouth of hell, 'Where I ere long (I feare) must goe to dwell.'

In contrast to this mundane effort, Richard Brathwait's first dialogue 'betweene *Death*, the *Flesh*, and the *Soule*' in *The Last Trumpet*[10] exploits the dramatic possibilities of the form in a new and exciting way. The whole is conceived dramatically and allegorically. Flesh (who, in a reversal of the usual situation, takes on the attributes of the physical body) is a damsel, the Soul her mistress. When Death knocks on their door, Flesh, the maid, is frightened and refuses to open it. The exchange that follows is a typical 'death and the maiden' piece, with Flesh refusing to submit her beauties to the embraces of Death, and Death insisting on his right:

> For smooth and soft conditions deare as *thou*,
> These, oft, I make to my embraces bow.   (p 5)

The maiden pleads her charms, but Death is impervious to them:

> I care not for thy *temples* faire and high,
> Though deckt with fragrant flowrs most curiously.   (p 6)

Death then catechizes the maiden on how she spends her time, and is told of her flirtations and her total possession by the world. Sometimes the Soul is angry with her, but the Flesh tempts and wins her. It is the Devil, curiously, who points the moral ('It seemes, then, that the maid her mistresse sways'), to which Flesh assents. But when the Devil seizes Flesh, she calls upon Soul to send him away. Soul begins by berating Flesh, reminding her that when she (Soul) leaves, Flesh will be nothing but a carcass 'on which, foule crawling worms must full be fed,' but she soon turns to comfort, saying that in the end death will be a boon to them both. She persuades Flesh that now sense must submit to reason, thus emphasizing the need for proper subordination that Flesh has overthrown. It is a mark of the lively characterization that distinguishes this dialogue that Flesh cannot resist pointing out to her mistress that this advice, coming from her, is a real about-face!

> O strange! then what have you (my Mistresse) done
> Who have bin still by my perswasions won,
> And, all this while, to them have lent your eare,
> Listning to *me* (your *Mayde*) without all feare,
> ...
> Why (then) doe you (now) *reason* so much presse?
> Which, you *you selfe*, so long, did thus transgresse.

(pp 26-7)

The soul responds by acknowledging her past faults, saying that this is why she is now so willing to leave the body, which she characterizes as 'this darke house of sin.' But even with this passing denunciation, there is no lasting bitterness between Flesh and Soul. The Soul instructs the Flesh and prepares it for death, reminding it of the grain of wheat that must die before it rises. Death, appropriately, has the last word: 'Thus (then) adeu / To *both* of *you*.'

This little piece is almost like a medieval morality play rather than a conventional dialogue. It is set at the moment of death, but the acrimonious charges and countercharges that one might expect are limited; there is still time for repentance. Nevertheless, though the form of this work is essentially medieval, there are features that link it to other body and soul literature in the seventeenth century. The incorporation of the allegory of the maid and mistress is unusual and looks forward to the analogical use of the body/soul relationship that is discussed in Chapters 7 and 8. The soul that comforts the body in the face of approaching death reappears in the work of Henry Vaughan, while the role of instructor that the soul assumes at the end is also to be found in later seventeenth-century works, notably in the dialogue by James Howell.

'Discussion' Dialogues between Body and Soul

The adaptability and consequent persistence of the body and soul debate in the mid-seventeenth century is shown by the way in which it assimilated characteristics of the 'discussion' dialogue, so popular in the period. James Howell's *The Vision: or a Dialog between the Soul and the Bodie*[11] is the chief work in this category. It is by far the longest of those in existence, the only one written in prose rather than in verse, and one of the least known. As literature it does not have a great deal to recommend it, but as evidence of the evolution of both a literary form and an idea it can claim our attention.

In its setting this work is quite close to the medieval debates and their direct seventeenth-century descendants. The framework is that of a vision which takes place while the author is lying in bed one night at the time of the summer solstice. Apart from the change of season (which may already show an imperfect grasp of the dialogue's original purpose) this is identical to the setting of 'Saint Bernard's Vision.' The soul is depicted in visual terms which almost equal those of 'Un samedi par nuit' in vividness and naïveté. 'Afterwards the fantasma [of the soul] varying, she took a shape, and the nearest resemblance I could make of it, was to a veild Nunn with a flaming cross on the left side of her breast ...' ('The Proem') Unlike 'Saint Bernard's Vision,' however, the debate does not take place after death. It is the author's own soul that appears, and while at the beginning and end of the dialogue the author functions as a third-person witness, at times he also seems to be identified with 'Body' which is, after all, *his* body.

The purpose of the dialogue is, like that of its medieval antecedents, ostensibly moral. The author expresses the hope that all those 'That read this Dream, thereby such profit reap / As I did *pleasure*, Then they have it cheap' (p 176). But in reality, the desire to discuss contemporary issues regarding the nature of the soul and theology predominates. *The Vision* opens with mutual recriminations between body and soul but quickly progresses from debate to dialogue. Under the pretext of discussing their own relationship, body and soul cover such varied topics as 'The Influxes and operations of the stars,' 'Of walking spirits, of the old Philosophers,' and 'Of sundry sorts of Christians throughout the world with many emergencies of new matter.' As the dialogue progresses, body and soul range farther from the subject of the medieval debates (their relative responsibility for sin) and the character of each determines very little of the content of what is said. The body, for example, discusses the different religious practices of the Greeks, Russians, and Nestorians (p 55); the soul, in its turn, considers the relative merits of prayer and praise as forms of worship (pp 69–74). In such passages the identity of the speaker is irrelevant to the content of the dialogue.[12]

The content itself is a curious mixture of classical philosophy, Christian theology, contemporary scientific knowledge, and superstition. Howell lists the 'Ingredients' whereof the 'Discours is compounded' as '1. Divinity, 2. Metaphysic, 3. Philosophy, 4. Poesie, &c.' Certainly all these elements are present, though the quality of some, notably that of the 'poesie,' is dubious to say the least.

After an introduction setting forth an essentially Aristotelian view of man – matter plus a trinity of souls – the dialogue proper begins with a complaint by the soul that the body has contaminated it. Here 'flesh' is used for 'body' in keeping with the negative connotations, and it is explicitly stated that this flesh (body) corrupts the soul, not merely that in conjunction with the body it cannot act as freely as it might otherwise.[13] None of this is new, although in the medieval debates there is more emphasis on the evil actions of body corrupting the soul than on the condition of union with the body itself as the cause of corruption. Howell's approach moves the argument closer to the philosophical emphasis we have already found in Donne's sermons and will find, in a more pronounced form, in the dialogues by Marvell and A.W.

The body replies to the charge with the argument commonly used in the medieval dialogues: it is 'but an unwieldie lump of earth, a meer passive thing ...' (p 2). This is supported by two familiar analogies, both of which are Platonic in origin and occur in the medieval body and soul debates, though not in the popular ballad versions of the seventeenth century. The soul is a pilot and the body its ship; the soul is a charioteer and the body, presumably, the two horses that it guides. In this latter analogy Howell, like the author of 'Als I Lay' and unlike Plato, makes the horses analogous to body, not to parts of the soul.[14] This reinforces the identification of the lower faculties of the soul with the body. The point of both analogies is then stated explicitly a second time. Whether the soul is a 'continual motion' (Heraclitus) or 'the perfection from whence all motion proceeds' (Aristotle), it is the agent that initiates action. Hence the body, which will suffer future punishment with the soul, has far more cause for complaint than the soul and repents the union between them. It expresses the common desire to have been inanimate, and sees man's very nature (the union of body and soul) as his greatest misfortune, not his greatest glory. 'Man of all creatures is a Heautontimorumenos, a self tormentor, a persecutor and crucifier of himself, all which are emanations from the Intellectual soul' (p 4).

Proper subordination is no longer observed; sense should be subordinate to reason, reason to faith, but now intellectual doubts trouble faith. This last, coming from body, is a real anomaly! The whole speech is remarkable for the wide variety of sources that have been drawn upon, and particularly the combination of medieval tradition and classical sources.

When the soul begins its reply by defining itself as 'undivisible, inextensive, without parts and inorganical, *Tota in toto, & tota in qualibet parte*' (p 5), we know Howell has ranged himself on the side of orthodox opinion against such writers as Henry More and Ralph Cudworth, who insisted that the soul had the property of extension. The soul is diffused throughout the body; the latter's actions are 'emanations' from it. (This Neoplatonic term, which recurs several times in the dialogue, is supported by nothing else in the context.) Despite this statement which, strictly applied, would mean the body's actions are wholly determined, it appears that it is more susceptible to some kinds of influence than others. The soul accuses it of giving more obedience to the sensual appetite and the will than to the intellect (reason). We have seen that many seventeenth-century theologians saw the will as the battleground of appetite and reason; here it has been taken over entirely by appetite and thus made congenial to the desires of the body. At the same time, both sensual appetite and will must, strictly speaking, be regarded as faculties of the soul if body is simply passive matter as it has claimed. Logically, therefore, Soul must still bear the responsibility for action, although Body does not use this argument in its reply. A result of the body's domination by the sensual appetite is the depravation of all the senses, which are given over to the service of evil. The soul then goes on to extend this depravation to the heart, fantasy, memory, understanding, and will, all of which are here attributed to Body! This inconsistency does not seem to have worried Howell at all.

In its reply the body betrays the prevailing ambivalent attitude towards itself. It admits that the rational soul is superior, the 'Queen of Forms,' but it itself is to be 'a *domicile* not a *dungeon* for [it]' (p 13) and quotes Scripture to prove its point. On the next page, however, it states that its smallness and slenderness are virtues since it thereby carries less corruption 'for the more flesh, the more corruption' (p 14), thus invoking the identification of literal body with figurative flesh and implying that this flesh (body) is of its very nature evil. The soul replies that not only does its intimacy with the body pollute it in this life, but even separation after death offers no hope of release. In a passage reminiscent of Digby's theory that after death the soul will become infinitely what it has been only partially during life,[15] it claims that once separated its pain and suffering for past evil will be far more acute than now when all sensation comes via the body.

Gradually the dialogue begins to move away from the 'debate' subject-matter and becomes chiefly a means of conveying information. The body deals with the process of conception in the womb and the infusion/ traducianism controversy. The soul commends the body on its self-knowledge and expands on the idea, borrowed presumably from Browne, that 'Man is that great *Amphibion* of Nature' (p 15). After another exchange between the two the body is completely subdued, and from this point on the relationship between them is not antagonistic but rather like that between a clergyman and his pastoral charge. While admitting its sin, Body still insists that it has impulses to good, which it illustrates by uttering 'a few ternaries of Stanzas' of praise. It then analyses its passions, describes their effect in physiological terms, admits the evil of an excess of some, but holds that an abundance of others, such as love, is a saving grace. Out of the discussion of love springs an appeal for tolerance, particularly for tolerance in religion. The relevance of this in 1651 when Howell himself was in prison is obvious.

The central section of the dialogue is taken up with contemporary religious problems. Here Body and Soul are not even distinguished to the extent of instructor and instructed. They discuss the issues as equals. Howell is against the new critical and scientific spirit that points out inconsistencies in Scripture and generally elevates human reason above the level of faith. 'I have always made *Reson,* and other sciences to truckle under *Divinity* their mistress' (p 116), the body states. Ancient authority is venerated (this time it is the soul speaking): 'Antiquity is venerable, therefore the older the Author is, the more to be valued, it being a maxim that may bear sway in divinity as well as in Heralday, *Tutius est cum patribus quam cum fratribus errare'* (p 96). These attitudes place Howell among the more conservative thinkers of the mid-century, and other ideas of his confirm this. Belief in an episcopal structure of church government is surely implied in the body's 'I have always inclined to love Order and degrees of respect, & to abhor confusion ...' (p 116). The 'confusion' and disorder throughout the world at this time are seen by both Soul and Body as signs of the end. Charles I's death is cited among other calamities, and the two, now partners in misfortune, commiserate with one another.

The discussion then moves back from political affairs to spiritual, and the dialogue concludes with the soul consoling the body by describing the joys of heaven. This contrasts with the corresponding section in the medieval dialogues in which the soul tells the body of the torments of hell, just as the summer setting of the whole contrasts with that of winter in the medieval debates. Here a joyous note is sounded as the body thanks the soul for its discourse on the Resurrection and the hope that both of them have in this. Like Philibert the hermit, the body promises to mortify itself and think on eternal things. The end of the *Vision* is a return to the concrete and naïve visual imagery of the opening section. The soul, once more depicted as a Nun, vanishes within the body and diffuses herself 'through the whole mass of blood among the spirits' (p 172). It is now dawn, and the author wakes.

The dialogue is obviously the product of an uncreative mind, one that assimilates rather indiscriminately. Its interest lies in its eclectic character, in the vast array of topical matters that have been crammed into the debate form. But why has Howell cast these ideas in the mould of a medieval form? The moral element in the medieval dialogues exerted some appeal, though to a lesser extent than it did for Crashaw. It seems rather that Howell perceived the dialogue could be used to reinforce a general religious and political conservatism, and that this was the decisive factor. The turmoil of the age demanded, he believed, a restatement of older values as well as a salutary reminder of death and the life to come, and the body and soul dialogue was easily adaptable to these purposes. The conservatism of his ideas has been shown in his insistence on the subordination of faith to reason, his emphasis on hierarchy and order in religious institutions, and his acceptance of the authority of Aristotle and Aquinas. The chief contemporary influences on him are Sir Thomas Browne and Sir Kenelm Digby, but he is less scientific and critical than either of these. His rather naïve imagination, evident in his visualization of the soul itself, makes it possible to see why the medieval poem, which he doubtless knew through Crashaw's translation if not directly, would appeal to him. But he was too much a man of his own times, too involved in contemporary affairs, to be content merely to reiterate the moral lesson of Crashaw. He used the form as a vehicle to convey something quite other than the medieval debate, and in so doing hopelessly divorced the form from the content, and the framework from the interior structure of the work.

This breakdown of the traditional structure of the debate is even more obvious in a work entitled *A Conference between the Soul and Body Concerning the Present and Future State* by Henry Nicholson.[16] In this dialogue, published just after the turn of the century, the author feels that he needs to justify making the body speak independently of the soul. He also takes care to explain that the debate is a parable, not to be taken too literally:

> But there must be some Objections found; perhaps 'tis odd the Body should speak distinctly from the Soul: If that be all, to give no other Answer, Jotham's Parable will bring me off, who makes the Trees speak, Judges 9.8. This being only a Parable too, of what a virtuous Man might say to convince a wicked; and the Day will certainly come, when these Objectors will find their Souls and Bodies reproach or congratulate each other in a stranger Dialect than this. ('The Preface to the Reader' iii–iv)

Soul and Body are characterized only according to their natures and desires; there is no visual description. Body is an Epicurean and longs for the pleasures of the senses; Soul stands for 'spiritual' values which are rather ascetic and spartan. The bulk of the dialogue deals with each of the seven deadly sins; Body is tempted, and Soul persuades it to resist. This conceptual framework is much simpler than that of the earlier debates, and within it the author, in the guise of Soul, finds scope to discuss many other issues. We learn that he is against priests who 'are turn'd boon Companions, and Buffoons in all Company' (p 75). 'Foolish jesting' and mirth are wicked; fighting for king and country are praiseworthy. After the conversion of Body it argues with Soul about whether hell and heaven have a particular location. The naïveté and literal-mindedness of the author is apparent in this exchange,[17] and his lack of sympathy for the new age is shown in his scorn for the Deists, whom he equates with atheists.

The emphasis on discussion in this 'conference' between body and soul is even more pronounced than it was in Howell's dialogue; accordingly, we find even fewer characteristics of the medieval debate. The lack of a specific setting and of the vision framework are noteworthy, and the content also differs markedly from the medieval debates. Mutual recriminations between body and soul are few. There is a reference to the need for proper subordination of the body to the soul, but this is not linked to any argument concerning their relative responsibility for sin. The author is obviously conservative, even reactionary; but in form and content his work confirms the development from debate to discussion dialogue found in the dialogue by Howell. When at the end of this eighteenth-century dialogue we find the soul giving a brief résumé of the content of the medieval body and soul dialogues, it appears quite incongruous and out of keeping with the rest of the work. The externals of the form have survived, but the moral questions that gave it life and urgency have not.

'Philosophical' Dialogues

The coupling of the medieval framework of the debate with a contemporary content was not happy or destined to last. A third line of development moved the dialogue away from the trappings of this framework with its emphasis on death and judgment to focus on the very nature of the body/soul relationship itself. These dialogues doubtless owe something to the medieval conventions, but they owe at least as much to some of the classical sources examined in Chapter 1. They are the most 'literary' of these works and depend for their effect not on the crudities of the terrors of hell but on the niceties of the apt turn of phrase and the witty, ironical thrust.

The first body and soul dialogue published in the seventeenth century, 'A Dialogue betweene the Soule and the Body' contained in *A Poetical Rhapsody*,[18] and the best-known dialogue of all, Andrew Marvell's 'A Dialogue between the Soul and the Body,'[19] both belong to this category. The author of the first dialogue is unknown. It is one of the many pieces in *A Poetical Rhapsody* attributed to A.W. which, it has been suggested by one editor, stands for 'Anonymous Writer.'[20] Whatever his true identity, A.W. was not interested in using this literary form in the manner of Crashaw, to present a moral treatise, or, as Howell did, to discuss contemporary issues. There is no vision framework; neither is there a third party, the author or Philibert, to be instructed, and no general moral is drawn. The setting of the poem is not defined. It must take place during life rather than after death, since the soul's complaint concerning its imprisonment is in the present tense, but we know nothing of the external circumstances other than this. The very fact that Soul and Body speak implies that they are concrete entities, but beyond this there is no pictorial characterization such as one finds in the medieval poems.

All this has its effect on the character of the dialogue. The striking setting of the medieval poems, often made more vivid by accompanying illustrations, was designed to impress forcibly on the mind of the reader the horror of the situation. The vision framework, as we have seen, enabled the author to show the transforming effect of the revelation on the life of a sinner and to draw the obvious conclusion: 'Go, and do thou likewise.' Its absence here means that the whole has a much more general application. This body and soul are not arguing about their own particular sin or the specific plight in which they find themselves. What emerges from the dialogue is a statement of the fundamental incompatibility of body and soul in this life. There is no solution to the problem; there is no moral to be drawn. Dualism emerges as 'the thing itself,' unmediated by doctrinal considerations.

> [Soule] Ay me, poore Soule, whom bound in sinful chains
> This wretched body keepes against my will!
> Body Aye mee, poore Body, whom for all my paines,
> This forward soule causlesse condemneth stil.
> Soule Causles? whenas thou striv'st to sin each day?
> [Body] Causles: whenas I strive thee to obay.
>
> Soule Thou art the meanes by which I fall to sin,
> Body Thou art the cause that set'st this means awork
> Soule No part of thee that hath not faultie bin:
> Body I show the poyson that in thee doth lurke,
> Soule I shall be pure when so I part from thee:
> So were I now, but that thou stainest mee.

The prison image predominates from the opening couplet. Connected with this image is an assertion of the essentially antagonistic nature of body and soul. Such a state of deadlock between the two, the recognition of an inherent incompatibility with no possible solution except divorce, finds no parallel in Christian literature except where this has been influenced by non-Christian sources. In the medieval dialogues body and soul are at odds with one another, but this state is not natural or inevitable. It is a specific result of sin, and there is usually some admission of mutual guilt and the expectation of a shared punishment. Although Christian assumptions are evident in it as well, this dialogue by A.W. seems to owe as much to classical philosophy as it was known during the Renaissance as it does to the medieval debates. Its dominant Platonism is obvious in the final assertion that soul will be pure only when separated from body.

Such debt as it does owe to medieval sources is chiefly evident in the references to sin. While the incompatibility between body and soul is not itself directly attributed to original sin, the debate makes the distinction between the cause of sin and the means by which it is effected, a distinction that is at the heart of the dispute. The soul accuses the body of being the 'means' by which it falls to sin – the means, presumably, in that only in the body does sin become manifest. The body retorts that it merely obeys the soul; the acts it carries out exhibit the evil intentions, the 'poyson,' lurking in the soul. This distinction between cause and effect is found both in medieval body and soul dialogues and in related debates, such as those between the heart and the eye.[21] The body's argument that its role is merely one of passive compliance is already familiar from the fourteenth-century debates. But the brevity of this poem means that these ideas are not explored in the detail they are in 'Saint Bernard's Vision.' There is no discussion of the roles of the various faculties of the soul; there is no suggestion that it is the body, as a sensuous agent, that originally tempts to sin. The idea of proper subordination is touched upon in lines 5–6 but is not developed. Yet this very omission of detail means that the line of argument presented is clear and precise. The poem is noteworthy as an expression of the incompatibility of soul and body in general and abstract terms. It exhibits an enjoyment of dialectic and the posing of an insoluble problem for its own sake.

Marvell's 'A Dialogue between the Soul and the Body' shows a further development away from the moral towards the philosophical dialogue. It shares many characteristics of A.W.'s dialogue – the lack of a specific setting, the fact that it takes place during life rather than after death, the general reference of the argument, the emphasis on mutual incompatibility without any attempt to provide a solution to the problem. In content it is even farther removed from the medieval dialogues; all references to sin have disappeared, and there is no distinction made between the internal cause and the external manifestation of an act, between will and action. The debt of the poem to classical philosophy is even more apparent than in that by A.W. Indeed, the closest parallel to the statement of incompatibility between body and soul in Marvell's poem that I have found is the passage from Plotinus, quoted in Chapter 1: 'But when two distinct things become one in an artificial unity, there is a probable source of pain to them in the mere fact that they were inapt to partnership ... Then the essential duality becomes also a unity, but a unity standing midway between what the lower was and what it cannot absorb, and therefore a troubled unity ...'[22]

The first stanza, spoken by Soul, is based on the prison analogy. The soul, a spiritual substance, is confined within the physical body. But Marvell develops this tired analogy in wholly new ways as he revels in exposing the paradoxical nature of a union which is necessary to each of the partners and at the same time injurious to them. The function of each of the body's senses is perverted so that it works ill to the soul rather than good. Thus the soul is 'blinded with an Eye' and 'deaf with the drumming of an Ear.' The implication is that intuitive knowledge received directly by the soul is superior to that which the body admits through the senses, a view that was prevalent, though not universal, among seventeenth-century divines.[23] The malice attributed to the body in thus hindering the soul, however, is Marvell's own. In the second stanza, the body replies that while the bondage the soul exerts over it is different in kind, it is no less oppressive. It has become 'A Body that could never rest, / Since this ill Spirit it possest.' Each involves the other in suffering. The soul, that could not of itself feel pain (since the faculty of sense can only be exercised through the body), now endures care and disease. A return to health just presages a longer period of torture by denying the release of death. The body, in its turn, suffers the psychical maladies of the soul. Hope, fear, love, hatred, joy, and sorrow alike disturb its former inanimate tranquillity.

The idea that body and soul each would be better off without the other is expressed in the medieval dialogues as well, although there, like everything else, it is linked to the problem of sin. Body wishes it had remained inanimate, for then it could never have sinned; Soul laments that it was ever joined to Body, for alone, as a pure spirit, it could not have been subject to temptation. These sentiments are expressed by other seventeenth-century writers, such as Henry Vaughan,[24] also. But in Marvell's poem, unlike these precedents, there is no definite frame of reference for the complaint. Neither is it counterbalanced by the Christian assumption that the union of body and soul is both necessary and, in ideal circumstances, a positive good. Much more than in the poem by A.W., the emphasis here is on the unsatisfactory condition of their unity itself, unrelated to any specific topic such as sin or to action of any sort. The problem is posed in general terms, and there is no attempt to resolve it.[25] Incompatibility arises out of the very nature of each. Only in the last couplet is the situation made at all specific, and even here it is expressed in the form of a rather ambiguous analogy. The soul will not allow the body to fulfil itself simply as a part of inanimate nature like the 'Green Tree' but must square and hew it to its own designs; the body will always be unmalleable material and will cramp and hinder the soul. It will never be able to be a fitting and concrete expression of the soul's vision.

While Marvell's and A.W.'s dialogues are indebted to the medieval debate, they can in no sense be termed a revival. They are not Puritan in inspiration; they cannot be explained in terms of a compatible climate of religious thought and expression since they are not specifically religious or, in the case of Marvell's, even moral. The impetus for the writing of these dialogues is to be found in the Renaissance revival of interest in Platonism. Marvell, along with many of his contemporaries, was attracted by the dramatic possibilities of that aspect of Platonism and Neoplatonism that saw a fundamental dichotomy between those things which were higher and those which were lower on the scale of being, between body and soul. Thus the drop of dew ('On a Drop of Dew,' 1.12–13), representing the soul, 'shuns the sweat leaves and blossoms green' to merge eventually 'into the Glories of th'Almighty Sun.' The straightforward nature of this poem, however, does little to prepare one for the wit of the dialogue between Body and Soul. Here the medieval tradition, with its ambiguities about the role and attributes of body and soul, provides a complexity of reference that enables him to use fully his gifts for paradox and irony. But apart from this, it is difficult to see much other than direct classical influence in Marvell's poem. The emphasis on the dichotomy between body and soul is compatible with the seventeenth-century Christian position not because it derives from it, but because it has returned to the very sources that were responsible for its introduction into Christian thought in the first place. The dialogue by A.W. bears some traces of the Christian heritage as well, but the inspiration for that by Marvell seems to have come in a purer form from the original classical sources of their later interpreters, bypassing the long route by which they were transmitted through the church. In this it is a typical product of the Renaissance.[26]

The dialogues by Marvell and A.W. had no direct descendants in the seventeenth century. They lacked the didactic function of the morality dialogue as well as the (to us) bizarre appeal of the terrors of hell and the last judgment. Neither could they function as a framework for a broader dialogue, in the manner of James Howell's work. In the case of Marvell particularly, the success of the dialogue depended to such a large extent on the wit and sophistication of his individual genius that it was, in the short term, inimitable. Yet it is this form of the dialogue that, precisely because it is general and divorced from anachronistic medieval concepts of sin and damnation, is still read and appreciated today and, indeed, has at least one twentieth-century descendant, loosely but recognizably related, in the works of W.B. Yeats. The eternal psychological conflict that man feels within himself is re-expressed in every age, and the more abstract that expression is, the less tied to concrete detail that dates it, the more likely it is to remain alive and vital as a literary force in succeeding generations.

Related Dialogues

Apart from the dialogues already discussed, there are two additional categories that are related to those between body and soul but do not conform wholly to the convention of a debate between two warring entities that are also genuinely part of the individual person. They diverge from this norm in opposite directions – those between the flesh and the spirit that portray the conflict between two rather abstract impulses within man and reinforce dualism, and those between a 'good' body and soul (both real parts of man) that are completely lacking in conflict.

The seventeenth-century flesh and spirit dialogues, like their medieval prototypes, are commonly grouped with body and soul dialogues, but it is just as incorrect to do so. The same distinctions that existed in the medieval works (they are between two abstract concepts, not two parts of a genuine person; they take place during life, not after death; they have no real philosophical interest) are still present.

The most typical flesh and spirit dialogue is that by Francis Quarles.[27] While 'flesh' and 'spirit' are visualized concretely in the accompanying illustration, they cannot be seen as comparable to body and soul since the dialogue deals with only one aspect of each – their differing perception. Spirit, pictured with a long spy-glass, can see much farther than Flesh. Therefore, while Flesh notices objects close at hand that delight the senses, Spirit has a vision of the Last Judgment and urges Flesh to leave its 'vain' 'present toyes' and to turn to 'those true, those future joyes.' In its moral purpose (emphasized by the prefatory quotation from Deuteronomy 32:29: 'O that men were wise, and that they understood this, that they would consider their latter end'), it is similar to the works of Prynne, Crashaw, and Howell. But in contrast to the personification of Body and Soul in those works, Flesh and Spirit here remain abstract entities in the sense of Galatians 5:17. 'Flesh' is in all respects inferior to 'Spirit'; there is none of the parallel treatment one finds, for example, in Marvell's dialogue. No mention is made of their interaction and effect on one another. Consequently, there can be no real argument between them about which is responsible for sin, the basic theme of the medieval debates, nor can there be a sense of mutual incompatibility, such as we find in Marvell's poem. They are seen as two opposed elements, not as two warring parts of one composite.

Another flesh and spirit dialogue by Richard Baxter ('Self-Denial: A Dialogue between the Flesh and the Spirit') is less literary and more determinedly theological.[28] It is didactic and moral in tone, lucid in its theological content, but confused imaginatively. The exchanges between Flesh and Spirit are catechetical (Flesh poses the questions and Spirit answers them) yet belligerent. At times Flesh takes on some of the attributes of Body, as when it objects to becoming 'nothing' – that is, in true biblical fashion, losing its life in order to save it.[29] In general, however, Spirit appears to be subduing an abstract principle. Spirit urges on Flesh the paradoxical ideas that pleasure is poison, that drudgery is pleasure, that prosperity is barren, that 'God's Cage' (the law) is better than the wilderness. Flesh reacts in a way that is wholly typical, opposing itself to the things of the spirit and insisting that the paradoxes are nonsense. When (confirming its sporadic identification with Body) it says, *'Nature made me a Man, and gave me sense: / Changing of Nature is a vain pretence'* (sig F2ʳ), the argument for the 'naturalness' of body's inclination leads to a rebuttal that pits the old meaning of 'nature' and 'natural' against the new. For a brief section in the middle of the dialogue the matter of the body and soul debates – the need for proper subordination, the horse and rider analogy – appear, but the poem concludes with the straightforward claims of the Flesh's hedonistic approach to life and the Spirit's rejection of them. There is no conversion; Flesh holds out to the end, fearful of death 'That laies our flesh to rot in loathsom graves' (sig F4ʳ), but refusing to be comforted. Rather cheekily, Flesh says it will not refuse Heaven if God offers it, *'But for my Pleasure here I'le not forsake it.'* The dialogue ends with the author's renunciation of Flesh, which is used here in a wholly figurative sense.

Finally, there is Marvell's 'A Dialogue between the Resolved Soul, and Created Pleasure' (1.9–12). While this dialogue displays all the verbal wit and sophistication of 'A Dialogue between the Soul and the Body,' it lacks its philosophical subtlety and is much farther removed from the mainstream of the debate tradition. Neither of the two opponents is fully characterized. In its antithesis of spiritual to sensual pleasures and its assertion of the superiority of the spiritual, the dialogue is closer to some of Marvell's pastoral dialogues than to that between Soul and Body. There is conflict here, but no real debate – simply temptation and reply. Wealth, glory, and knowledge are all offered to the resolved soul and rejected with the concluding paradox that one mounts to heaven only through humility. The verbal skill that in 'A Dialogue between the Soul and the Body' was used to expose the complex and ambiguous state of their union is here used to opposite effect. Soul replies to Created Pleasure in rhyming couplets whose neat conclusiveness denies the very possibility of ambiguity.

In marked contrast to these works that highlight the opposition between body and soul (or flesh and spirit) are three dialogues by Henry Vaughan – 'Death. *A Dialogue'* (pp 399–400), 'Resurrection and Immortality' (pp 400–2), and 'The Evening-watch. *A Dialogue'* (p 425). Unlike the medieval debates, these do not take place between a sinful soul and body but between a good soul and an obedient body. Consequently, there is no 'strife' between them; the only dramatic element comes from the time they take place – the moment of death – thus giving an urgency to the body's questions about its future state. The soul responds by comforting the body and assuring it of the Resurrection. Although there is a precedent for this in the addresses of a good soul to a good body in both the Exeter Book and the Irish Homily, there is no evidence that Vaughan could have known these works or patterned his own on them. In any case, one does not need to presuppose a model to explain Vaughan's poems. His emphasis on the love that body and soul bear for one another, their closeness and intimacy, is quite in keeping with the general tone of his work. God's tenderness towards the body, expressed in such poems as 'Buriall' (pp 427–8) is here reflected in the loving concern the soul has for its own body.

Vaughan's interest in Hermetic lore doubtless influenced his belief that body and soul were of equal importance and not innately antagonistic. According to Hermetic writers, *all* things – even gross matter – are immortal; thus there is no absolute distinction between matter and spirit, body and soul.[30] While Vaughan conceives of body and soul imaginatively as concrete beings, they are never warring entities. Both are part of a whole creation permeated and sustained by God's spirit. In 'Resurrection and Immortality' we find an omnipresent 'preserving spirit' that assures the body's survival after death. The soul claims that 'death' is merely a name, 'a meere mistake':

> For a preserving spirit doth still passe
> Untainted through this Masse,
> Which doth resolve, produce, and ripen all
> That to it fall. (ll 31–4)

And in the poem 'Death' the soul assures the body that though it will not lose all sense with its (the soul's) departure, it will not find the long wait in the earth unendurable.[31]

The Hermetic lore is, however, incorporated into a specifically Christian frame of reference. Body will not merely be preserved as part of the whole material universe, but will rise individually to be reunited with its own soul.[32] 'The Evening-watch,' in particular, is specifically Christian in content and incorporates no direct references to hermetism. Soul simply comforts the dying body with the assurance that they will meet again at the last day.

These dialogues are not debates; they teach no moral lesson and give no warning. In their question/answer format they have certain things in common with the dialogues of instruction, but in their emotional warmth they are quite different from those works. Marvell's dialogues reinforce dualism by removing it from a specific setting of outmoded assumptions and refining it to a new verbal subtlety. Vaughan retains the classical Christian setting of the deathbed, but, influenced by hermetism, emphasizes the interdependence of body and soul. Thus the general direction of his thought is more in keeping with developments in the latter half of the seventeenth century, though in its source and certain specific ingredients it is not.

The variety of uses to which the medieval dispute between body and soul was put in the seventeenth century has been amply illustrated. After 1660, however, it gradually disappears and, with the exception of some ballads, there are no body and soul dialogues based directly on the medieval tradition after 1705. The reasons for this are various, but they are probably more easily explained than those for the reappearance of the dialogues in the first place.

Crashaw's direct translation of the medieval debate, although in some respects anachronistic when it was made, was the most likely to proliferate of the three types of debate. Its moral lesson could be readily grasped by the simplest, and the form was easy to imitate. The fact that it survived in ballad form until the nineteenth century shows that it retained its appeal among the relatively uneducated. However, the serious theological writings of the Puritans show that even they were too sophisticated after the mid-century to accept morality in this naïve form, and the whole idea was incongruous in the era of the Royal Society.

As for James Howell's 'Vision,' it is already in a state of transition between the medieval body and soul debate and the discussion dialogue, so it is not surprising that it has no successors in the debate tradition. We have seen the incongruities resulting from Howell's attempt to include his views on current theological and political problems within the debate form and the consequent divorce of framework from content in his work. The dialogue between body and soul has here become extraneous, a cumbersome device largely irrelevant to the real point of the work. The moral lesson is still present, but it is not the chief reason for writing the dialogue. The natural line of development from Howell's dialogue is towards discarding the medieval framework altogether, so that the work becomes purely a discussion dialogue. This is what has happened in the early eighteenth-century 'A Conference Between the Soul and the Body.' More commonly, the abstract soul and body disappear altogether, giving way to real people (though often with allegorical names) who express views that are compatible with their imaginative characterization. The body's reference to its 'intellectuals' in Howell's dialogue, its translation of psalms, its knowledge of Aristotle – these things are not likely to have been read without a smile in Howell's own day. A later age would not have tolerated them.

The reasons for the lack of successors to the 'philosophical' dialogue have already been touched upon. Precisely because of the refinement of these dialogues in form and argument, and because of their philosophical rather than moral bias, they are not readily imitable, at least in the short term. The threat of death and the fear of hell do not depend on literary excellence for their effect; the paradoxical argument of Marvell's poem does. A moral lesson can be repeated, with slight variations, indefinitely. A philosophical argument presented in a form as polished as that of Marvell's dialogue does not lend itself easily to such repetition. Once the paradoxical nature of the relationship between body and soul – their interdependence and incompatibility – has been expressed thus eloquently, there is nothing more to add. Then too, in the latter half of the century, wit and irony such as we find in Marvell's dialogue were focused more often on political than philosophical matters. Absalom and Achitophel succeed the soul and the body. It was only in a much later age, with the rise of different modes of poetic expression and a new understanding of dualism, that the perennial theme could again be taken up by a poet with gifts not inferior to those of Marvell.

In addition to these specific reasons for the disappearance of the various types of body and soul dialogue, certain general trends in the thought and literary consciousness of the period, discussed in Chapter 2, must be taken into account. First, the theme of the medieval debates, the relative responsibility of body and soul for sin, coupled with a reminder of the terrors of hell and judgment, lost much of its appeal in the second half of the century with the decline of Puritanism and the rise of an optimistic Deism.

Second, the mainstream of religious thought was moving away from a reliance on revelation and authority alone to a reliance on reason as well. This rational inquiry caused a reaction against the extreme dualism prevalent in the first half of the century. Indeed, we have seen how the first statement of this dualism presented in rational and philosophical terms – that by Descartes – served, paradoxically, to provoke a reaction among both philosophers, such as Hobbes, and theologians, such as the Cambridge Platonists. There was a parallel movement away from dualism among the poets of the period, notably Henry Vaughan and Thomas Traherne. Unlike Marvell, who selected the elements in Platonism and Neoplatonism that emphasized the difference between body and soul, Vaughan and Traherne emphasized their fundamental unity. This emphasis was partly due to the influence of contemporary philosophers such as the Cambridge Platonists, and partly inspired, particularly in the case of Vaughan, by such ancient authors as Hermes Trismegistus. Milton's affirmation of the unity of body and soul and his denial that they are separated even at the time of death – the basis of the fiction of the medieval debate – was more purely theological in inspiration, but nevertheless in keeping with the general trend.[33]

A third factor of even greater relevance to the literary presentation of body and soul than the recognition of their unity on the rational level was the gradual disappearance of their imaginative representation as concrete entities. To some extent, this was a result of scientific inquiry into their method of interaction. Once they were analysed in this way they became, naturally, less 'imaginable' as individuals. Changing literary taste was also responsible. The vogue for personifying abstractions, so popular in the first half of the century, gradually disappeared in the second. In some cases allegorical representation of a more abstract nature than that of the sixteenth century came back into fashion and took its place. It is perhaps significant that Henry More, who in his philosophical works attempted to bridge the gap between body and soul, should, in his poetry, turn to allegory rather than to direct personification. The Platonic discussion dialogues, which were growing in popularity, also often had casts of characters with allegorical names. But the fiction now was always a conscious one. There was none of the 'blurring' that occurred earlier when soul and body could be at once abstract qualities and yet concrete parts of man, each with a voice and being in its own right. Soul and skeleton talking together in the dead of a winter's night were no longer credible or relevant to the age.

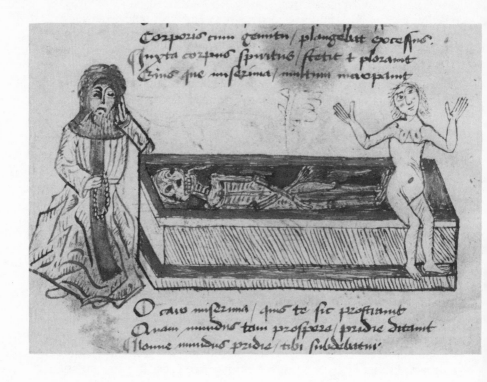

Philibert the Hermit has a vision of Soul and Body debating in the dead of a winter's night. (From Cambridge University Library MS Add 3093, 1ᵛ)

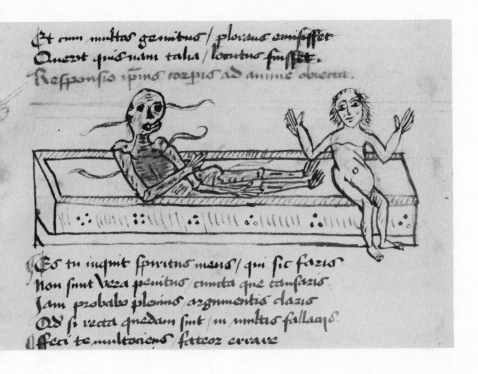

The Body raises itself with groans and replies to the Soul's accusations. (3ʳ)

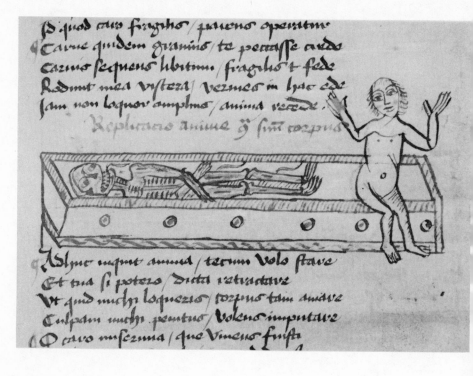

The Soul replies to the Body. (3ᵛ)

Devils appear to carry off the Soul to Hell. (5ᵛ)

The Soul is dragged towards Hellmouth. (6ᵛ)

Part Three

Body and Soul
in Seventeenth-Century
Literature

CHAPTER SIX

Aspects of Body and Soul in Seventeenth-Century Poetry

If the literary importance of the body/soul relationship in the seventeenth century were limited to the relatively small number of dialogues that were produced, it could be dismissed as a purely esoteric interest. But such is not the case. The nature of the relationship is a pervasive undercurrent running through much of the sacred and secular poetry, informing its assumptions while at the same time being subtly shaped itself by the demands of poetic expression. The interchange of literal and figurative uses of body and soul, so noticeable in both religious writings and the dialogues, informs the poetry of the period as well, but here the shifts of meaning are usually not just unhappy accidents, but are exploited positively to produce startling effects of irony and paradox.

Secular and Sacred

Up to this point, the body/soul relationship has been viewed primarily from a theological and moral standpoint. The dialogues themselves are preoccupied exclusively with this aspect of the matter. However, the love relationship in secular poetry provides a new focus for reflection on the relative merits of body and soul. While the emphasis is changed, and the end of the discussion is terrestrial, these reflections are by no means unrelated to the theological considerations already discussed.

Renaissance love poets were keenly aware of two kinds of love – one earthbound, the other heavenly. These could be identified as *eros* and *agape*, or alternatively as *cupiditas* and *caritas*. The attitude of writers to these two types of love differed greatly. They could be seen as diametrically opposed – the first associated with the body, lust, and inordinate desire; the second with heavenly love – warring against one another in yet a further manifestation of the universal struggle between flesh and spirit. In this case, embracing one must involve rejecting the other, as, for example, in Sidney's sonnet, 'Leave me, O love, which reachest but to dust.' But according to the second, more common attitude, earthly love and heavenly are not opposed but at different points on the same continuum, with the lower a means of ascent to the higher. Both attitudes have their roots in Neoplatonism and represent an extension of the contrary elements already noted in that philosophy (those that emphasize the separation of matter and spirit and those that emphasize their continuity) into the realm of secular love.[1]

Parallel to the Neoplatonic notion of continuity was the Christian concept of nature and grace as continuous orders, an idea first expressed by Aquinas (see Chapter 1, p 16) and brought into seventeenth-century thought by way of the scholastic tradition. Here, as in Neoplatonism, there are optimistic and pessimistic strains; the Calvinists would give a much less positive role to 'nature' and a correspondingly larger one to 'grace' than either Catholics or moderate Anglicans.[2] But in general, these latter branches of Christianity reinforced the elements in Neoplatonism that emphasized the interdependence of the two types of love, and it is this view that predominates in the secular poetry.

I shall also argue that there is a third type of relationship between 'physical' and 'spiritual' love – that in which the former is the necessary external manifestation of the latter. This view, which derives from the Aristotelian concept of the body as the instrument of the soul, enabling the soul to exercise its faculties (see Chapter 1, pp 6–7), lacks the implicit value judgments of the other two attitudes and suggests a reciprocal action between the two forms of love rather than a conflict or movement from one to the other. This attitude is found primarily in the poems of Donne; whether it is used with serious intent or as a witty game is a matter of debate.

It is with the poems of Donne that one begins, for no other writer has examined the body/soul relationship in love with such a combination of cerebral reflection and bodily passion. Despite the sharp distinction he makes between the physical and spiritual in his work, the connection between them is always an intimate one. Indeed, it has been argued that the primary purpose of Donne's 'wit' is to bridge the gap between apparent opposites.[3] In that startling image of the 'bracelet of bright haire about the bone' ('The Relique'), he suggests that the physical token may be taken for a device of the lovers 'To make their soules, at the last busie day, / Meet at this grave, and make a little stay.'[4] Similarly, the scratched name in the window glass of 'A Valediction: of my Name in the Window,' becomes the lover's 'ruinous Anatomie,' the 'rafters of [his] body, bone,' and, in a curious fancy, the focus for the return of his souls (which are emparadised in the beloved) as well as for the rest of his body, 'Muscle, Sinew, and Veine' (p 65).

Nevertheless (and contrary to much that has been written about Donne's love poetry), if one disregards such lighthearted jests as 'The Indifferent' and some of the 'Elegies,' Donne insists on the primacy of a spiritual love that is able to exist independently of the physical. In 'The Anniversarie,' contemplating the 'divorce' of the lovers that death must make, he asserts that 'soules where nothing dwells but love / ... then shall prove / This, or a love increased there above,' and ends with the famous line that links this particular assertion about lovers to all those general statements that would make the body, in this life, the prison of the soul: 'When bodies to their graves, soules from their graves remove' (ll 17–20, p 71). The well-known 'A Valediction: forbidding Mourning' makes a similar point – the possessors of a 'love so much refin'd,' 'Inter-assured of the mind, / Care lesse, eyes, lips, and hands to misse' (ll 17, 19, 20, p 63).

Yet along with this assertion of the primacy of the soul in love, there is an insistence on the importance of the body as well. The lovers in 'The Anniversarie' (cited above) who can contemplate the divorce of death in the future, nevertheless enjoy the pleasures of physical love in the present, and the love of 'A Valediction' has surely grown strong enough to survive separation through the caresses of the very 'eyes, lips, and hands' that can now be dispensed with. If the essence of love is spiritual, its actuality, on earth, can only be expressed through the body. Love cannot survive as mere essence of potentiality, which is too often equivalent not to 'idea' in the Platonic sense, but to a flimsy abstract notion – 'some lovely glorious nothing,' as Donne calls it in 'Aire and Angels' (p 75). The analogy with soul and body is made explicit as he asserts that, just as the soul takes limbs of flesh, so must love, the child of the soul, do likewise:

> But since, my soule, whose child love is,
> Takes limmes of flesh, and else could nothing doe,
> More subtile then the parent is,
> Love must not be, but take a body too. (ll 7–10)

Thus the action of love is linked to the action of the soul, both of which must have an organ in order to perform their function. In the case of the poet's love, this organ is not the physical body but the love of the woman, less pure than his, and therefore analogous to air, not angels, 'corporeal enough' to be appropriate for human beings 'who are neither all soul nor all body.'[5] There is possibly an intended double meaning in line 10, contrasting the state of mere 'being' with the 'doing' of line 8. Love can 'be' but can 'nothing doe' without a body, and in this earthly realm the two must be combined.

The most explicit description of the progression of love from 'being' to 'doing' is found in 'The Extasie' (pp 59–61). So much has been written about this poem that one hesitates to add to the mass of criticism. Yet if one can avoid beginning with such tempting preoccupations as the startling imagery, the 'ecstasy' experience, the narrow moral questions as to whether what is being advocated is 'right' or 'wrong' – or even precisely what *is* being advocated – 'The Extasie' emerges as a much simpler poem than most critics would allow it to be. Without denying its indebtedness to the earlier poems cited so persuasively by George Williamson,[6] it appears to rest, fundamentally, on a much more ancient foundation. It does not deal so much with two kinds of love, the physical and the spiritual, as with a description of the logical and inevitable progression from thought to act, from spiritual intention to physical execution. The image of the body as the 'spheare' governed by the soul as the 'intelligence' of that sphere, as well as the assertion that even heaven's influence works on man only through a physical medium, the air, takes one directly back to 'Aire and Angels,' thus encouraging the application of the more abstract statements about love in that poem to the complex particulars of love in this one.[7] To fail to take the step from the 'love' between souls to the 'love' between bodies is to leave 'a great Prince in prison' (l 68). This movement from 'spiritual' love to physical is neither progression nor regression, ascent nor descent; indeed, movement itself is probably a misleading way of thinking of it. It is merely the external manifestation of what, in reality, already exists. This is why it can be asserted with such confidence that there is 'small change, when we'are to bodies gone' (l 76). In this context, that final line ceases to sound like special pleading, and the moral issue as well falls into place. There is 'small change,' theologically at least, between an action of the mind and an action of the body. If this interpretation is correct, then Donne is not writing here primarily within a Neoplatonic framework which, even when it emphasizes the continuum between the physical and the spiritual, does make a real distinction between them. He is rather using a more Aristotelian distinction, which lacks the value judgments of Platonism between thought and act.[8] Combining this with a rather sophistical version of the Christian view that a sin in thought is equivalent to a sin in act (Matt 5:28), he can argue that what is *not* a sin in thought cannot be a sin when acted out. Thus, if there is a moral issue, it must be pushed back well beyond the situation of the lovers at the beginning of the poem.[9]

The strongest claims for physical love without any spiritual overtones are found not in the works of Donne, but in the large body of poems influenced by the philosophy of *carpe diem*. They lack the subtle analysis of the physical and spiritual elements of love and their relationship that one finds in Donne, and there is no attempt to soften the antithesis between the two. Love is physical love, and whether the poems are seductively persuasive like Herrick's, or harshly logical, like Marvell's, their message is the same: death will come all too soon; therefore let us experience the joys of life while we can. Thus they present a remarkable antithesis to Crashaw's statement in the introduction of the *Visio* that men must live well in order to die well. They do not deny the premises of the medieval poems; they simply draw different conclusions from them. The awareness of death invites the poet not to prepare for it but to turn more vehemently to life. All those medieval warnings in the *ubi sunt* tradition do not lead to a rejection of those things that are transitory but to a conviction that to embrace them is the one way to hold off, if only for a little, the deprivations that will inevitably come with death. Only in that anti-*carpe diem* poem, 'Vertue,' by George Herbert do we find the transitory nature of pleasure used in the traditional way, as an argument to turn to those spiritual qualities that will endure.[10]

The sharp dichotomy between the things of the body and those of the spirit that one finds within the *carpe diem* tradition is blurred when modified by the assumptions of the pastoral. The wholly *carpe diem* poem assumes nothing beyond the world it describes; its adherence to the 'rough strife' of pleasure is made in the face of an overwhelming sense of the brevity of that pleasure. This is not the case with the pastoral which, while firmly rooted in physical pleasure, seeks to assert the timelessness and ideal nature of it. These assumptions are so finely displayed in Marlowe's 'The Passionate Shepherd to His Love' if only to be denied in Raleigh's 'Nymph's Reply,' that it is unnecessary to elaborate on them. But Raleigh's poem also shows just how deceptive the simplicity of the pastoral's assumptions is. The ideal world conjured up by it often raises more questions than it can answer as Marvell's two pastoral dialogues, 'Clorinda and Damon' (1.18), and 'Thyrsis and Dorinda' (1.19) demonstrate.

At a casual glance, 'Clorinda and Damon' appears to be a secular version of the 'Dialogue Between the Resolved Soul, and Created Pleasure.' Clorinda presents Damon with all the delights and beauties of nature, and Damon opposes to these his own spiritual values. When Clorinda describes the enticing beauties of nature, Damon reminds her of their transiency: 'Grass withers; and the Flow'rs too fade.' To this Clorinda gives the typical *carpe diem* reply: 'Seize the short Joyes then, ere they vade' (ll 7–8). This, however, is *not* the reply of the poem as a whole. The very neatness of the antithesis seems to show the interrelationship of the two, the physical and the spiritual, as opposite sides of the same coin. This impression is reinforced by the double sense of words such as 'Temples,' the double significance of such things as the cave and fountain, and finally of Pan himself. The 'Temples' that the flowers are to adorn may be either a part of Damon's body or a place of worship – the two, in Clorinda's eyes, probably related! The fountain too may refresh either soul or body, and the resolution of the poem is not through the victory, by means of logic or conversion, of one or the other, but through the uniting symbol of the god Pan, half goat and half man, representing the union of the physical and the spiritual.[11]

In 'Thyrsis and Dorinda,' the world of the pastoral is from the first touched by time, as Dorinda begins by asking what will happen when Death parts them from the joys of their present life. Yet there is, again, no sharp antithesis between the world of sense and that of spirit. Indeed, because Dorinda can only conceive of one through the other, it is in physical terms that Thyrsis describes to her the heavenly Elizium. The final resolution to leave the earthly for the heavenly paradise is not a wrenching act of self-denial but a plausible progression to a state that contains everything in the earthly paradise except vicissitude and death. 'There, alwayes is, a rising Sun' (l 35), Thyrsis asserts – and that element of eternity, here claimed as a definite fact, not a mere assumption as in the secular pastoral of Marlowe – simply perfects what, even in its earthly form, is an existence containing a large element of the ideal.

The same lack of opposition between physical and spiritual is conveyed through the symbolism of 'The Garden' (1.48–50), which combines elements of both Eden and the garden of contemplation. Passion (the 'white' and 'red') is rejected, but not the sensuous delights of nature itself. The withdrawal of the mind (in stanza 7) implies not a rejection of the things of the body, but a parallel treatment of mind and body according to which each, soul and body, finds its appropriate pleasure. Neither oppresses the other, and the soul does not wholly leave the garden but, like a bird uncaged and content, sits on a bough suspended

between earth and heaven. The return to time and the world of 'th'indus-
trious Bee' in the last stanza reinforces this sense of a happy balance
between the sensual and the spiritual in this life.[12] The harmonious
relationship between the body and the soul in 'The Garden' can be
seen as the counterpart of that between the warring antagonists in 'A
Dialogue between the Soul and the Body.'

Both the nature of earthly love and the assumptions of the pastoral,
which lay behind so much sixteenth- and seventeenth-century love
poetry, prevented the secular poetry in general from exhibiting the
extreme dichotomy between body and soul that existed in many of the
works of religious writers and in the body and soul dialogues. The same
is not true of the sacred poetry, where many of the ideas and images of
the theological writings are taken over with little modification, and
dualism flourished, unmodified by secular ideas. Most of the assumptions of this dualism are by now so familiar that they need only be
mentioned briefly in this new context. The body as the prison of the
soul is found in countless poems ranging from the direct statement of
Quarles's 'My Soul is like a bird, my flesh the cage' (5.x, p 285) to the
implicit acceptance of the idea in George Herbert's 'Home':

> O loose this frame, this knot of man untie!
>   That my free soul may use her wing,
> Which now is pinion'd with mortalitie,
>   As an intangled, hamper'd thing.[13]

Donne, who in 'The Extasie' could argue for the necessity of the body,
finds in 'The second Anniversarie' that it is the prison of the soul –
conflicting points of doctrine between which 'no reconcilement can be
made.'[14] Elizabeth Drury's body is made an exception, but chiefly
because it possesses 'soul-like' qualities.
   Most poets accept the comonplace Aristotelian doctrine of the three
souls – the vegetative, sensitive, and rational – although again it is
Donne who is most explicitly philosophical in his poetic statements
about the subject:

> Wee first have soules of growth, and sense, and those,
> When our last soul, our soule immortall came,
> Were swallowed into it, and have no name.[15]

We know from his sermons that Donne believed the body to have been created before the soul[16] and this, coupled with the order of the creation of souls cited above, leads one to suspect that this is another instance of a writer, subconsciously at least, associating the two lower souls with the body. The only poet (apart from Milton) who mentions traducianism as a possibility at all is William Cartwright, and he only cites it as an hypothesis, not a fact.[17] In general, as one might expect, the poets are more conventional and less speculative in their views than the theologians.

The most notable discrepancy between theology and poetry is found in relation to original sin. While Donne's sermons make it clear that it is neither body nor soul alone that is responsible, but their union, in his poetry the simpler view that body corrupts soul prevails:

> This curded milke, this poore unlittered whelpe
> My body, could, beyond escape or helpe,
> Infect thee with Originall sinne, and thou
> Couldst neither then refuse, nor leave it now.[18]
> ('The second Anniversarie,' ll 165–8, 1.256)

With regard to actual sin, there is more latitude. Negative references to the body in general often seem to make it culpable yet, on the whole, Donne acknowledges the prime responsibility of the will and reason, faculties of the rational soul. This is frequently coupled with the nostalgic wish, found in the medieval debates, that man had been created a simple creature without the addition of the rational soul and hence 'further from corruption.' At other times he passionately disputes the justness of the guilt that besets man because, in him alone, the will assents to evil. It is this knowledge that the 'highest' of God's creatures is, in fact, the least fortunate, that is behind the outpouring of 'Holy Sonnet IX':

> If poysonous mineralls, and if that tree,
> Whose fruit threw death on else immortall us,
> If lecherous goats, if serpents envious
> Cannot be damn'd; Alas; why should I bee?
> Why should intent or reason, borne in mee,
> Make sinnes, else equall, in mee more heinous?
> (ll 1–6, p 8)

The lack of proper subordination as a cause of sin is also stressed, and in 'The Litanie' Donne acknowledges the dangers inherent in a situation 'When senses, which thy souldiers are, / wee arme against thee, and they fight for sinne' (ll 181–2, 1.345). The close parallels between the theology and sacred poetry show the latter as very conservative. Originality was scarcely a sought-after quality in these poems; from that point of view the secular verse, where there is a less high premium on orthodoxy, is intrinsically more interesting.

In the works of later poets, particularly Vaughan and Traherne, there are parallels of a different nature. Here the lessening of the dichotomy between body and soul is similar to the trend noted in the works of other writers of the same period, particularly the Cambridge Platonists, whose work was familiar to both poets. Their direct influence on Vaughan was slight, in part because of certain differences in temperament and approach between them. Vaughan would have been opposed to the Puritan views of the Platonists and, unlike them, was quite uninterested in scientific developments. The exchange of pamphlets between Thomas Vaughan (Henry's brother) and Henry More reveals only animosity between the two, and when Henry Vaughan likens the soul to light or air, More accuses him of materialism.

While to us Vaughan and Henry More appear to be less widely separated in their views than their acrimonious conflict would indicate, Vaughan's chief impetus for seeing body and soul as part of one continuum came from a more ancient offshoot of Platonism – the Hermetic writings. Their influence, whose importance has already been mentioned in the previous chapter in connection with Vaughan's body and soul dialogues, extends to his poetry in general.[19] Closely related to Neoplatonism, the Hermetic writings embody the same paradoxical attitudes towards body and the physical world but with a more mystical cast. Physical things are 'lower' than spiritual on the scale of being, but this must not be confused with the belief of the Gnostics that 'matter' is a separate principle that is actively evil. For the Hermetic writers there is a kind of mystical correspondence uniting all things, higher and lower. The 'sydereal spirit,' which unites the spiritual and terrestrial, endows nature with a primitive sense so that all creation literally waits 'with earnest expectation' for 'the manifestation of the sons of God.'[20] Man's body is part of this world of natural things, and after death, when the soul has fled, this primitive spirit still pervades it:

> So murthered man, when lovely life is done,
> And his blood freez'd, keeps in the Center still

> Some secret sense ...   ('The Timber,' ll 21–3, p 498)

Such poems as 'And do they so?' (p 432) show that this spiritual presence throughout all nature is, on its highest level, associated with the immanence of God himself. Vaughan's sense of God's immanence, however, is coupled with that of his transcendence, which is eloquently expressed in such a poem as 'Disorder *and* frailty':

> O, is! but give wings to my fire,
> And hatch my soul, untill it fly
> Up where thou art, amongst thy tire
> Of Stars, above Infirmity!   (ll 46–9, p 446)

The two, immanence and transcendence, are really two aspects of one process. Immanence, God's presence in nature, leads man to transcendence, God's presence above and outside earthly things. In the course of this process, the qualitative distinction between body and soul, which exists on earth, disappears entirely. Clay becomes 'a spirit' and 'true glory' dwells in the physical 'dust, and stones' ('The Check,' ll 34–6, p 444).

This perfect union between the material and spiritual worlds should, ideally, exist throughout creation. But in his own variation on the theme of man's troubled dual nature, Vaughan laments that the one creature who contains both worlds does not find this perfect union realized in himself. The 'spirit' that informs the lower creatures guides them to do right instinctively; the beings without human bodies that are above man on the scale of creation are not subject to his limitations:

> All have their *keyes*, and set *ascents*; but man
> Though he knows these, and hath more of his own,
> Sleeps at the ladders foot.   ('The Tempest,' ll 37–9, p 461)

Man remains bound by the limitations of natural things. He thinks of and loves the physical, and when this disappears, as in death, neither his spirit nor his body can retain a sense of communion with the departed. As the body dissolves

> Love languisheth, and memory doth rust
> O'r-cast with that cold dust.
>   ('Sure, there's a tye of Bodyes!' ll 3–4, p 429)

He lacks the elementary contact that herbs and animals share with one another and with nature. 'Imaginary flights' carry him 'wide of a faithfull grave' (ll 15–16). Yet the perfect state of spiritual communication in which 'the spirit, not the dust' would be his brother eludes him also. Vaughan is at one with his contemporaries in recognizing that man's dual nature thus prevents him from enjoying the effortless communion with God that both the lower creatures and the higher have, and that it is this same dual nature than makes him able to sin. But this recognition lacks the passionate bitterness of Donne's 'Holy Sonnet IX,' and the overwhelming impression given by the body of Vaughan's work remains that of the interdependence of body and soul, united by an all-pervading spirit.

In the works of Thomas Traherne, the same Neoplatonic strain prevails, untouched by the more explicit elements of hermetism in Vaughan's work. Here the influence of the Cambridge Platonists is more certain and direct. Traherne took up a chaplaincy with the Bridgeman family in 1669. Sir Orlando was interested in the thought of the Cambridge Platonists and another chaplain of his, Hezekiah Burton, was a minor member of the group and a friend of Henry More.[21]

The interrelationship between the physical and the spiritual is most clearly seen in Traherne's treatment of perception – the connection between concrete objects and the abstract ideas about these objects. Things in themselves are dead and are only conveyed to our minds by 'thoughts' that are God-sent and bear similarities to Neoplatonic emanations.[22] Yet God does not choose to enlighten man directly, bypassing objects, and so thoughts cannot be communicated to us unless they are expressed in terms of the concrete. All things must 'borrow Matter first, / Before they can communicate.' The title of the poem from which this line comes, 'The Circulation' (ll 38–9, II.153), aptly indicates the nature of the process. Thoughts illuminate things; things, in turn, give concrete expression to thoughts. The relationship between things and thoughts, the world of sense and the world of ideas, is analogous to the relationship between body and soul. The circular movement between thought and object is paralleled by that between the glorified body and soul. Joys shall

> Affect the Soul, though in the Body grow.
> Return again, and make the Body shine
> Like Jesus Christ, while both in one combine ...
> ('Thanksgiving for the Body,' ll 437–9, II.226)

The above passage is, as it happens, referring to the relationship between body and soul after death, but it cannot therefore be dismissed as untypical, because this state of harmony that all acknowledge as the reward of the just is, to Traherne, the norm. Original sin plays a very small role in his thought. Each child enters the world in a state of pre-lapsarian innocence or 'felicity,' and only falls from this state through its impressionable nature and the bad example of others. Thus the harmony that one perceives between body and soul in his work is not so much the result of a unique perception of body and soul themselves, as of his general view of man's state in relation to God.

This close, harmonious relationship between body and soul that one finds in the works of Vaughan and Traherne is something quite different from the explanations of their communication via the 'spirits' that one finds in Donne, for example. In Donne's work, despite their intimacy, they remain essentially separate with a strong tension existing between them. The lessening of this tension, and the perception of body and soul not as opposites but as part of one continuum in the mid-century works of Vaughan and Traherne (although it derives primarily from unique influences on them), is wholly in keeping with the general trend of the period.

Imagination and Belief

No analysis of statements about the body/soul relationship in this literature can give an adequate picture of what happens to them as they function within the poetry of the period. For poetry is not versified theology or philosophy; the demands of the imagination are as pressing as those of belief. Poetry and other forms of literature must be 'imagin-able' in Hobbes' sense of the word; theological works need not be so. But in making religious poetry 'imaginable' one inevitably alters the content somewhat. Poetic images do not simply illustrate theological beliefs; they subtly help to form them.

At the most basic level, poetry affects the description of the soul itself. While Donne and his contemporaries did not believe the soul to be visible, they just as certainly did *imagine* it to be so. In 'Resurrection, imperfect,' Donne speaks of those 'whose credulous pietie / Thought, that a Soule one might discern and see / Goe from a body ...' (ll 17–19, p 28). Yet his poetic images suggest just such a visible soul:

> Oh my blacke Soule! now thou art summoned
> By sicknesse, deaths herald and champion;

> Thou art like a pilgrim, which abroad hath done
> Treason, and durst not turne to whence hee is fled.
>
> ('Holy Sonnet IV, 'll 1–4, p 7)

Herbert asks God to 'furnish & deck my soul' ('Christmas,' l 13, p 81), and refers to doomsday as a time 'when souls shall wear their new array' ('Death,' l 19, p 186). The whole of Crashaw's 'To the Name Above Every Name'[23] involves an elaborate personification of the soul. It must 'traverse round / The Aiery Shop of soul-appeasing Sound' and 'beat a summons in the Same / All-soveraign Name' (ll 33–6). Sermons provide examples as well. Although one might assume that here theological concerns would be paramount, the need to hold the attention of an audience and to make the sermon a 'literary' work worthy of God,[24] dictated other priorities as well. And such personification need not conflict with meaning but could convey it more vividly, happily combining abstract ideas and concrete presentation: 'What would a dejected Spirit, a disconsolate soule, opprest with the weight of heavy, and habituall sinne, that stands naked in a frosty Winter of desperation, and cannot compasse one *fig leafe*, one colour, one excuse for any circumstance of any sinne, give for the *garment of Righteousnesse*.'[25] The richness of association here enhances the theological impact as the disconsolate soule, looking in vain for a 'fig leaf' in the frosty landscape, is a new Adam, cast out of the Garden of Eden.

Parallels to these verbal images are not to be found in the literal explanations of the soul's extension in the works of Hobbes or More or Cudworth, but in the art of illuminated manuscripts and emblem books. There too we find the soul represented in concrete form, usually a naked, sexless figure, rather childlike, clearly related to the medieval illustrations that accompanied manuscripts of the *Visio*. In Quarles' *Emblemes*, the woodcut illustrations reinforce the verses' depiction of the soul as a human form. The close relationship between verbal description and emblems at this time is further illustrated by Thomas Jenner's *The Soules Solace or thirtie and one Spirituall Emblems*,[26] a collection of emblems based entirely on verbal illustrations in sermons.

The concrete representation of the soul in art and literature was nothing new, but in the early seventeenth century it acquired added vigour as it coincided with the tendency, manifest in the dialogues of the period, to personify abstractions in general. Examples of this kind of personification are everywhere. Two poems on death, one by Lord Herbert of Cherbury, and one by his more famous brother, George Herbert, show the dramatic effect it could produce:

Methinks Death like one laughing lyes,
Shewing his teeth, shutting his eys.[27]

Death, thou wast once an uncouth hideous thing,
  Nothing but bones,
  The sad effect of sadder grones:
Thy mouth was open, but thou couldst not sing.
('Death,' ll 1–4, p 185)

While this sort of personification had a long history, that of the early seventeenth century differs from that of earlier ages in that it was, by this time, largely divorced from the elaborate systems of correspondence that had originally fostered it. In the sixteenth century such personifications were typically embedded in sustained allegory as, for example, *The Faerie Queene*. The incipient breakdown of the modes of thought that fostered this allegory, as well as the literary movement away from it to more direct and dramatic modes of presentation gave, for a brief period, a new direction to the use of these personified abstractions. Their separation from the systems of thought that gave rise to them meant their own ultimate disappearance as well, but for a while, in the interim, they survived to be used with unprecedented vigour and freedom. The startling effects of much of the imagery of the metaphysical poets can surely be traced to just this freedom. Thus Donne's 'Holy Sonnet v' (p 13), which begins with the conventional image of man as a little world, continues in a most unconventional manner, through an allusion to the discovery of 'new sphears' and 'new lands' to beg that 'new seas' may be poured into his eyes so that they can then 'drowne' this world with weeping.[28]

The needs of dramatic presentation fostered not only the concrete representation of the soul but the portrayal of it in situations of conflict. After tracing the long history of body and soul as antagonists, it would be absurd to argue now that, really, their strife is merely a literary game, but equally the literary elements cannot altogether be dismissed. When Herbert writes, in 'Affliction (1),' 'My flesh began unto my soul in pain ...' (l 25, p 47), he is not envisaging a scene of conflict such as those depicted in the body and soul dialogues but is merely dramatizing for the reader the physical woes that follow on a life of pleasure and excess.

Donne typically casts the soul in a situation of conflict. The approach of death in 'Oh my blacke Soule,' quoted above, becomes the summoning of the soul 'by sicknesse, deaths herald,' which calls it to the bar of judgment. The whole is made more vivid by a series of comparisons in which the soul becomes a pilgrim that has committed treason or a prisoner hauled to execution. The discrepancy noted between Donne's views on the body's role in the transmission of original sin in his sermons and in his poetry may well be due to just such perceived literary demands. Thus the careful theological explanations of the sermons give way to the charges of 'infection' against the body in 'The second Anniversarie.' The fact that the body and soul dialogues themselves, with the sole exception of Vaughan's, deal with the warring relationship between an evil soul and body rather than with that between a good soul and body (for which there are also medieval precedents), shows the perennial appeal of the more dramatic situation. Conflict is always more interesting that mutual congratulation.

All these factors come into play in the most notable example in the period of a work formed by the dual demands of theology and imagination – *Paradise Lost*. When Raphael says to Adam and Eve,

> ... And what surmounts the reach
> Of human sense, I shall delineate so,
> By lik'ning spiritual to corporeal forms,
> As may express them best ...[29]

he is stating the method of Milton himself. But *Paradise Lost*, unlike the shorter poems by Donne and Herbert cited above, is a major work with a purpose of such ultimate importance – to 'justifie the wayes of God to men' – that its method cannot be dictated by literary considerations alone. These must be in harmony with the aims of the epic as a whole.

It is the ancient Christian doctrine of accommodation that provides the needed theoretical framework to unite the theological and imaginative demands of Milton's work. Briefly, accommodation recognizes man's intellectual limitations and sanctions the likening of spiritual things to corporal not on the grounds that it makes them 'imaginable' but that it makes them 'knowable.' Its roots are at least as ancient as Augustine[30] and, since it sprang from an acceptance of the limitations of man's fallen nature, was readily adopted by such churchmen as Calvin and John Colet. Insofar as it is a theory of communication, accommodation may well have been implicitly behind the use of imagery in the sermons and poetry quoted above, but its theological basis is given a new importance by Milton in *De Doctrina Christiana* where he states that God 'is exhibited not as he really is, but in such a manner as may be within the scope of our comprehensions.'[31] Man's own conception of God should be guided by the descriptions (themselves accommodations) that he finds in scripture.[32] Accommodation has philosophical implications as well. There must be a 'higher' reality for which the 'lower' is the accommodation. This fits beautifully with the Platonic scheme of the universe with its scaled levels of being, and there is evidence that, at an early stage, Milton was very much a Platonist.[33] But he was always very much aware of those aspects of Christianity, particularly the Incarnation, that troubled the early Christian Platonists,[34] and in his maturity seems to have opted for something closer to the Hebraic monism, which also had a continuous intellectual tradition. Thus Milton concludes: 'Man is a living being, intrinsically and properly one and individual, not, according to the common opinion, made up and framed of two distinct and different natures, as of soul and body, but that the whole man is soul, and the soul man, that is to say, a body, or substance, individual, animated, sensitive, and rational ...'[35]

This leaves the central question still unresolved. If the theory of accommodation fits essentially with a Platonic frame of reference and Milton, by the time he wrote *Paradise Lost*, had rejected this framework for the more ancient Hebraic one, how can one argue that accommodation remains the essential poetic mode of *Paradise Lost*? In response to this I would claim that here Milton allowed himself to be swayed by the demands of poetry rather than adhering strictly to doctrine. Accommodation as a theory may imply a dualism in which Milton no longer wholly believed, but as a poetic and dramatic device it was essential – not simply in the way it was necessary to theologians or preachers as a means of condescending to lesser intellects but as the very basis of epic sructure. Thus, in a rather different sense, theology and Hebraic monism must themselves be 'accommodated' or reconciled to the needs of poetry and Platonic dualism.

Milton's task in *Paradise Lost* went far beyond that of Donne and Herbert, who made concrete the abstract in the single situation of the short poem. The epic deals with process and history, and it is therefore these large-scale ideas that must be embodied in recognizable, physical events. Yet this must be done in such a way that the physical events themselves will not be taken for the complete action.[36] A wholly allegorical approach might make for a clearer solution (though not a richer one), but Milton does not have this option since for him, and most of his contemporary audience, the actual events of his biblical source are literally true. In any case, the relationship between event on the physical level and event on the spiritual is, as many critics have demonstrated, more complex than this or, indeed, than anything inherent in the simple theory of accommodation. For behind this lies the rich tradition of fourfold biblical interpretation.[37] Thus the fruit of the tree is also the 'fruit' of all our woe,[38] and the action in the Garden of Eden has its analogues not only in the heavenly rebellion, but in the life of every man. One is dealing with physical action that is at once 'real' in itself, not merely an external manifestation of spiritual action, but that at the same time does embody a spiritual action that transcends it.[39]

The account of the War in Heaven, to which Raphael's statement specifically refers, presents the greatest challenge to Milton's ability to unify action and meaning, poetry and doctrine. This colossal struggle between good and evil is to be localized, made specific, made, to some extent, corporal. Only thus can it be recounted to those who, of necessity, measure 'things in Heav'n by things on Earth' (vi.893) – though it is worth noting that Milton, like More and Cudworth, did genuinely believe that spirits have airy bodies, so their presentation in a visible form is not *merely* a fictive necessity. On one level, the battle of the 'Spirits that live throughout / Vital in every part' (vi.344–5) may be felt an inadequate 'objective correlative' for the theological concept. On another and more profound level, however, the conjunction of the earthly and heavenly in this context points to the deeper conjunction of the two throughout *Paradise Lost*, as the War in Heaven is reflected in the rebellion of Adam and Eve. 'Accommodation' in this instance both serves the needs of poetry and, through its emphasis on correspondence (the other aspect of difference) reinforced by the multiple meanings of biblical exegesis, it implies an underlying monism compatible with Milton's theology. Thus the demands of literary expression, in this case, lend themselves to an explicit statement of great theological importance: earth and heaven *are* linked, and the likening of spiritual forms to corporal has a significance far beyond that of human poetic necessity.

The other point at which the interplay of the demands of theology and literature is most complex is Milton's description of the Fall and original sin. For Milton's stated views on these matters become subtly changed when conveyed through his interpretation of Genesis. Soul and bodies are not separate entities in the Platonic sense; consequently the body cannot be 'evil.' Man was created in the image of God 'not only as to his soul, but also as to his outward form.'[40] Insofar as there is division it is one of function, and in this sense all the faculties of reason, fancy, and the senses, belong to the soul, which therefore must bear all responsibility for sin. As in the works of Aquinas and Hooker, sin occurs not because the body tempts the soul, but because Reason, though created 'right,' can be deceived by the senses and, in this way, misinform the Will. Adam is surprisingly well informed about the psychology of temptation when he expounds it thus to Eve:

> But God left free the Will, for what obeyes
> Reason, is free, and Reason he made right,
> But bid her well beware, and still erect,
> Least by some faire appeering good surpris'd
> She dictate false, and misinform the Will
> To do what God expresly hath forbid.   (IX.351–6)[41]

Once original sin, of which Milton predictably takes a serious view,[42] has overthrown the proper subordination within soul and allowed passion to run riot, succeeding sins inevitably follow:

> For understanding rul'd not, and the Will
> Heard not her lore, both in subjection now
> To sensual Appetite, who from beneathe
> Usurping over sovran Reason claimd
> Superior sway ...   (IX.1127–31)

The whole process still takes place within the soul, however; body is not implicated. Indeed, his refusal to denigrate the body leads Milton directly into his famous unorthodox view that the soul dies with the body. Adam, contemplating his fallen state, concludes:

> It was but breath
> Of Life that sinn'd; what dies but what had life
> And sin? the Bodie properly hath neither.
> All of me then shall die ...   (X.789–92)[43]

Milton's acceptance of traducianism rather than the more common belief in infusion was also part of the same insistence on the unity of soul and body, although it was compatible with his serious view of the Fall and original sin as well.

These theological beliefs, many of which (as the quotations above show) are included as theoretical statements in *Paradise Lost*, are modified by what actually happens between Adam and Eve in Book IX. The role improper subordination plays is not in doubt, as Eve first refuses to take Adam's wise advice to stay with him, and he, as the superior partner, fails to compel her obedience (IX.370–2). But other elements of the action do not fit so closely with Milton's theology. Given the established context of seventeenth-century views on body and soul, it is difficult to avoid seeing elements of a body/soul conflict in the tempta-tion scene. The serpent's appeal to Eve's vanity (IX.531–48) and the role that physical desire plays in her decision to eat the fruit (IX.735–44) which is 'Fair to the Eye, inviting to the Taste' (l 777), both suggest her identification with body. Even if one argues that these attributes could be applied equally well to sense, the poetic demands for concrete representation and dramatic conflict militate against that more abstract solution. And Adam, finally, does not behave like the higher faculties of the soul described in Milton's theory of sin. He is 'not deceav'd' but, like an all-too-human husband, 'fondly overcome with Femal charm' (IX.998–9).[44] After both have eaten and the recriminations begin, their 'mutual accusations' are remarkably similar to those uttered between soul and body. Eve accuses Adam of not having forbidden her to leave him; he, she argues, permitted her temptation and sin. Adam, furious, replies that he warned her and hence is not responsible. This dispute about whether the rebellious subordinate or the controlling superior is chiefly responsible for sin sounds very familiar indeed. The final lines of Book IX might be the conclusion of any medieval or seventeenth-century debate:

> Thus they in mutual accusation spent
> The fruitless hours, but neither self-condemning,
> And of their vain contest appeer'd no end.   (IX.1186–8)[45]

One can see this account of the Fall deviating in two distinct direc-tions from the simple couching of Milton's views on original sin in the mythology of Genesis. It deviates first in the direction of a purely human drama played out between husband and wife. Second, it deviates in the direction of a struggle between warring abstract entities, such as body and soul, sense and reason. But because this latter struggle is superim-posed on the human drama attached to the very real husband and wife, they cannot function precisely as an acting out of the theoretical aspects of temptation and sin.[46] These purely theoretical statements are found, instead, incorporated into the text as descriptions of the process of temptation taking place within Adam and Eve as individuals. Thus, in addition to the large acting out of the Fall, in which Adam and Eve function as objective aspects of man's nature, we have a non-dramatic *description* of the process of temptation and the Fall within each of them. The first, the large drama of the Fall as played out by Adam and Eve, has its analogues in the dramatic war in Heaven in Book v and the plotting of Satan in Books I and II. Here the demands of epic with its need for conflict and the theory of accommodation with its dualistic assumptions militate against the abstract, monistic beliefs about sin and temptation of Milton's maturity. The second, the description of temptation, derives from classical accounts as they have been interpreted by the Church Fathers and adapted by Milton himself. It would be difficult to find in seventeenth-century literature a more complex example of the interaction of literary expression and theological dogma. Yet, apart from the ambiguous role of 'body,' neither account necessarily contradicts the other but rather complements it – conflict and rebellion as it is immediately felt and acted out is illuminated by a careful analysis of its origins and progress within the individual. 'Truth,' for man at least, is neither one nor the other, but a combination of the two.

Literal and Figurative

The literal and figurative uses of body and soul discussed in Chapter 2 are, on one level, a specific example of the discrepancy between factual statement and literary expression. Yet they become more than that, because the two uses coincide with two different theological views, and even the figurative, therefore, can be seen as grounded in Christian belief. When, for example, Herbert says of man, 'In soul he mounts and flies, / In flesh he dies ('Mans medley,' ll 13–14, p 131), he is objectifying the two abstract impulses within man described in Galatians 5:17, the Old Man versus the New, and, at the same time, expressing a belief that these two impulses are connected with the two literal components of man's nature as indicated in Romans 7:22–4 – the law of sin is associated with the body. The assumptions underlying this use, and much of the manner of the usage itself, are identical with those discussed in relation to the theological writings and sermons, but in the poetry the literary effects produced by the superimposition of one meaning on the other or by deliberate shifts between literal and figurative meaning are unique.

On the literal level, a poet like Herbert reveals a positive affection for the body, an affection that is justified by the Incarnation and most eloquently expressed when he contemplates the brutal treatment suffered by the earthly body of Christ:

> O Blessed bodie! whither art thou thrown?
> No lodging for thee, but a cold hard stone?
>
> ('Sepulchre,' ll 1–2, p 40)

When he turns to the purely human body in 'Church-monuments' (pp 64–5), his attitude is still one of tenderness. Even though the 'lesson' it is set to learn is the harsh one of its own mortality, it is addressed as 'Deare Flesh,' and accorded a treatment parallel to that of the soul and as appropriate for its end. The use of 'flesh' for 'body' in this poem, however, signals a slight shift away from the wholly positive attitude to the 'blessed bodie' of 'Sepulchre.' This body or flesh is potentially 'wanton in [its] cravings' and must be schooled to subdue its baser impulses. It is the 'flesh' that sin has 'turned to stone,' not the 'innocent earth' that we possessed before the Fall. When we turn to other passages in which Herbert characterizes 'body' as 'flesh,' we find that the negative, figurative connotations come more fully into play, as they do in the passage from 'Mans medley' quoted above. When in 'H. Baptism (II)' he says, 'The growth of flesh is but as blister: / Childhood is health' (ll 14–15, p 44), there is a fusion of the two uses of 'flesh.' Arising out of the perception of childhood as a state of pre-lapsarian innocence, it links the growth of the physical body with that of evil impulses, making the growth of the literal and figurative 'flesh' coincide. In 'Coloss. 3.3,' the delicate balance between literal and figurative has been overturned, this time on the side of figurative interpretation:

> One life is wrapt *In* flesh, and tends to earth:
> The other winds towards *Him* ... (ll 5–6, p 84)

Herbert is here speaking primarily of the two abstract and contrary impulses within man, and only secondarily is one of these wrapt 'in flesh,' the physical body.

This movement from literal to figurative usage illustrated by Herbert's work coincides with a shift from the term 'body' to 'flesh,' but such is not universally the case. Donne, for example, uses 'body' with all the negative connotations of 'flesh,' a hindrance to the soul, when he says,

> As dead low earth ecclipses and controules
> The quick high Moone: so doth the body, Soules.
>
> ('To the Countesse of Bedford,' ll 41–2, I.196–7)

On occasion other terms as well, such as 'clay,' 'dust,' 'earth,' are also used figuratively to denote man's baser nature. Thus Vaughan can ask, 'Are we all stone, and Earth?' ('Christs Nativity,' II, l 14, p 443) and state that the way to reach God is not through 'th'applause, and feat / Of dust, and clay' ('Retirement,' ll 30–1, p 463), but through a retreat from these things.

The coincidence of literal and figurative use extends to 'soul' and 'spirit' as well. When Vaughan exclaims, 'O that I were all Soul' ('Chearfulness,' l 17, p 429), it is obviously the figurative meaning that is uppermost although, like his contemporaries, he believes that the soul is a very real part of man's being. And when Traherne says, 'I felt a Vigour in my Sence / That was all *Spirit*' ('Wonder,' ll 20–1, II.8), he is attributing to part of his physical being sensations so pure that they can only be characterized as 'spiritual.'

The superimposition of literal and figurative meanings of body and soul, flesh and spirit, on one another is theological in origin, rooted in the conflicting Hebraic and Hellenic ways of viewing the body, and only secondarily used to provide a richness of association in literature. The deliberate shifts from one to the other, in contrast, while deriving from the same theological ambiguities, were exploited in the period primarily as a literary device. At the most superficial level, such a shift can create the kind of 'wit' in which the metaphysical poets revelled. In 'Satyre III' ('Flesh [it selfes death] and joyes which flesh can taste, / Thou lovest; and thy faire goodly soule, which doth / Give this flesh power to taste joy, thou dost loath.' [ll 40–2, 1.156]), Donne is, in the first instance, using 'flesh' that is 'it selfes death' primarily in a figurative sense; but the 'flesh' through which the power to taste joy is exercised, must be primarily the physical body. It is from this identical terminology but changed meaning that the paradox arises. Flesh is loved to the exclusion of that power which enables it to be lovable. But the 'flesh' that is loved is only in part and verbally the same as the 'flesh' through which the powers of the soul can be exercised.

The verse letter to the Countess of Bedford, 'T'Have written then,' provides further evidence of the literary effects Donne achieves through the subtle balance of literal and figurative usage. Here it is 'body' rather than 'flesh' that is the term at issue, but the shifts in meaning are effected with the same agility:

> Let the minds thoughts be but transplanted so,
> Into the body, 'and bastardly they grow.
> What hate could hurt our bodies like our love?

Wee (but no forraine tyrants could) remove
These not ingrav'd, but inborne dignities,
Caskets of soules; Temples, and Palaces;
For, bodies shall from death redeemed bee,
Soules but preserv'd, not naturally free.

(ll 51–8, p. 197)

The transplanting of the mind's thoughts into the body does not, of course, signify chiefly the soul's literal implantation, but rather its inordinate preoccupation with bodily matters. Yet in the succeeding lines, this figurative use of body gives way to an argument, leading from the premises of these first lines, for the removal of the soul from the physical body. By preserving our physical bodies we keep our souls enclosed as in caskets, though the assurance that they are not thereby 'ingrav'd' (with the obvious pun on the word) points the way to the transition that can, potentially, take place after death, when the bodies that are redeemed become 'Temples and Palaces.' The condensation of meaning in the passage, bringing together the contrary attitudes towards body (casket, Temple) that coincide with the contrast between the body in this life and the body in the next, combined with an implicit argument for assisting the transition from one to the other is made possible through the shifting, double use of the term 'body' itself. This complexity, nevertheless, cannot disguise the fact that in both this poem and the passage from 'Satyre III,' the end result is chiefly sophistical rather than profound.

It is in Shakespeare's 'Sonnet 146' that one finds these same devices used for an end that surpasses the clever. Although chronologically it precedes the poem by Donne and, indeed, most of the works cited, this sonnet brings together all the assumptions about the antagonism between body and soul in this life that were prevalent in the age.

The soul is the 'centre' of the sinful earth or body in at least two senses. It ought to be the 'centre' in the sense of a governing force and the focus of caring but, instead, its position, enclosed within the body, only serves as a literal sign of its figurative captivity, '[thrall to]' the 'rebel pow'rs' that array it. The contrast between the excessive care for the external and the total disregard for the internal is couched in the imagery of a mansion and its inhabitant. Yet this mansion, merging again with the physical body, is itself transitory, and will be eaten up by worms. In the remarkable final quatrain the soul is urged, figuratively, to consume the body, thus buying 'terms divine in selling hours of dross,' and bringing about a reversal of the situation at the beginning of the sonnet, so that the inner man, the soul, is fed while the external body is consumed.

Then, in a final and dramatic shift, the figurative Death becomes identified with the literal body. Thus to feed on 'death, which feeds on men' is to consume the physical body as the concrete representation of abstract death, St Paul's 'body of this death.' This is not vindictive but redemptive – and redemptive, paradoxically, for the body itself.[47] In the climactic final line, Death, now wholly a powerful abstraction, is destroyed, thus preparing the way for the resurrection of the literal man, body and soul. The solution posed to the body / soul dilemma in the sonnet places it firmly in the Christian context of losing one's life in order to find it, and the dual meaning of 'death' in the penultimate line makes the Soul's action neither cannibalism nor a merely symbolic gesture against evil. Nowhere are the theological ambiguities inherent in the body / soul relationship turned to the uses of literature with greater effect.

CHAPTER SEVEN

Body and Soul
Analogies

The relationship between body and soul, functioning both as an explanation and a reinforcement of man's dualism, was seen from ancient times to be similar to a wide variety of other relationships. These similarities come from the deep-seated belief that God, man, and creation itself all correspond in certain fundamental ways. Some of the comparisons are thus 'true' analogies,[1] but most frequently this is not the case. Their authors are not seeking to establish a consistent, theological relationship between two levels of being, but are using the assumption of such a relationship to illuminate a specific point of similarity. Thus these similes, metaphors, and 'analogies' (in the general sense of the word) frequently work only on one level or in relation to a particular aspect of the things compared.

Some of these comparisons, which occur in the dialogues themselves, have already been encountered. The active and passive natures of soul and body are like flame and wood;[2] the classical comparison of the body to a prison takes on a homely medieval aspect when, in *Complaynt of the Soule*, the prison becomes a sack, enclosing the soul.[3] The issue of proper subordination is reflected in such analogies as that of the horse and rider, or the servant and mistress. And as early as Hildebert's 'De Querimonia et Conflictu Carnis et Spiritus,' we find the most versatile analogy of all, that which sees the soul as the husband (Adam) and the body as the wife (Eve).[4]

Not only did these analogies survive in seventeenth-century literature; they flourished in new adaptations. In the end, it was probably in this guise, rather than more directly, that the body/soul literature had its most lasting influence. Analogies do not demand precise belief; hence they could survive and flourish in the midst of factors that made the debates anachronistic. Yet if the analogies do not demand belief, they imply a kind of assent as to the nature of the relationships they assume, and they foster the survival of those assumed relationships in at least an 'underground' way. Thus the use of these analogies in the seventeenth century tells us much not only about the richness and variety of associations that the body/soul relationship could express, but also about the extent to which the beliefs concerning it remained implicit in the age.

Standing on the borderline between the concrete and the abstract, body and soul can function analogically either to objectify relationships between abstractions (which is essentially what happens in the dialogues themselves, where they externalize an internal, psychological struggle) or they can function to add an abstract and ideological dimension to relationships that are themselves objective and/or human as, for example, between an instrument and its music or between husband and wife. This division is a very important one in terms of the way the analogies can function, but it is not particularly helpful in organizing the range of analogies because very often a single analogy may move in both directions at once, comparing body and soul first with two abstract qualities, and then with two concrete entities that are seen to embody the same abstract relationship. Thus John Welles, in *The Soules Progresse*, sees body and soul as analogous to matter and form, and also to a house and its tenant.[5] And in J. Guillemand's 'A Combat betwixt Man and Death,' a whole list of concrete analogies for body and soul (horse / rider; ship / pilot; lantern / candle; cage / bird; shell / egg)[6] are designed to express certain abstract aspects of the relationship – controller / controlled; light / enlightened; prisoner / prison, and so on. I therefore deal with the analogies not according to the ways in which they function, but according to their topic and content. The range of comparisons is very broad indeed and moves in ever-widening circles from the purely personal level, through the social and political, to the macrocosmic. Also, as the relationship between body and soul is not simple and static, but complex and dynamic, so the analogies, even within a single category, can express such differing qualities as mutual help or mutual antagonism, proper subordination or rebellion.

External/Internal Relationships

The most obvious feature of the body/soul relationship as it was conceived in the Renaissance is essentially spatial – the body, in this life, contains the soul; the soul is the inhabitant of the body; the body is the external manifestation of the soul. From these relatively simple perceptions arise comparisons, some of which merely restate them, others of which add new dimensions through their own connotations. The two most common analogies of the first sort are those that see the body as the clothes or the house of the soul. The first analogy is very ancient, attributed to Galen by J. Woolton, Bishop of Exeter, in 'A Treatise of the Immortalitie of the Soule'[7] and to Aesop by J. Guillemand in 'A Combat betwixt Man and Death.'[8] Yet the variations and elaborations are seemingly limitless. Donne, expanding on the basic simile of the body as a house of clay, describes the bones as timbers, the walls as flesh, the windows as eyes.[9] Adams provides a moralized allegory; after the initial comparison stating that bodies are to souls as houses are to the goods within them, he goes on to describe the senses as doors and faith and prayer as the locks to those doors. These must be maintained fast against the 'Day of the Lord,' which will come as a thief in the night.[10] In a more secular vein, he uses a body/soul analogy to inveigh against the common practice of selling land (with the hardship this imposed on retainers) to buy clothes to maintain social position. Here the land is equated with true substance, the soul, and the garments with mere external, bodily show. 'Akers of land are metamorphosed into trunks of apparell: and the soul of charity is transmigrated into the body of brauery.'[11] By a further extension of the basic analogy some writers, notably Donne, see the grave in the same relationship to the body as the body is to the soul. Just as the body is the house of the soul, so the grave is the house of the body.[12] Or, to change the terms slightly, the body is the garment of the soul, and the grave is its wardrobe. Thus the faithful shall lay up 'the garments of [their] soules, [their] bodies, in the wardrobe the grave, till [they] call for them, and put them on again, in the resurrection ...'[13]

These analogies, based on the external/internal nature of the body/soul relationship, do not necessarily imply value judgments, yet they are usually implicit unless one genuinely believes that the clothes *are* the man! Indeed, in many cases, the value judgment is the chief point to be made. While characterizing the soul in the body as an inhabitant in an unclean inn or living tomb and as a precious jewel in a cabinet[14] are not different in terms of the functional relationship described, they are worlds apart in the value assigned to body and the felt aspects of the relationship. Thomas Beverley compares the body to a garment to show the ease with which it can be cast aside; the soul 'values the Body no more, than the Body does a Garment ...'[15] In contrast, when Adams compares the mortal body to the skin of a serpent, he is not thinking primarily of its ability to be cast aside but, recalling the significance of the serpent in bestiaries, of its capacity for renewal. Just as the serpent, by shedding its skin, gains perpetual youth, so we 'shall put off, not the skinne, but this *mortall body*: and so be *clothed with immortalitie* and eternall life aboue ...'[16]

Yet Adams also used the much more familiar and negative view of the relationship, echoing Donne's comparison in saying that our bodies are to our souls as graves are to our bodies.[17] And when the soul leaving the body is compared to a child entering the world,[18] it is the confining nature of the womb/body that is being emphasized, as it is in that most common of all body/soul analogies that compares the body to a cage or prison and the soul to a captive bird. Even apparently neutral analogies can, through the ingenuity of the writer, take on moral connotations. Donne's comparison of the soul in the body to a letter in a box, though unusual, would seem, on the surface, merely to indicate the internal/external aspects of the relationship. But Donne develops it thus: 'Is your soule lesse than your body, because it is in it? How easily lies a letter in a Boxe, which if it were unfolded, would cover that Boxe? unfold your soule, and you shall see, that it reaches to heaven ... whereas the body is but *from* that earth, and *for* that earth, upon which it is not; which is but a short, and an inglorious progresse.'[19]

The soul in the body may also be perceived as the active agent in an inert habitation. Thus the soul is in the body as a candle in a lantern, and when the candle is removed from the lantern, the lantern (body) is dark, but the candle (soul) burns more brightly.[20] In contrast, when Edward Reynolds describes the confinement of the soul in the body, he compares it to a man in a coach, who can only receive such motions as the coach (body) affords.[21] Both of these analogies emphasize the confining nature of the body and have certain affinities with the familiar prison metaphor, but while in the first case the emphasis is, conventionally, on the moral aspects of the relationship, in the second, along with the notion of the limitations imposed on the soul by the body, comes an awareness of the psychology of perception, and one can see older ways of thinking being adapted to encompass the new concerns of the age.

It is not surprising that the ambivalent attitudes towards body expressed in the theological writings should also find their parallels in these analogies. The body may be an element opposed to the soul, or the body may be the external manifestation of the soul. Two macrocosmic analogies, superficially similar, express these essentially opposite views. The first, by Nathaniel Culverwel, takes as its point of departure Plato's notion that God is the soul of the world and Nature but the body. Yet

Culverwel goes on to chide Plato for not reforming 'the abuse of this word *Nature*; that he did not scrue it up to an higher, and more spiritual notion.'[22] Thomas Adams, on the other hand, changing the terms 'Nature' and 'God' to 'Earth' and 'Heaven,' alters the implications of the analogy completely. Earth is not seen as the physical manifestation of heaven but as an element absolutely opposed to it: 'The *soule* is; at all parts more precious than the *Body* ... The *soule* is compared to heauen, the body to earth. The heauen is glorious with Sun, Moone, Starres; so the soule with vnderstanding, memory, reason, faith, hope, &c. The body like the earth, wherof it was made, is squallid with lusts.'[23] It is no coincidence that the first of these comparisons comes from a minor member of the Cambridge Platonist school, while the second is from a clergyman with decidely Puritan leanings. Even figures of speech bear the all-pervasive stamp of the theology of their users.

Variations on those positive analogies that see the body as the external manifestation of the soul give rise to a particular group dealing with liturgy and worship. The train of associations here links the general notion of the physical as the outward sign of the spiritual to the distinction between execution and intention in church worship. Within this context, the ambiguities in attitude towards the bodily, external elements disappear; they may not be qualitatively equal to the internal aspect, but they are a necessary complement to it. Thus Joseph Meade, in a Cambridge University sermon, can say, 'As the outward worship without the inward is dead, so the inward without the outward is not complete, even as the glorification of the soul separate from the body is not, nor shall not be consummate till the bodie be again unite unto it.'[24]

Donne showed particular awareness of this relationship between the external and the internal in church worship and of its application to our own constitution. He claims that the soul is to the body as Christ himself and his merit are to the clear and outward profession of his truth.[25] In a sermon preached about three months later, he goes much farther than this to assert that the liturgy itself is as the mystical body of Christ, appliable to our souls: 'The Son of God is ... *The word*; God made us with his word, and with our words we make God so farre, as that we make up the mysticall body of Christ Jesus with our prayers, with our whole liturgie ...'[26] The implications of this passage go far beyond its specific application to this topic. It sets forth Donne's theology of preaching and worship, with its emphasis on the incarnational aspects of the sermon itself, so that the word preached is like the will of the Father manifest in the Son. With these comparisons between the body of Christ and the liturgy, we have moved from the realm of mere simile or metaphor, 'analogy' in the popular sense of the word, to 'true analogy' in which the one element actually corresponds to and partakes of the nature of the other.[27] It is in this more profound sense that Lancelot Andrewes also sees the word in the mind and the word spoken as analogous respectively to the eternal generation of the son and his generation in time, and so to soul and body: 'His generation eternal, as *Verbum Deus*, is as the inditing the word within the heart. His generation in time, *Verbum caro*, is as the uttering it forth with the voice. The inward motion of the mind taketh unto it a natural body of air, and so becometh vocal ...'[28]

The variations on this theme are endless, and do not all by any means operate on this higher level of 'true analogy.' Donne's ingenuity makes doctrine be to language as the soul is to the body or essence is to existence.[29] None of this is to the detriment of the body or, indeed, of preaching and the liturgy. Just as in his secular poetry the 'love's mysteries' that grew in souls must be manifest in the 'book' of the body, so here the external elements of worship are the necessary end of purely spiritual adoration, just as faith, if it is genuine, will result in works.[30] Even the distinctions between the two elements of expression – thought and language – are brought into play, and the church is seen to be to the soul as rhetoric is to logic – the external manifestation of an internal truth.[31] The ancient comparison of the body to the temple of the soul is transformed into an analogy linked to Donne's own calling, that sees our bodies as the temples to which our souls are the priests.[32]

In all these analogies, the external elements of worship – language, rhetoric, the liturgy, the church building itself – are seen to be analogous to body, wholly distinct from, though not necessarily inferior to, the soul and its analogues. There is another category of analogies, however, that compare these same external elements of worship not to body but to the elements uniting body and soul. That remarkable passage already quoted, in which Donne asserts that 'we make up the mystical body of Christ Jesus with our prayers, with our whole liturgie,' points the way to the transition between the two categories. Here the liturgy is analogous to Christ, himself *Verbum*, the external manifestation of the will of the Father. But Christ is also a union of God and man, indeed, the bridge between God and man. At this point, therefore, one moves into a series of analogies based on similarities between the word preached, the Word manifest by God (Verbum, Christ), poetry itself, and the animal spirits that unite the two elements of man, body and soul. Thus the ceremonies of the church become 'those Spirits that unite soule and body together,' and so, by implication, peculiarly necessary to man, a creature composed of this union of the celestial and the terrestrial: 'So great a care had God, of those things, which though they be not of the *revenue* of Religion, yet are of the *subsidy* of Religion, and, though they be not the *soule* of the Church, yet are they those *Spirits* that unite soule and body together.'[33]

Poetry as well shares this 'middle nature' and consequent ability to speak to man. Its use is therefore justified both as an instrument of God ('*God* by *Moses* made the children of *Israel* a *Song*, because, as hee sayes, howsoever they did by the Law, they would never forget that *Song*, and that *Song* should be his witnesse against them')[34] and as an instrument of man, appropriate to keeping fame as the grave keeps bodies and heaven souls:

> Verse hath a middle nature: heaven keepes soules,
> The grave keeps bodies, verse the fame enroules.
> ('The first Anniversary,' ll 473–4, p 245)

In this way Donne implicitly exalts his own vocation as preacher/poet, while at the same time effecting a kind of metaphysical union between the disparate elements of man through the offices of that dual vocation.

The variety of these comparisons derived from this first and most basic relationship between body and soul illustrate not only the ingenuity of these seventeenth-century writers, but the way in which they are capable of moving beyond analogies based on superficial similarities to those grounded in perceived theological truths.

Accomplices/Antagonists

The analogies based on the internal/external relationship between body and soul perceive that relationship, essentially, as a passive one. Therefore, they can only illustrate a few facets of a union between two partners that were frequently cast in an active role, either working together as accomplices in good or evil or warring against one another as deadly enemies. These aspects of the relationship find expression in other analogies of the period.

One of the most striking analogies portraying them as evil accomplices, in the manner of the dialogues, is Donne's characterization of them as Herod and Pilate, who concur in the planning of sinful acts: 'It is when this *Herod*, and this *Pilat* (this Body, and this soule of ours) are made friends and agreed, that they may concurre to the Crucifying of Christ.'[35] In contrast to this are analogies that emphasize their mutual dependence on one another. The faculties of the body are to the soul as ministers and conveyors of information are to Princes,[36] and have the same ability to help or, if indisposed, to hinder the soul by providing inadequate or false information.

Most of the comparisons, however, do not deal with body and soul as partners but with the more dramatic possibilities of the two in conflict. In the guise of flesh and spirit, they war against one another as did Esau and Jacob. The frequency with which these brothers are seen as a particular, historical manifestation of this most basic conflict is striking. The following passage, depicting their strife in the womb, is typical: 'As soone as God limited his Couenant to the Family of *Abraham*, of two children that hee had, hee that was borne after the flesh, did hate him that was borne after the Spirit. *Jacob* and *Esau* representing two contrary Nations, struggled together in the belly, and their quarrell began before their life.'[37]

Ishmael and Isaac, the son of the bond woman and the son of the free, are similarly analogous to flesh and spirit.[38] One must inherit; the other must be cast out. In a more unusual variation on this Old Testament theme, Simon Harward sees the ram offered in place of Isaac as the body, the irrational part that must be killed, while Isaac himself, who is bound awhile, but ultimately saved, is the soul.[39] The self-tormenting and mutually destructive nature of the body/soul antagonism is well illustrated by an analogy, previously noted, in which the soul kills the body as a sword cuts its own scabbard.[40]

More complex and interesting than these figurative interpretations of biblical events is a whole category of analogies based on the moralization of planetary motion. In their various manifestations, these macrocosmic analogies both illustrate some fascinating aspects of the history of an idea and show the strange blend of scientific interest and moral significance so characteristic of the period. An understanding of them is essential to a major metaphysical poem like Donne's 'Goodfriday, 1613. Riding Westward,' where they form the very basis of the argument.

There are two distinct versions of the analogy – that which sees the opposite motions of the *primum mobile* and the planets as analogous to the motions of soul and body, and that which places the opposition within the faculties of the soul itself – each corresponding to one of the two theories about the *locus* of the internal struggle that man feels within himself. Sacrobosco's moralization of the heavenly system avoids the issue by simply referring to 'rational' and 'irrational' motion,[41] but in Lydgate's translations of Guillaume de Deguileville's *The Pilgrimage of the Life of Man*, the conflict takes place between the 'spryt' and the body.[42] Both versions of the moralization survive in seventeenth-century literature. In addition to this discrepancy, there was uncertainty about whether the outer sphere, whose motion is westward, should be identified with the 'good' movement of the soul or rational part, and the inner, eastward motion of the planets with the 'evil' movement of the body or irrational part, or whether the identification should work in precisely the opposite way. Sacrobosco made the motion of the *primum mobile* that of the rational element, but in John Lydgate's work it is associated with the strivings of the body, and the inner, eastward movement is associated with the soul. This latter identification is still found in a letter from the mid-seventeenth century written by James Howell:

> Thus my soul still moves Eastward, as all the heavenly Bodies do; but I must tell you, that as those Bodies are over-master'd and snatch'd away to the *West, raptu primi mobilis*, by the general motion of the tenth Sphere, so by those epidemical infirmities which are incident to man, I am often snatch'd away a clean contrary course, yet my Soul persists still in her own proper motion. I am often at variance, and angry with myself ...[43]

The discrepancy between the two moralizations is almost certainly the result of the tension that existed between the positive classical associations of the First Mover, and the positive Christians ones that were attached to eastward motion. Since in the received system of planetary motion the two did not coincide, a choice had to be made, and in many cases the Christian association prevailed.[44] There is no consistency, however, and in a version of the analogy that places the conflict in man within the soul itself, E. Reynolds, unlike Howell, opts for the classical associations. Thus the sense, will, appetite, and passions are to Reason as the planets are to the *primum mobile*: 'The Will it selfe is stubborne and froward; the Passions Rebellious, and Impatient of Suppression; the Senses and Sensitive Appetite thward and wayward, creeping alwayes like those under Coelestiall Orbes into another motion, quite contrary to that which the *Primum Mobile*: Illightened Reason should conferre upon them.'[45]

It is quite predictable that Donne, on the contrary, should choose the Christian moralization rather than the pagan one. The great significance of the east in his own symbolic thought is not only apparent in his sermons ('The East, that is the fountain of all light and glory ...'),[46] but is enshrined in his own epitaph. His use of the analogy in 'Goodfriday, 1613. Riding Westward' is in keeping with these positive associations. The poem is based on the interweaving of two sets of contrasting motions – the one internal, the other external, analogous to the contrary movement of the spheres. The internal contrary motions are confined to the poet's soul, which is like a sphere governed by its 'intelligence,' which is devotion, and the 'forraigne motions' of pleasure or business, which function as 'first movers.' These internal and abstract motions are made objective through the poet's physical movement westward, which contradicts the movement of his 'Soules forme,' which 'bends toward the East.' The macrocosmic imagery here is not merely a straining after effect; Christ, the contemplation of whose death is the real subject of the poem, is he whose hands 'span the Poles / And tune all spheares at once ...' (ll 21–2, p 31). The historic event was indeed macrocosmic, and therefore to use such allusions to portray its reenactment within the individual is not hyperbole. The tensions between the contrary motions of the spheres have their counterparts not only in the 'rise and fall' of Christ which, for Donne, marked the culmination of the struggle between good and evil, but in the constant struggle within the soul of man. The resulting use of the analogy is a superb example of the richness of meaning that could be derived from these complex associations.

Actor/Agent; Form/Matter

Distinct from those analogies that see body and soul as partners or antagonists are those that see them in terms of their differing functions, jointly making up a complete action or object. The relationship here may be the Aristotleian form/matter one, or it may be that of actor and agent, with the soul as the means through which that action is effected.

The form/matter analogy, though both ancient and commonplace, is surprisingly versatile. Often it appears in company with other analogies, and its precise force varies according to these secondary associations. Thus when Donne says, 'That though in my matter, the earth, I must die; yet in my forme, in that Image which I am made by, I cannot die ... the Image of God himselfe'[47] he is using the analogy to underline the distinction between the eternity of the world of forms (the image of God in the soul) and the transient nature of the form's embodiment in particular matter (the body). In contrast, when he describes the soul as 'the forme of that body, the King of that Kingdome,'[48] he is thinking, in rather un-Aristotelian terms, of a hierarchy of form and matter, soul and body, in which the former controls the latter. We have already seen how the same analogy is linked to Donne's comparisons of body and soul and the external and internal elements of worship, where it signifies primarily a distinction between controlling design or intention and its manifestation in worship.[49] In fact, the extremely commonplace nature of this particular analogy means that it is often used carelessly, yoked to ideas that convey aspects of the body/soul relationship that are quite different from those originally intended by it. In some cases a writer altogether misunderstands the significance of the analogy he is trying to use. Thus when Samuel Haworth indignantly asserts that the soul is *not* the form of a man as a mariner is of his ship, because no one could be so arrogant as to assert that a Mariner is the form of the ship,[50] he is missing the point of the soul/body:Mariner/ship analogy, which is not linked to form and matter at all but to the actor/agent or director/directed aspects of the relationship.

This actor/agent relationship is behind another common analogy that compares body and soul to a tool or instrument and the art that directs that instrument, or the artificer himself. 'The body, and the senses are but the tooles and instruments, that the soule works with; But the soule is the art, the science that directs those Instruments.'[51] Other analogies arise from the perception of similar relationships between a part and the whole of both soul and body. Thus the heart is to the body as the will is to the soul – the chief seat of 'morality' or 'felicity,' evil, or good;[52] or the eye is valued by the body as the understanding is by the soul, as the most important and directing faculty.[53] The fluidity of such analogies is shown by a comparison of these statements, which rest on the assumption that heart and eye are the most important parts of the body, with the medieval heart and eye debates, where the argument rests on a distinction between internal agent (the heart) and external actor (the eye) which are, in that case, analogous to soul and body respectively. The perception of relationships changes all too readily in accordance with the point to be illustrated.

A large group of analogies based on the actor/agent distinction are linked to the use of musical instruments and the making of music. The most common form of this analogy sees a likeness between the body and a musical instrument and between the soul and one who performs on that instrument. This is similar in import to the artificer/tool analogy. Just as the soul gives life and action to the body, so the player strikes the instrument into harmony.[54] The variations possible on this apparently simple theme are surprisingly numerous. The analogy may be used to emphasize the closeness of the body/soul relationship. The soul enjoys 'contentments' by the senses just as a musician gains pleasure from his instrument, and to be without the body is to be like a lutenist without his lute.[55] With only a slight change of emphasis, the analogy also can explain why the soul leaves the body at death. 'As the Musitian ceaseth to play when the Instrument is vnstrung, so the soule ceaseth to giue life vnto the body, yea, flyes out, when it is destroyed ...'[56] The lute remains, like the body of a dead man, when a song is not being played on it.[57] Another minor variation on the analogy makes it compare body and soul not to musician and instrument, but to the two strings of an instrument that vibrate together in this life, and uses this to explain certain psychological effects that arise through the distemperature of the body:

> The Soul and Body in the present conjunction mutually sympathize. As two things that are unisons, if one be touch't and moves, the other untouch't, yet moves, and trembles ... Thus the Soul and the Body are two strings temper'd to such a correspondence, that if one be mov'd, the other resents by an impression from it. If the Body be Sanguin, or Cholerick, or Melancholy, the Soul by a strange consent feels the motion of the humors, and is altered with their alterations.[58]

Yet the same writer, in another musical analogy, asserts the ultimate superiority and independence of the soul. While its mental operations may be hindered by the 'ill habit' of the body, the mind still retains its intellectual powers just as a musician's ability to play remains undiminished, though his instrument may be out of tune.[59]

Just as the body is the soul's instrument, so man may be the instrument of God, as Donne writes in 'Hymne to God my God, in my sicknesse':

> Since I am comming to that Holy roome,
>   Where, with thy Quire of Saints for evermore,
> I shall be made thy Musique; As I come
>   I tune the Instrument here at the dore,
>   And what I must doe then, thinke now before.
>
> (ll 1–5, p 50)

This analogy, like that based on the opposed motion of the planets, is rich in allusions. It can be used to signify either harmony or discord and implicitly calls into play a host of Platonic associations with the order of the universe and the music of the spheres as well as with man's place in that total pattern. Donne's particular use of it in this instance also links it with those analogies of his that see worship and the liturgy as the external manifestation of the mind or heart. Here the whole man becomes this external manifestation of the will of God, an harmonious instrument, played upon by Him and designed to resound His praise everlastingly with the 'Quire of Saints.'

While these multiple associations are what give the analogies their chief literary interest, they also make it impossible to divide them into rigid categories. Just as the music analogies are linked to certain aspects of the cosmological ones, so this whole division, based primarily on the distinction between actor and agent, or form and matter, is implicitly one of director and directed as well, and thus leads to those analogies that are based on the hierarchical nature of the body/soul relationship and the need for proper subordination between them.

Subordination

The emphasis on hierarchy and subordination is a pervasive one, and the analogies based on this aspect of the relationship exist on all levels – the personal, the domestic, and the political. Fundamental to it is the concept, also originating in the Aristotelian form/matter distinction, that everything, while a limited 'end' in itself, functions as a means to an end for something higher on the scale of being. Thus John Davies of Hereford states with great certainty that the world is made for man, man for the soul, soul for the mind, and the mind for God.[60] This hierarchical 'tidiness' finds expression in analogies that liken man to a well-governed house. The use of the analogy here differs from the house/ tenant one examined earlier in that the emphasis is not on the house as the external enclosure of the tenant, but on its order and good government. Adams, preaching a sermon on the text 'I will goe into thy House, with burnt offerings: I will pay thee my vows' (Psalm 66.13), makes the order within man akin to the ordered house of God itself: 'Mans body is closed vp within the Elements: his blood within his body; his spirits in his blood, his soule within his spirits; and the Lord resteth in his soule.'[61] The enclosure imagery here suggests a microcosmic universe in which, as in the Ptolemaic one, the centre is the place of chief importance.

The essentially domestic analogy of man as a house is capable of expansion and elaboration so that the house becomes a household with the analogy based on the actual relationships between the people living and working there. In this context, the soul may become the mistress and the body the servant, as Richard Braithwait's dialogue has shown.[62] Adams embroiders the basic concept in another sermon where the servant and mistress are no longer anonymous types but are linked to biblical prototypes, Hagar and Sarah. Hagar is, of course, flesh; Sarah is spirit; and the Christian listener is predictably chastised for ornamenting the one at the expense of the other.[63]

The added dimension that comes from the identification of abstract qualities with biblical characters, deriving from the medieval fourfold interpretation of Scripture, is beautifully exemplified by the moralization of Jacob's household in 'A Verray deuote treatyse' by Richard of Saint Victor. Here the simple soul/body:mistress/servant relationship is expanded to include the hierarchical relationship among many of the faculties within the soul. Jacob is analogous to God, Rachel to Reason, and Lya [Leah] to Affection. The maids to Rachel and Leah signify Imagination (which is servant to Reason) and Sensuality (which is servant to Affection).[64] The whole is worked out in interminable detail and with great seriousness.

No less elaborate, though divorced from specific biblical associations, is the household analogy in a 1640 funeral sermon by William Sclater. Here there are three 'levels' of houses – the external house of the body, the spiritual house within, and the mystical house of the Church of God. The second of these deals with relationships among the faculties of the soul; mind, spirit, and understanding run the household and guide the inferior faculties, the servants. Of these, will is the chief steward, and the concupiscible and irascible faculties are inferior servants. Just like ordinary servants, they may either execute the will of the steward or frustrate it. The affections are peasants, lackeys to execute orders and bring tidings. Finally, the hands and other organs of the body are like field servants, doing the active business of the house.[65]

The kingdom, perceived either as a large-scale household, or a smaller version of the kingdom of God, functions analogically in ways that are similar to those of the household, with the emphasis on proper subordination – the King is to the kingdom as the soul is to the body. 'In man there is a *kingdome*, 'Adams asserts. 'The minde hath a Souereignity ouer the body. Restraine it to the *Soule*: and in the Soules kingdome ... Reason hath a dominion ouer the affections.'[66] This passage also shows that, like the household analogies, those based on the kingdom can relate to faculties within the soul as well as to soul and body. The Mind (Reason) is King; the Will is a Privy Counsellor, and the Heart is the obedient community. Will imparts to Heart those things which Reason has appointed.[67] The relationship is not always harmonious; in *The Soules Progress* the kingdom is a court and the man who, soul and body, is a prisoner, finds his various faculties functioning both as witness and judge. Conscience is the accuser, memory produces the witnesses, and judgment gives the sentence.[68]

While the need for proper subordination provides the chief focus of these analogies, some have other connotations as well. Donne uses the kingdom analogy, for example, to show the care that the soul has of the body and, perhaps, subtly to remind the sovereign of his duties: 'My soule may be King ... but it neglects not the remoter parts of my body.'[69] Just as the body cannot be cured without the cure of the soul, so in States no ills can be cured without the cure of the Prince, and he (extending the analogy one step upwards) is himself dependent for health on pure Religion.[70] When all the parts are healthy and in accord with one another, then the kingdom will flourish like a healthy man. It will be a state 'as hath the best Body, (best united in it self, and knit together) and the best Legs to stand upon, (Peace and Plenty) and the best Soul to inanimate and direct it, (Truth of Religion) and the best Spirits to make all parts answerable and useful to one another, (wisdom and Vigilancie in the Prince, Gratitude and Chearfulness in the Subject).'[71] The equation between the parts of man, the elements of a kingdom, and abstract, spiritual qualities invests the first and second with a new significance, while giving a practical basis for the application of the last.

The habit of mind that proceeded from the microcosmic to the macrocosmic – from the faculties within man's mind to his soul and body, to his household, to the kingdom, seeing similarities and analogies at every point – is too well documented to need more extensive illustration. Yet one can become so complacent about these relationships that one fails to realize any longer that, believed in rather than functioning merely as decorative figures of speech, they endowed both life and literature with unique meaning. This is particularly evident in two additional groups of analogies that, because of their multiple associations, cannot be categorized according to the abstract relationships on which they are based, and must therefore be considered according to their subject-matter.

Analogies with the Church and the Trinity

Analogies between soul and body and the Church or Christ are based on one of two similarities – the unique union of the physical and the spiritual in each (akin in its external/internal aspects to the analogies with worship discussed above), or the relationship between an enlightening principle and enlightened subject. Christ's Incarnation made him a being, like man himself, composed of two distinct elements – his Godhead and his manhood. Thus, on the simplest level, these two are commonly seen as analogous to soul and body: 'Our soul is not turned into nor compounded with the body, yet they two though distinct in natures grow into one man. So, into the Godhead was the manhood taken, the natures preserved without confusion, the person entire without division.'[72] Man's peculiar station in the chain of being is therefore sanctified by the dual nature of Christ himself. There is only one distinction – but one that is sufficient to explain the difference between divinity and troubled humanity. The soul suffers with the body, while the divinity of God does not participate in the frailties of the earthly nature to which it is joined.[73]

The basic analogy is frequently extended to include the church as well, which is 'the body of Christ.' Then soul is to body as God is to man or as Christ is to the Church, each union forming a new whole. 'Beyond all this, God having thus married soule and body in one man, and man and God, in one Christ, he maries this Christ to the Church.'[74] The creation of man is like Christ's establishment of the Church on earth – both are formed of earth and spirit, body and soul.[75] And Baxter, linking the intricate whole to an analogy with the kingdom as well, notes that the love of the soul to the body is like the love of Christ to his 'mystical political Body,' the Church. Indeed, not only is man *like* a church; the proper union of soul and body may, figuratively, *be* a church.

> It is not only a concurring of men, a meeting of so many bodies that makes a *church*: If thy soule, and body be met together, an humble preparation of the mind, and a reverent disposition of the body ... if all thy senses, and powers, and faculties, be met with one unanime purpose to worship thy *God*, thou art, to this intendment, a Church, thou art a Congregation, here are *two or three met together in his name*, and he is in the midst of them, though thou be alone in thy chamber.[76]

The emphasis of these analogies in general and this last passage in particular is on the harmonious union of the separate elements within man. But in those analogies based on the light/enlightened distinction, while both elements are still integral parts of a whole, there is greater emphasis on their differences. These are essentially sacred versions of the candle/lantern analogy; the soul is to the body as God is to the soul – the principle that animates and enlightens it. Just as the body dies when the soul leaves, so the soul dies when it loses God.[77] The soul is in man as the Holy Ghost is in the world,[78] and the office that the soul performs in the body, the Holy Ghost performs in the body of Christ, the Church.[79]

This last statement is appended to a much more complex analogy that posits a relationship between soul, body, and spirits/Father, Son, and Holy Ghost/and the triple work of Creation, Redemption, and Sanctification. The identifications here are not to be taken completely literally so as, for example, to link Christ exclusively to body, but rather to indicate the general correspondence between the acts of God to man and specific persons of the Trinity, and also between the uniting function of the spirits and that of the Holy Ghost.[80] Just as the external forms of worship could shift from being analogous to body to become analogous to the spirits uniting body and soul, so here, when it is the members of the Trinity rather than God as a unity that is the subject, the Holy Ghost is placed in this intermediate position.

The Holy Ghost is the union of the Father and the Son. As the body is not the man, nor the soul is not the man, but the union of the soul and body, by those spirits, through which the soul exercises her faculties in the Organs of the body, makes up the man; so the union of the Father and the Son to one another, and of both to us, by the Holy Ghost, makes up the body of the Christian Religion.[81]

This correspondence between the trinity in man and the Trinity in God is based on the account of man's creation in the image of God in Saint Augustine's *The Trinity*. In origin these analogies 'are not merely illustrative parallels of the Trinity; they are embodiments of the archetypal trinitarian pattern.'[82] But while rooted in the work of the Church Fathers, they are pursued with unprecedented vigour and ingenuity in the Renaissance. Adams points out that while in God there are three persons in one essence, so in man there are three essences in one person – 'an elementary body, a diuine soule, and a firmamentall spirit.'[83] He then goes on, moving in an ever smaller compass, to link these to the trinity of powers in the soul itself – the vegetative, the sensitive, and the rational.

Spiralling still inward, the Trinity becomes analogous to the three faculties within the rational soul itself. There are two common forms of this analogy. The first, attributed to Saint Bernard, makes the three persons of the Trinity analogous to Reason, Memory, and Will[84] which, like the Trinity, are both separate and interdependent. The second substitutes 'understanding' or 'cogitation' for memory and, as it is expounded in the following passage, depends for its validity on the way in which each member of the group proceeds from the previous person or faculty in that group:

> As our understanding proceeds from our reasonable soule, so the second Person, the Son, proceeds from the Father, therefore we attribute Wisdome to the Son: And then, because the Holy Ghost is said to proceed *Per modum voluntatis*, That as our soule ... and our understanding, proceeding from that soule, produce our will, and the object of our will, is evermore *Bonum*, that which is good in our apprehension, therefore we attribute to the Holy Ghost, Goodnesse.[85]

The comparisons based on the 'true' Augustinian analogy were also turned, with typically Renaissance ingenuity, to other more far-fetched correspondences. To Donne, always preoccupied with the business of words, the emphasis on process in the preceding quotation enables the stages of thought and speech also to become analogous to the Trinity. 'The understanding of man (that is as the Father) begets discourse, ratiocination, and that is as the Son: and out of these two proceed conclusions, and that is as the Holy Ghost.'[86]

Even more complex, however, is the analogy based on Saint Bernard's version that takes quite other comparisons as its point of departure. This seventeenth-century adaptation goes far beyond the significance of its original by adding to it two corresponding manmade and God-given trinities, depicting man's turning away from God through the temptations of the flesh and his return to him through the gifts of the spirit. Thus we have within ourselves 'A Creating and a Created Trinity: A Trinity, which the Trinity in Heaven, Father, Son, and Holy Ghost, hath created in our soules, Reason, Memory, and Will; and that we have supercreated, added another Trinity, Suggestion, and Consent, and Delight in sin; And that God, after all this infuses another Trinity, Faith, Hope, and Charity, by which we return to our first.'[87]

The linking here of the actual faculties and abstract qualities within man, and the balancing of the 'trinities' leading to sin and to salvation is so ingenious that one can scarcely suppress a smile when, in the same sermon, Donne frankly acknowledges, 'And therefore it is a lovely and a religious thing, to finde out *Vestigia Trinitatis*, Impressions of the Trinity, in as many things as we can ...'[88] Yet one must not confuse this habit of mind with the romantic and post-romantic searching for 'symbols' or 'significance' in natural phenomena. The significance and the correspondences deriving from the Church Fathers were there, real, believed in, divinely ordained, for these seventeenth-century writers; it only remained for man 'to finde [them] out.'

Soul and Body; Husband and Wife

Of all the analogies for the soul/body relationship, the most pervasive and resonant was that with husband and wife. The two basic components of man and the basic unit of society were seen to correspond in many ways both as ideal types and as fallen, sinful counterparts. The marriage relationship, believed to be divinely ordained, but observably imperfect and fallen from its original state, was ideally suited to present this dual perspective on the condition of man himself. It also combined, to an unusual degree, elements of stark realism with abstract concepts. Unlike the purely abstract comparisons in the previous section, marriage was not merely a theoretical relationship but an actual one with all its passion and pettiness as well as its joy. When writers thought of body and soul as living friends or antagonists, indissolubly bound together for good or ill, rather than as theological concepts, it was in terms of marriage partners that they envisaged them. And just as the analogy with marriage gave an added concreteness and 'imaginability' to the soul/body relationship, so the soul/body relationship gave an archetypal significance to that between husband and wife.

The ideal pattern of the marriage relationship is set forth in terms of other relationships already recognized, in their own right, to be analogous to soul and body. Thus marriage is 'a mystical representation of that union of two natures in Christ and of him to us, and to his Church ...'[89] And Cudworth, linking the Christian notion of types to the Platonic one of forms, says of the relationships between husband and wife, Christ and the Church, that there is not only 'a bare Similitude between the union of Man and Wife by Marriage, and the mysticall union of Christ and the Church,' but that one is a '*Real Type*' of the other, and the other an *Archetypall Copy*, according to which that was limmed and drawn out,' and reinforces this view by stating that to the Platonists material things 'are but Ectypall Resemblances and Imitations of spirituall things which were the First, Primitive, and Archetypall Beings.'[90]

If the ideal and unchanging type of the marriage relationship is that between Christ and the church or Christ and the believing soul, the historical archetype is the relationship between Adam and Eve. Here, in place of the assertion of a static, unchanging union, we have a dynamic partnership that is capable of objectifying the immense variety of experience within marriage and within man himself. Created perfect, but yet fallen, Adam and Eve present both an ideal and a counter-ideal, and the latter can be measured by the gulf between it and the former. Their actions provide not only a pattern for the diverse relationships between soul and body, but an historical explanation for those that are antagonistic. The Fall of Adam and Eve is the cause of our own fallen nature, and their struggle and discord has become internalized in our own being:

> And so the Serpent robbed the Woman, and robbed her Husband, and robbed all their Posterity, of that godly affection, that holy appetite and desire, which the Lord had furnished Mans nature withall. Ever since which ... all the whole many of us are peruerted in our wills, and so corrupted in all our desires, that now the inclinations of our nature are no longer desires ... but they are lusts and concupiscences, nothing els but lewd and inordinate affections.[91]

The exact point of the comparison between the fallen Adam and Eve and the fallen soul and body varies from writer to writer. To John Randall, in the same sermon quoted above, it is the weakness of Eve, who is therefore most susceptible to temptation, that is analogous to the flesh: 'It is the olde pollicie of Satan, to seeke first to overcome the weakest, that afterward he may overcome the strongest; he set first upon *Eve*, that so he might overcome *Adam*; and so still he sets first vpon our flesh, which is the weakest and most inclinable to sinne, that afterward he may overcome the spirit ...'[92] For Jeremy Taylor, whose interpretation of the Fall agrees with Milton in this, the analogy lies in the uxoriousness of Adam that is akin to the inordinate love of the spirit for the flesh: 'For the flesh complains too soon, and the spirit of some men like *Adam* being too fond of his *Eve*, attends to all its murmurs and temptations ...'[93]

All the variations on theories of the Fall and responsibility for sin noted previously emerge again through these analogies. Thus John Randall assumes that it was Eve (flesh) that by tempting Adam (soul) was chiefly responsible, while Jeremy Taylor assigns responsibility to Adam, who was 'too fond of his Eve.' The eternal argument of the body/soul debates is perpetuated, unresolved. Also, just as some writers place the struggle between temptation and virtue within the soul itself, so in terms of the analogy Adam and Eve may be compared to the higher and lower faculties of the soul. It is in this context that Browne questions 'whether the temptation of the Man by the Woman, be not the seduction of the rational and higher parts by the inferiour and feminine faculties,'[94] and Sir John Hayward frankly equates Adam with reason and Eve with sensuality.[95]

The one consistent feature in all this is that, whatever the precise point of the analogy, it is always the body or sensuality that is identified with Eve (woman), and the soul or reason that is identified with Adam (man). This is perfectly explicable within the context of the Adam/Eve story where it was, after all, Eve who, like sensuality, was attracted to a physical object and thus moved to disobedience. It is extended, however, not only to other wily biblical women (appetite fights against reason as Delilah against Samson, putting out sight)[96] but to husband and wife in general. This is the more remarkable when the soul in isolation is typically portrayed as feminine, an identification that is reinforced by the gender of the word itself in Romance and Germanic languages. Indeed, the one example I have found that does not conform to this pattern is in the French 'Un samedi par nuit.' Even here, however, woman gets the worst of the argument, since in keeping with the general tenor of this debate, it is soul that is primarily responsible for sin. Thus she is the evil, controlling mistress, and Body accuses her,

> Tu estoies my dame, si me carchas la soume,
> Que je ne puis soufrir, le quer me fist partir.[97]

In English, however, three factors combined to make the woman the body and the man the soul. The first was, of course, the identification of soul and body with Adam and Eve. Less important, but still a factor among the more learned writers, was the Aristotelian belief that, at conception, the father contributed the soul, while the mother gave only the matter or body. This took on a new significance in Christianity as it enabled those theologians who believed in traducianism to explain the absence of original sin in Christ. Finally, and probably most important, was the fact that this form of the analogy reinforced the hierarchical nature of each set of relationships and the proper subordination that ought to exist between soul and body, husband and wife.[98]

This last, the need for proper subordination, is usually the point of the analogy when it is used in general terms, divorced from specific biblical associations. 'The Dominion of a man over his Wife is no other than as the Soul rules the Body ...'[99] writes that most moderate of Anglican preachers, Jeremy Taylor. Just as the weakness and imperfection of the body are supported by the strength and relative perfection of the soul, so the wife must lean on her husband for support. As this rule of proper subordination is carried out or ignored, so the union of soul and body or the marriage may be happy or wretched:

> For the Woman that went before the man in the way of Death, is commanded to follow him in the way of Love ... For then the Soul and Body makes a perfect Man, when the Soul commands wisely, or rules lovingly, and cares profitably ... [for] that Body which is its partner and yet the inferiour. But if the Body shall give Laws, and by the violence of the appetite first abuse the Understanding, and then possess the superiour portion of the Will and Choice, the body and the soul are not apt company, and the man is a fool and miserable.[100]

The analogy may be extended to embrace the familiar King/kingdom relationship as well, both in terms of proper subordination and in terms of the indissolubility of the unions. The King is the husband and soul of the Kingdom, Donne asserts, and then concludes: 'Man and wife, soule and body, head and members, God hath joyned, and those whom God hath joyned let no man sever.'[101]

This irrevocable element in the relationships is potentially a source of great torment to an ill-suited soul and body, as in Marvell's dialogue. Like a bad marriage, each partner is doomed to suffer the foibles and contrary impulses of the other's nature. Yet the happy marriage as well finds its counterpart in the same analogy. From one point of view, body and soul may be 'inapt for partnership,' but from another their unequal natures serve to emphasize their mutual need for each other. In this context, soul and body complement and receive perfection from one another, even as husband and wife do:

> And as the feminine Sex is imperfect, and receiveth perfection from the Masculine; so doth the Body from the Soul, which to it is in lieu of a Male: And as in corporal generations the Female doth afford but

gross and passive matter, unto which the Male giveth ... prolifical vertue; so in spiritual generations ... the Body administreth only the Organs which, if they were not emplyoyed by the Soul, would of themselves serve to nothing.[102]

Even the implications of inequality present in the above passage disappear in the ideal relationship between body and soul as it is found in the Resurrection. Here they are no longer analogous to the middle-aged, warring husband and wife, or to that of the already fallen Eve tempting her husband to sin, or even to the inadequate, imperfect wife being 'completed' by the man, but to that of the beautifully adorned bride and her husband:

As the appearance of the Bride newly come from her Chamber in the daies of her Espousals, on the Solemnity of her brideale and other Nuptial Rites, bedecked and adorned with all the Ornaments both of body and mind that may render her gratious, and Amiable in the eyes of her Betrothed ... Even such is the inward grace and outward Magnificence, Pomp and State of the body in the morning of her Resurrection and Ascension from the Chamber of death, to be Espoused again to the Soul in an everlast [sic] Wedlock ...[103]

The soul/body:husband/wife analogy provides a range of possibilities both in terms of conceptual parallels and of human situations far beyond any other of the period. It remains to show how this and other analogies were used not just explicitly as illustrations in sermons and religious writings but to enrich certain aspects of the drama as well.

CHAPTER EIGHT

Body and Soul
as a Motif in
Jacobean Drama

The two prime motivating forces in Jacobean drama are lust and the desire for power – forces that occur sometimes in isolation, as in *The Dutch Courtesan* or *The White Devil*, and sometimes in combination, as in *The Tragedy of Bussy d'Ambois* and *The Malcontent*.[1] The conflicts involved in the working out of these powerful forces are both external, between the various characters in the plays, and internal, between the passions struggling within the protagonists themselves. Despite the widespread contention when the plays were produced and subsequently, that they are immoral or, at best, amoral, they give a vision of life which, if it is 'nasty, brutish, and short,' has at least the redeeming feature of being significant. Tales 'full of sound and fury,' their cry is made to reverberate beyond a mundane level.

Since many of these dramas, unlike most Shakespearean tragedy, do not provide a moral norm for the audience through one or more characters within the play itself, the external conflicts, as they function on the literal level, cannot be the prime means of expressing this significance.[2] There are moral *issues* in these plays (the contrast between Stoic reason and tragic passion, or between fortune and nature, for example),[3] but these are frequently not integrated adequately into the literal and political elements of the play.[4] It is therefore through the literal, external conflicts as seen in a metaphoric light, and the internal conflicts, often similarly viewed, that the significance of the plays is primarily manifested.[5] And one of the chief groups of analogies that, in their many permutations, function in this way are those deriving from the body/soul relationship.

The many implications of the relationship have already been examined. We have seen how they move ever outward from their starting point as a simple externalization of the internal conflict that man feels taking place within himself (the chief function of the body and soul dialogues) through the social implications of the marriage analogy and the political ones of the King/subject or King/kingdom analogies, to the religious implications of the analogy with Christ and the Church. The struggle for superiority that is at the heart of the body/soul relationship is intrinsically dramatic, with ultimate salvation or damnation dependent on the outcome. It is a drama played out within every man on the stage of this world, but with the final act reserved for the judgment day and the stage of either heaven or hell. The relationship thus serves naturally as an analogy to underlie and enrich many other conflicts within the theatre. It consistently reminds the audience that the petty power struggles they are witnessing on the stage – the pursuit of debauched mistresses and the rejection of unworthy wives – are not simply random examples of man's bestiality and of a universe gone awry. They have their analogies in timeless actions and in a theatre of ultimate moral conflicts, and these analogies add a resonance to the action that it would not possess otherwise. The analogies are found both as isolated figures of speech, similar to those in the poetry and religious writings of the period, and as pervasive motifs permeating the action of certain plays as a whole.

Themes and Images

The analogies in the drama are based on the same literal assumptions about body and soul as those in other literature of the period, but they gain a new force and poignancy as they relate to a particular dramatic situation. On a large scale, many of these dramas deal with the problem of the 'good' or potentially good man who is forced to live in a corrupt world.[6] The situation thus set up presents obvious similarities to the plight of the soul in the body – or at least to that view which sees the soul in the body as the Christian in the world. The conflict between the impulses of passion and reason, action (revenge) and Stoic resignation are thus naturally expressed in terms of the soul/body dichotomy. When Charlemont, in *The Atheists Tragedy*, returns to the funeral of his murdered father only to find himself reported dead as well, he describes himself as tortured 'between the passion of / My blood and the religion of my soul' (iii.ii.35–6). Potentially, this metaphoric stance can be (and in some cases is) extended to underline situations of temptation and conflict throughout entire plays. But the same body/soul relationship may be used in more limited ways as well. In Marston's *Antonio's*

Revenge, for example, it is used not to indicate internal conflict but to assert, defiantly, the paucity of Pandulpho's enemies' power. They can reach to his body but not to his immortal soul, he asserts to the Duke:

> The earth's my body's, and the heavn's my soul's
> Most native place of birth, which they will keep
> Despite the menace of mortality.   (ii.i.158–60)

Always, however, such statements are modified by the situations in which they occur. Thus later in the same play, when Piero says to Mellida, 'The flux of sin / Flows from thy tainted body' (iv.i.127–8), the dramatic context tells us that it is Piero's evil perception, not Mellida's body, that is really stained, and a fine irony shows through the commonplace.

The ambivalence of the values assigned to body and soul gives them the necessary versatility to aid dramatic invention in a wide variety of situations. The body, which is earthly, may in its own way be 'good' if it serves the divine ends of the soul. By the same token, its potential for evil, if it does not, is immense. Vittoria in *The White Devil*, though scarcely the person best qualified to utter moral platitudes, lays out the choice before Zanche, her servant, thus:

> Are you grown atheist? will you turn your body
> Which is the goodly palace of the soul
> To the soul's slaughter house?   (v.vi.56–8)

Here the corruption of the body, by analogy, becomes a forsaking of the proper use of the world itself, as Vittoria continues:

> ... O the cursed devil
> ...
> Makes us forsake that which was made for man,
> The world, to sink to that was made for devils,
> Eternal darkness.   (v.vi.58, 62–4)

Similarly, the soul, the heavenly part of man, may become more debased than a corrupting body:

> ... The poison of
> Your breath, evaporated from so foul a soul,
> Infects the air more than the damps that rise

From bodies but half rotten in their graves.
                    (Castabella in *The Atheist's Tragedy*, IV.iii.150–3)

The versatility of the body/soul relationship with its consequent variety of uses does not mean that it functions randomly as an extraneous piece of decoration. The very reversal of normal values in the above quotation, for example, is used to underline the amoral values of the world of most of the characters in the play while at the same time asserting, by implication, the norm from which they are a deviation. Furthermore, Castabella's accusation against D'Amville's proposed incest, couched not simply against the act but against his person, is but one example of the way in which the external action of the characters, the 'plot' of the drama, is a visible manifestation of the invisible condition of their being. The court and its doings find their analogies in the internal states of the individuals who live there. In *Women beware Women*, Leantio compares the possibility of the redemption of a woman's body from the palace of the Duke to the redemption of a soul from hell (III.ii.376–8), and the comparison is borne out by the fate of the doubly-doomed Bianca. Private wrongs and public are similarly linked in *The Dutch Courtesan*, where the selling of bodies and the selling of souls invites an implied comparison between whores and politicians or nobles:

> They sell their bodies; do not better persons sell their souls?
> Nay, since all things have been sold – honor, justice, faith,
> nay even God Himself –
> Ay me, what base ignobleness is it
> To sell the pleasure of a wanton bed?   (I.i.118–22)

Thus the internal world of corruptible man finds itself writ large in the corruptible court.

This correspondence between internal and external is most apparent in those actions dealing with temptation and man's response to it, which are at the very heart of these plays. In another analogy linked to the court, Malevole describes the sexually corrupt life there as the social equivalent of the familiar progress of temptation from the lower to the higher faculties, from the senses to the mind, through imagery that reinforces its physical origins. 'Strange delights,' like the exotic, debauched women he is describing, are used to beguile the soul to evil: 'Strong fantasy tricking up strange delights, presenting it dressed pleasingly to sense, sense leading it unto the soul, confirmed with potent

example, impudent custom, enticed by that great bawd, Opportunity'
(III.ii.40–4).

This last example, in which women are equated with the tempting
lower faculties of the soul or with the body, introduces the richest of all
the sources of analogy that link internal states and external drama in
these plays about the relationship between men and women as they
pursue one another for lustful or political ends. Here the diversity
of forms the analogy takes is linked to the diverse views of women
themselves. Like the body, which can be either 'the goodly palace of the
soul' or 'the soul's slaughterhouse,' women may be either an influence
to good or a temptation to evil. Nowhere are both aspects of their nature
shown more clearly than in *The Dutch Courtesan*, where the whore
Franchesina and the virtuous Beatrice are diametrically opposed in their
nature and influence. Thus Malheureux, who is attracted to Franchesina, acknowledges that he is 'passions slave,' while Freevill, who follows
Beatrice, claims his soul has placed his affection on this 'lawful lady.'[7]
These two views of women are by no means evenly balanced in Jacobean
plays. For every Bassanes who, somewhat belatedly, describes his wife
as a 'temple built for adoration only' (*The Broken Heart*, IV.ii.32), there
are ten Vindicis who, in the words of the proverb he quotes in *The
Revenger's Tragedy*, believes that 'Wives are but made to go to bed and
feed' (I.i.132). And even Bassanes, it must be remembered, does not
take that flattering view of Penthea, his wronged wife, throughout the
play; that, indeed, is his tragedy.

Whether viewed positively or negatively, women (as in the non-dramatic literature) are seen within the context of the analogy as body, not
soul. Passages supporting the identification of flesh/body with a negative
view of women are predictably numerous. In *The Dutch Courtesan*
Freevill, taunting Malheureux, describes Franchesina as 'a body without
a soul, a carcass three months dead' (II.i.133–4), and in a passage
from *The Malcontent*, where the rhetoric seems to owe something
to Shakespeare's 'Sonnet 129,' Mendoza says women are 'extreme in
desiring, slaves unto appetite ...' (I.ii.89). Women's souls are at best
blind (*The Malcontent*, II.v.20), and the Duke, in *Women beware
Women*, only concedes that they even have a soul at the height of his
flattery of Bianca (III.iii.25). Against these identifications must be set
the passage cited above from *The Broken Heart*, in which Penthea is
perceived as a 'temple' to be adored and ruled:

> ... I, who was made a monarch
> Of what a heart could wish for, a chaste wife,

> Endeavor'd what in me lay to pull down
> That temple built for adoration only,
> And level't in the dust of causeless scandal.   (IV.ii.29–33)

The positive tone of this passage cannot obscure the fact that Penthea, as the temple to be inhabited and directed by her Lord, is still placed in a role corresponding to that of body, not soul. Very occasionally women are identified with soul as, for example, when Pietro addresses Aurelia as 'poore lovèd soule' (v.vi.82), but this, as we have seen, is normally limited to situations where they are viewed alone, apart from the context of their relationship with men.[8]

It is when their identification with body is combined with their role as controllers that women's influence is seen at its most malign. Then unlike Penthea, who allows Bassanes unquestioned rule of 'his' Temple, they usurp power and invert the proper order of subordination. They themselves are governed solely by appetite:

> Sooner hard steel will melt with southern wind,
> ...
> Then women, vowed to blushless impudence,
> With sweet behaviour and soft minioning,
> Will turn from where that appetite is fixed.
>   (Pietro in *The Malcontent*, IV.iii.32, 35–7)

Since they display improper subordination within themselves, their effect when they are in control extends this improper subordination into a larger sphere. Monsieur, in *Bussy d'Ambois*, recognizes this when he says

> ... Women that worst may
> Still hold men's candles: they direct and know
> All things amiss in all men; and their women
> All things amiss in them ...   (III.ii.147–50)

Here the inverted order of things extends from the servant to the mistress to the man in an expanding chain of evil.

The image of the ruling woman has certain affinities with the medieval mistress who commands fealty and obedience, and there are still occasional traces of this ancestry in the Jacobean drama. It is outside the context of marriage, for example, that both the virtuous Beatrice and the whore Franchesina in *The Dutch Courtesan* wield their power.

Penthea, in *The Broken Heart*, makes the distinction between the ruling mistress and the obedient wife when, in response to Bassanes who says 'Rule me as thou canst wish,' she answers, 'I am no mistress, / Whither you please, I must attend' (II.i.107–8). This distinction is surely also behind the following exchange in *The Revenge of Bussy d'Ambois*. Montsurry says, in injured tones, to Tamyra who has cuckolded him, 'I us'd thee as my soul, to move and rule me,' to which she replies tartly, 'So said you, when you woo'd' (I.ii.62–3). The latter passage is one of the very few in which the ruling mistress is characterized positively as 'soul.' For the most part, such positive connotations of rule by one's mistress as existed in the courtly love tradition have disappeared, and rule by women, both within and outside marriage, is an evil. Women, when they strive to rule, become malign influences, and the men who allow them to rule are doomed. The general issue of proper subordination thus raised is an extension of that in both medieval and seventeenth-century body and soul dialogues.

Women may not only rule men improperly on the external level, but can instigate improper subordination among the faculties of men on the internal. The man who succumbs to this improper subordination and who cannot, therefore, subject the lust and desires of the body to the government of the soul is lost. 'Know, sir, the strongest argument that speaks / Against the soul's eternity is lust, / That wise man's folly and the fool's wisdom,' says Malheureux to Freevill in *The Dutch Courtesan*. This is a conventional sentiment, but action proves its truth when later, as Malheureux is hopelessly controlled by that same lust, he exclaims, 'Passion, I am thy slave!' (II.ii.111). Still later, he remonstrates with himself in a delightfully ironic passage, which turns on the double meaning of the word 'sense': 'My lust, not I, before my reason would; yet I must use her. That I, a man of sense, should conceive endless pleasure in a body whose soul I know to be so hideously black.' (III.i.234–6)

Malheureux is astounded that he, a man of 'sense' or reason, has just promised to murder his friend, Freevill, in order to please his mistress and to gratify his lust. Yet it is precisely because he is a man of 'sense' or appetite that he is powerless to overcome what he knows to be a wrong resolution. The fouled soul and body of his mistress become, by extension, his own, and the conventional wisdom he recites at the beginning of the play takes on greater depth as it is confirmed by experience. As Langbeau succinctly expresses it in *The Atheist's Tragedy*:

> The flesh is humble till the spirit move it,
> But when 'tis rais'd it will command above it.   (IV.i.92–3)

The conflict between flesh and spirit, passion and reason, is not merely a medieval survival here, but is given new impetus by the seventeenth-century realization that man's 'natural' (instinctive) impulse is definitely *not* rational. There is nothing completely deterministic in all this, however. Soul, coupled with will, always has the ultimate ability to choose good or evil, and if Malheureux allows himself to be the slave of passion, Freevill takes the opposite course, in which soul legitimately rules body. 'I lov'd her with my heart until my soul show'd me the imperfection of my body, and placed my affection on a lawful love, my modest Beatrice ...' (I.ii.89–92).

It is noteworthy that once more the resolution of the subordination issue is coupled with attachment to the 'right' woman. In these cases (admittedly rare) when love is 'pure,' the relationship between man and woman is analogous not to the warring soul and body but to the mutually dependent union of the two. Thus Aurelia in *The Malcontent* can say of her husband:

> As the soule loved the body, so loved he,
> 'Twas death to him to part my presence,
> Heaven to see me pleased.   (IV..v.32–4)

The woman is still the body, but not a body that suffers any detraction in comparison with the soul.[9]

This distinction between corporal and spiritual love may take on all the implications of the body/soul dichotomy rather than, in each case, being analogous to two different types of body/soul relationship. While the distinction is usually a figurative one, it acquires a literal and practical application in the action of *The Atheist's Tragedy*, when the evil Levidulcia urges Castabella to prefer the present and available physical love, represented by Roussard, to the spiritual love that she shares with the absent Charlemont. In addition, by becoming an argument for the supremacy of body over mind or soul, and hence for a subversive inversion of universal order, it is linked to the theme of proper subordination.

> Prefer'st the affection of an absent love
> Before the sweet possession of a man,

> The barren mind before the fruitful body,
> Where our creation hath no reference
> To man but in his body, being made
> Only for generation which, unless
> Our children can be gotten by conceit,
> Must from the body come. If reason were
> Our counsellor, we would neglect the work
> Of generation for the prodigal
> Expense it draws us to of that which is
> The wealth of life. Wise Nature, therefore, hath
> Reserv'd for an inducement to our sense
> Our greatest pleasure in that greatest work,
> Which being offer'd thee, thy ignorance
> Refuses for th'imaginary joy
> Of an unsatisfy'd affection to
> An absent man ... (1.iv.79–96)[10]

It is appropriate that such an argument for the supremacy of the body and lust should be urged by the wanton Levidulcia, and it is a beautifully ironic stroke of Tourneur's that makes Rousard, the object of Levidulcia's pleas, impotent, and therefore as incapable of fulfilling the physical rites of love as the absent Charlemont.

The orthodox position, in which physical love (analogous to body) must be subject to rational love (analogous to soul), is expressed by Leantio in *Women beware Women*:

> But love that's wanton, must be ruled awhile
> By that that's careful, or all goes to ruin:
> As fitting is a Government in love,
> As in a Kingdom: where 'tis all mere lust
> 'Tis like an insurrection in the people,
> That raised in self-wil wars against all reason. (1.iii.41–6)

Here the theme of proper subordination, related to lust and reason, body and mind, is further extended to make it analogous to proper subordination in a Kingdom. Thus the individual and personal is firmly linked to the social and political, as the internal action within the minds of the characters is linked to the external action on the stage.

Finally, this fusion of internal and external action in the drama is shown in the way the commonplace idea of the shared fate of body and soul is used to underline the catastrophic conclusion of many of these tragedies. There is no doubt that, although the pleasures of the body are transient, their effects are not. The Cardinal in *Women beware Women* may question why 'lust' *should* 'bring man to lasting pain, for rotten dust' (iv.i.251), but there is no doubt that it most certainly does. Thus when Bussy d'Ambois comes to die, he suddenly realizes that not only is the body merely 'penetrable flesh,' but also that the mind itself must 'follow [his] blood.' As he cries out, 'Can my divine part add / No aid to th'earthly in extremity?' the implied answer is 'No' (v.iii.125–8). These are not merely theoretical statements; they function as both an explanation and a justification of the unprecedented carnage at the end of these plays where revenger and victim, corruptor and corrupted, actor and agent of evil fall in one scene of common destruction – often a banquet or masque, symbol of the vanity and pride of life to which all have succumbed.

The Second Maiden's Tragedy, The Malcontent, and Bussy d'Ambois

In some Jacobean dramas the use of the body/soul relationship is not restricted to a few scenes or a particular situation but functions as a pervasive motif throughout. Three such plays urge examination in some detail – *The Second Maiden's Tragedy, The Malcontent* by Marston, and *Bussy d'Ambois* by Chapman. While analysis of them in this light may not provide a total interpretation, it does not give a merely peripheral one either. The tragedies are not didactic morality plays, but the pattern of events in them cannot be fully understood if the elements of morality are ignored.

The *Second Maiden's Tragedy* is at once the simplest of the three, in that relationships are presented in the most schematic, abstract fashion, and the most complex in the variety and interweaving of these relationships throughout the plot and subplot.[11] The main plot presents the reader with certain obvious identifications between the characters and abstract, moral qualities. The Lady, in contrast to the woman's usual role, is clearly spirit. She is, first of all, the reversal of everything expected in a woman. 'O she's a woman, and her eye will stand / Upon advancement ... ,' Govianus says. But even he underestimates his beloved. She is heavenly, not earthly, and has the added perfection of not desiring dominion over either kingdoms or men. It is this last attribute that excites greatest wonder in the Tyrant.

> ... There stands the first
> Of all her kind that ever refused greatness

> A woman to set light by sovereignty! –
> ...
> 'Tis their desire most commonly to rule
> More than their part comes to: sometimes their husbands.
>
> (I.i.182–4, 186–7)

Even when tempted by her own father to accept worldly greatness and marry the Tyrant, she resists.

The Lady, as her appellation suggests, is not 'woman' as she is normally characterized. Although she is sought by men and might, under happier circumstances, have become the wife of Govianus, she does not really enter into relationships with them but remains apart, more akin to those isolated female forms in literature such as Philosophia or Beatrice who personify all goodness and perfection, functioning as an inspiration and ideal, not as an earthly partner.

There is, of course, a terrible irony in the treatment of the Lady. Although she is, demonstrably, pure spirit, she is perceived and used by the Tyrant as if she were mere flesh. (The flesh/spirit opposition here is the correct one, since there are none of the complexities of the body/soul relationship present, as there are in the subplot.) Indeed, she seems to function as a touchstone of the character of those who love her, so that Govianus is willing to sacrifice and kill her body to save her soul, while the Tyrant clings to that same body even after the spirit has fled.[12] Although the Tyrant *claims* that he has exhumed the Lady's body so that he might clasp it 'for the spirit that dwelt in't / And love the house still for the mistress' sake' (IV.iii.111–12), the scene in which he dresses up the body of the dead Lady and makes love to it emerges as one of the most literal and bizarre exaltations of purely physical love in drama. The Tyrant can, in fact, only relate to that aspect of the Lady that is uppermost in himself. As he acknowledges,

> In vain my spirit wrestles with my blood;
> Affection will be mistress here on earthe.
> The house is hers; the soul is but a tenant.   (v.ii.1–3)

This acquiescence to improper subordination within himself is a virtual acknowledgment of his depravity, which is then given concrete expression in his preparation to make love to a corpse. None of this, however, affects the true identification of the Lady with Spirit. Indeed, the fact that her spirit appears on stage during the scene of her flesh's dishonour, emphasizes the extent to which the 'house' the Tyrant has so lovingly decked is empty; the true Lady is elsewhere.

The adoration of the flesh also provides an ideal opportunity for the dramatist to remind us of its ultimate vanity and fragility, themes that are inextricably linked to the dialogues as well.

> O, what is beauty, that's so much adored?
> A flatt'ring glass that cozens her beholders.
> One night of death makes it look pale and horrid;
> The dainty preserved flesh, how soon it moulders.
>
> (v.ii.14–17)

This emphasis, in turn, prepares us for the destruction of the fleshly Tyrant. The connection is made explicit when it is, appropriately, the kiss given to the dead body that causes his own death. The triumph of Spirit, not only in theory but in fact, as the Tyrant falls dead and the Ghost of the Lady is welcomed as a 'blessed spirit' by Govianus, is complete.

Set against the infallible Lady, we have the fallible Wife. If the Lady is spirit, the Wife is body – not intrinsically evil, but weak, subject to temptation. Indeed, the temptation motif is made explicit in the Garden of Eden imagery of her second encounter with Votarius.[13] The Wife, ideally, is a 'pleasant garden / Where all the sweetness of man's comfort breathes' (i.ii.188–9), but, like the Garden of Eden, she holds hidden dangers.

> ... I praised the garden,
> But little thought a bed of snakes lay hid in't.   (i.i.231–2)

Tempted by Votarius, who is acting as the agent of Anselmus, her husband, she is unable to resist, and blames it on the general weakness of woman's nature and the specific vulnerability of her situation.

> *Wife*. It is not honest in you to tempt woman;
> When her distresses takes away her strength,
> How is she able to withstand her enemy? (i.ii.242–4)

This excuse of weakness is, one notes, precisely that of the body. The evil of Anselmus, on the other hand, is one that derives from mind or soul rather than from bodily passion, as Votarius points out:

> Man has some enemy still that keeps him back
> In all his fortunes, and his mind is his,
> And thats a mighty adversary. I had rather
> Have twenty kings my enemies than that part. (i.ii.158–61)

This relationship between tempter and tempted has its analogues in that contemporary body and soul literature that sees the malign soul as the instigator of evil and the body as the weak and malleable material on which it works. To Votarius, however, the issue is not clear-cut. Once he has taken on the despicable role of tempter in which Anselmus has cast him, he finds himself tempted as well by the Wife. The ambiguity about who really bears chief responsibility in this situation is very similar to that in the dialogues. And, as in the dialogues, ultimately it does not matter: the destruction of all the parties – Anselmus, Votarius, and the Wife – is complete. The snake in the garden brings not only exclusion from paradise, but death and eternal damnation.

We thus have in this play an example of the man/woman: soul/body analogy in the subplot, and the rarer identification of woman with spirit in the main plot. As one would expect, the two coincide with woman's role in relation to man, and her role in isolation from him respectively.

If *The Second Maiden's Tragedy* gives the impression of a court world where normal activity has stopped, frozen, while certain terrible choices and actions are highlighted, both *The Malcontent* and *Bussy d'Ambois* present us with courts where good and evil struggle within the context of noisy business, only to be observed when some particularly terrible action surfaces, catching everyone off-guard.

The world of *The Malcontent* is 'the only region of death, the greatest shop of the devil, the cruellest prison of men' (IV.iv.27–8). In other words, it is hell. The dominant note is discord, struck overtly by the music that sounds from Malevole's chamber at the beginning of the play, and manifested through the actions of the characters throughout. The two chief forces that cause this discord are the dominant impulses cited at the beginning of the chapter – the twin lusts for women and power. These ends are pursued through a combination of unbridled bodily appetite and craft. The two attributes are sometimes combined in a single character, but frequently the collusion of the two or the use one makes of the other is displayed through the relationship of two people on the stage. Unlike *The Second Maiden's Tragedy*, there is nothing of the primal significance of the Fall in the acts of these men and women, who have long since lost any innocence they possessed, but there are certainly elements of the post-lapsarian Adam and Eve, as they eternally repeat the pattern of temptation and acquiescence to sin, accusation, and counter-accusation.

One cannot fail to notice how the women, except for Maria, are characterized as weak, sensual, dominated by the body, lust, and appetite. Mendoza, who does not hesitate to use them, nevertheless despises them, saying, 'Their blood is their only God; Bad clothes and old age are onely the devils they tremble at' (I.vi.95–6). Women's dependence on their bodies for all good is argued explicitly by the panderess Maquerelle. She points out that if men 'lose youth and beauty, they gain wisdom and discretion; but when our beauty fades, good-night with us' (II.iv.48–50). It is, perhaps, a long step from saying that women depend solely on their bodies to identifying them with body in the abstract, but in terms of the action of the play there is only one woman, Maria (and she appears only in Act v), who is ruled by any consideration other than the affections and lusts of her body. Aurelia takes not one lover, but several; Maquerelle is an acknowledged panderess, and Emilia and Bianca, Aurelia's attendants, lap up Maquerelle's whorish wisdom with eagerness. 'O powerfull blood, how thou dost slave their soul!' Pietro exclaims.

The men in the play are by no means morally superior. Just as the women are 'slaved' by their blood, so a man like Ferneze is 'slaved' by Aurelia. Characterized as a goat, he is completely subject to lust, with no object beyond the gratification of his senses.

> Now treads Ferneze in dangerous path of lust,
> Swearing his sense is merely deified.   (Mendoza, II.i.2–3)

Thus the chain of improper subordination moves ever up the scale.

Most of the men in the play execute their depravity with less instinct and more craft. If the women are analogous to debauched bodies, then the men are their evil, directing souls – souls which have already succumbed to the baser elements within themselves. They are both tempted by the women, and use them as instruments in their designs. Mendoza is the supreme example of this. His evil is primarily intellectual in origin. 'My brain is in labour till it produce mischief,' he says (I.vii.84–5). Unlike Ferneze, he is not 'slaved' by Aurelia, but uses her as the bait and instrument by which he can undo both Ferneze and Pietro, her husband. He arranges for Pietro to find Aurelia and Ferneze in bed together in order (1) to deflect Pietro's wrath from himself, for Pietro suspects, rightly, that Mendoza has cuckolded him; (2) to ingratiate himself once more with Aurelia by killing Ferneze, protesting his undying love for her, and finally plotting with her to kill Pietro, her troublesome husband. Then, (3) with Pietro out of the way, he will become Duke himself and wed Maria to consolidate his position. Aurelia is a victim (once she is enmeshed in Mendoza's plot she has little chance to escape), but she is by no means an innocent one. She has, after all, given herself not only to Mendoza but to Ferneze as well, and is unrepentant. When, after her exposure, Pietro urges her, 'Weep not too much, but leave some tears to shed / When I am dead,' she replies, 'What weep for thee? my soul no tears shall find.' To this Pietro rejoins, 'Alas – alas, that women's souls are blind!' (II.v.17–20). Her reward for allowing herself to be governed by passion, as she herself says, is that she has 'lost soul, body, fame, and honour' (IV.v.40). Having used Aurelia, whose lust makes her a willing instrument, to save himself from Pietro and to eliminate Ferneze, Mendoza proceeds with the third stage of his plot, to fulfil his political ambitions. Once Pietro is believed to be murdered, Aurelia, as if to confirm her 'instrument' status, must be banished so that he can marry Maria, the wife of the former Duke (in reality the disguised Malevole). Even Maria is not, for him, an end in herself. Mendoza admits that his love for her is primarily politic (III.iii.102–4), and when she refuses to reciprocate his feigned affection, he is quite prepared to fasten on her the suspicion of having poisoned Pietro, 'on which she dies, or loves us' (IV.iii.135).

One must recognize in this action close similarities to the warring body and soul of the dialogues. Both types of relationship depicted there – that dominated by the tempting body, and that by the evil, directing soul – are illustrated by those between Aurelia and Ferneze and between Aurelia and Mendoza respectively. While it is unlikely that this play was influenced by the revivals of the dialogues, since it predates most of them, Marston must have been familiar with the archetypal relationship as described in so many sermons and religious tracts of the period. The specific issue of subordination, so key in the dialogues, is raised by Malevole himself when baiting Pietro. Pietro, he claims, has made Aurelia 'commandress of a better essence / Than is the gorgeous world, even of a man' (I.iii.113–14). His predictable reward is that he has been cuckolded.

Against this pattern of men and women as accomplices in evil, set in a world that is, figuratively, hell, we have a pattern of their happy union, living together in trust and harmony. Mendoza's 'use' of women as instruments and, indeed, his whole Iago-like progress, comes to a halt when Maria, the one virtuous woman in the play, refuses to be used in this way. She will not marry him, but remains faithful to Altofront (Malevole). Her love, as she says, is 'still in her soul' (V.vi.25). And Aurelia, finally recognizing Pietro's love for her and repenting her unfaithfulness, sees the ideal pattern of their relationship as analogous to the union between body and soul in the key passage already cited:[14]

> As the soul loved the body, so loved he;
> 'Twas death to him to part my presence,
> Heaven to see me pleased.   (IV.v.32–4)

But if Aurelia, about to be reconciled with Pietro, provides an explicit statement of the body/soul: husband/wife analogy in the play, it is Maria and Altofront, united, who are its concrete representation. The dance of death in which Maria thinks she is going to participate when invited by Malevole ('With you I'll dance.' Maria: 'Why then you dance with death' [v.vi.72]), changes to one of joy and concord as she recognizes her husband.

The multiple meanings that the analogy can bear do not always function strictly as alternatives. Superimposed on one another, they give a richness and ambivalence to a particular passage or situation that it would not possess otherwise. When Mendoza extends that remarkable invitation to Maria, saying, 'Come, let's love; we must love, we two, soul and body' (IV.iii.120–1), he is ostensibly alluding to the conventional use of the analogy with husband and wife, that which describes a close and happy relationship. But given the reality of the way in which he is plotting to use her, it is the evil, directing soul and the instrumental body that are also connoted. The ambiguity that is inherent in the analogy adds an ironic double meaning to his words.

Malevole's cynical and misanthropic remarks link the sexual corruption of the court to its political corruption. The two are beautifully joined in his image of the 'pigeon-house that was smooth, round and white without, and full of holes and stink within' (I.iv.85–7). He is speaking to Bilioso, who assumes the allusion is to women only when he replies, 'O, yes, 'tis the form, the fashion of them all' (I.iv.88). But Malevole clearly intends the metaphor to extend to include Bilioso himself and the whole world his 'court-friend' inhabits as well.

The improper subordination that is so characteristic of relations between men and women is also present on the political level. Malevole is really a deposed ruler, Pietro is a usurper, and Mendoza's villainy has as its ultimate aim not the possession of women but the possession of the dukedom. The evils of the life of the court are ingrained in the very action of the play, and linked to the corruption both within the individual and between the sexes. The warring soul and body, in their various guises, are analogous to the play's whole world of craft and lust.

The link between political and sexual corruption is even more explicit in Chapman's *Bussy d'Ambois*. The play opens with Bussy railing

against the vices of the court, and insisting 'I am for honest actions';
yet before the end of the scene he has succumbed to the glitter that
accompanies the reward of these vices. Hell, which is figuratively the
whole world of the play in *The Malcontent*, is here literally portrayed
when Bussy, accompanied by the Friar, rises from a pit into Tamyra's
bedroom to woo her as his mistress. The conjuring of spirits, and the
appearance of the ghost of the Friar later in the play, assist in the
creation of an infernal other-world.

In this macabre setting, Bussy connives to fulfil his political ambitions through the use of women such as the Duchess of Guise. Bussy, a
man of great ability but little lasting virtue,[15] functions as the controlling
element in this relationship, using a woman as a mere instrument in
his design. The rhetoric of the play invites us to regard Bussy himself
as pure spirit, proud and noble. In the speech after his death by the
ghost of the Friar, he is linked with star and fire and likened to Hercules.
These attributes, however, are often in conflict with his character as it is
revealed through action. And when he becomes involved with Tamyra,
whom he genuinely seeks for herself, not as a means to some other end,
the man of spirit is no longer fully in control. It is in this central complex
relationship that the body/soul motif of the play is most completely
realized. Tamyra, rather like the Wife in *The Second Maiden's Tragedy*
(and unlike Aurelia in *The Malcontent*) begins by being a virtuous wife,
but as Bussy pursues her, she takes on the role of tempting flesh. She
is dominated by body and the senses and admits, speaking of women
in general.

> Our bodies are but thick clouds to our souls,
> Through which they cannot shine when they desire;
> When all the stars, and even the sun himself,
> Must stay the vapours' times that he exhales
> Before he can make good his beams to us –
> O how can we, that are but motes to him,
> Wandering at random in his order'd rays,
> Disperse our passions' fumes, with our weak labours,
> That are more thick and black than all earth's vapours?
>
> (III.i.59–67)

(The imagery of the motes, subject to passions fumes, harks back to
Bussy's own comparison in Act I of great men to motes that play in the
sun, thus further interweaving the sexual and political themes of the
play.) Women who cannot 'disperse their passions fumes' nevertheless

attempt to rule men, and in this they are like the capricious moon, symbol of change themselves and cause of change in others:

> ... 'Tis not like, my Lord,
> That men in women rule, but contrary,
> For as the Moon (of all things God created)
> Not only is the most appropriate image
> Or glass to show them how they wax and wane,
> But in her light and motion, likewise bears
> Imperial influences that command
> In all their powers, and make them wax and wane;
> So women, that (of all things made of nothing)
> Are the most perfect images of the Moon,
> (Or still-unwean'd sweet Moon-calves with white faces),
> Not only are patterns of change to me:
> But as the tender Moonshine of their beauties
> Clears or is cloudy, make men glad or sad.   (IV.i.7–20)

This moon is in sharp contrast to the constant and spiritual star identified with Bussy, and the apparent compliment of the comparison between women and the moon turns into an indulgent indictment of these 'tender Moonshine' beauties, who are yet able to make men glad or sad.

If Bussy, in the passage above, looks on the rule of women with tolerance, even this he has reason to regret before the end of the tragedy. When in Act v Tamyra, under duress, summons Bussy to her, the message has all the elements of a temptation of the spirit by the passions.[16] Ironically, Bussy perceives it quite differently. Despite what he has said about the rule of women in general, he sees Tamyra here as life itself, a force that must not be resisted, that can legitimately control him through a chain of command stretching through will to motion.

> Should not my powers obey when she commands,
> My motion must be rebel to my will,
> My will to life.   (v.ii.70–2)

The action of the play proves how wrong he is. Everything else has pointed to the identification of Tamyra not with life or soul but with body and death. Nevertheless, Bussy obeys her and, as he enters her room, is slain by assassins. His error has been a fatal one.

Bussy's dying thoughts turn from the external body/soul drama to the internal one that is being played out within himself. He begins by contemplating the body/soul relationship in literal terms. He is incredulous that he, who has perceived himself and been perceived by others as spirit, must die because his body has been slain.

> ... Is my body then
> But penetrable flesh? And must my mind
> Follow my blood? Can my divine part add
> No aid to th'earthly in extremity?
> Then these divines are but for form, not fact.   (v.iii.125–9)

The pun on 'form' – the divine part or soul is the form of the body in the Aristotelian sense, but if it cannot save the body, then its existence is merely for form, not real – is characteristic of Bussy's wit, even in death. The passage then moves outward through analogy to extend the reference from a merely personal one to embrace the whole world of the court that Bussy has first condemned, then embraced, and now must leave forever.

> Man is of two sweet courtly friends compact;
> A mistress and a servant: let my death
> Define life nothing but a Courtier's breath.   (v.iii.130–2)

Not only do we have here an explicit analogy between soul and mistress, body and servant, but it is implied that these are two 'courtly' friends whose sweet love in life lacks the hard substance necessary to sustain one another in death. The final line that defines life as 'nothing but a courtier's breath' extends the fickleness of the body/soul relationship to those relationships with his false friends in the court and to that with Tamyra, that fickle and moon-like woman through whom he has lost his life. The fusion of personal, sexual, and political connotations is complete.

The body/soul relationship, as it functions here, cannot be reduced to an academic or theological formula. It draws on the philosophical beliefs of centuries, but links them to the passion and conflict of the moment. Associated as it is in Jacobean theatre with the revival of other medieval motifs such as the dance of death and the themes of *ubi sunt* and *contemptus mundi*, it adds a curious blend of ancient horror and morality to these dramas of a depraved world.

Othello and Measure for Measure

Shakespeare's plays do not yield such clear-cut schematic links to the body-soul literature as does the minor Jacobean drama; nevertheless, two in particular are informed by the same underlying ideas. Thematically complex, they show the subtlety and depth the body/soul motif could assume.

Both Othello and Measure for Measure[17] contain a dominant male figure who embodies 'soul' in that he is at once directing and passionless. He is also evil, or becomes so. Thus we return to the evil, directing soul as perceived by the body in the medieval debates.

Iago, in Othello, is a notoriously cold-blooded creature who insists that 'power and corrigible authority ... lies in our wills' (I.iii.325–6). The image of the body as garden and the will as gardener reinforces the idea that it is easy for soul to be totally in control; 'we have reason to cool our raging motions ... our unbitted lusts' (I.iii.331–2). Roderigo's passion for Desdemona is 'merely [italics mine] a lust of the blood, and a permission of the will' (I.iii.335–6). Iago himself claims he does not love Desdemona 'out of absolute lust ... but partly to diet my revenge.' He thus presents himself as the most malign of controlling souls (the kind of influence the body of the medieval debates believes but can never prove the soul to have been) both over his own instincts and over the passions of others.

Yet the irony of Iago's position is that he knows all too well the power of physical weakness and passion. If he does not know it from experience, he has learned it from observation. He thrives by understanding perfectly how to play upon the sensual vices of others, and controls Roderigo, Cassio, and Othello himself through exploiting their various physical weaknesses.

Roderigo's excessive passion for Desdemona makes him an easy tool in his plot, and Cassio's weakness for drink is similarly exploited. He then uses Cassio's debauchery to initiate Othello's downfall. For it is, significantly, Othello's confrontation with the drunken Cassio that leads proper subordination to be overthrown within himself, as passion begins to rule reason.

> ... Now by heaven
> My blood begins my safer guides to rule
> And passion having my best judgement called
> Assays to lead the way ...   (II.iii.195–8)

Iago's recognition of this incipient 'passion' in Othello then enables him to play further on another aspect of that passion – jealousy.

Othello's own failure to see what is so clear to Iago – his vulnerability – makes him an easy victim. He begins by identifying himself with soul ('My parts, my title, and my perfect soul, / Shall manifest me rightly' [I.ii.31–2]), and both he and Desdemona show a certain naïveté in downplaying the physical nature of their attraction, though its lustful element is assumed by others. 'She lov'd me for the dangers I had pass'd, / And I lov'd her that she did pity them' (I.iii.167–8), Othello asserts, thus removing their love far above the physical plane. And later in the same scene, when Othello begs Desdemona's presence with him on the voyage, he claims he does so not 'to please the palate of my appetite / ... But to be free and bounteous of her mind' (I.iii.262–5). Even at the end, Othello tries to present his murder as motivated by pure idealism ('It is the cause, it is the cause, my soul'), though the manner of the killing (suffocation in bed) speaks of jealousy and frustrated lust.

The other element in this tragedy is provided by Desdemona. She combines the passive innocence of the 'good' body with its unwitting qualities of temptation. Only in Iago's perverted eyes is she one who loves 'with violence,' whose eye 'must be fed' (II.i.221–4). But like the 'good' body she is susceptible to direction:

> ... For 'tis most easy
> The inclining Desdemona to subdue,
> In any honest suit ...   (II.iii.330–2)

And when that direction comes from an evil source (Iago via Cassio, whom he makes his instrument), her fate is sealed. As for Othello,

> His soul is so infetter'd to her love,
> That she may make, unmake, do what she list,
> Even as her appetite shall play the god
> With his weak function.   (II.iii.336–9)

Desdemona then, though innocent, nevertheless represents to Othello the temptations of the flesh and can complete in him the overthrow of proper subordination of passion to will begun by Cassio.

If Iago in this play represents the soul in its evil, directing guise – a soul imposed on a medieval Vice figure – and Desdemona the body, chaste in actuality though unwittingly a temptress, then Othello himself is the battleground of soul and body, the meeting point of idealism and lust. His tragedy is that he confuses the two, believes body to be soul, passion to be idealism. Thus he recognizes the potency of the body too late to avoid succumbing to its claims.

The latter could be said of Angelo in *Measure for Measure* as well, but there the similarity ends. For Angelo, in his cold, domineering stance, is more akin to Iago than Othello, though he lacks Iago's actively evil impulse. Angelo begins as pure will. He 'scarce confesses / That his blood flows; or that his appetite is more to bread than stone' (i.iii.51–3). He is 'one who never feels / The wanton stings and motions of the sense' (i.iv.58–9).

Against this 'purity,' Isabella, whom Lucio calls 'a thing enskied and sainted,' 'an immortal spirit' (i.iv.34–5) appears as a temptress, who 'corrupt[s] with virtuous season' (ii.ii.168). Like Desdemona, her evil influence lies not in herself, but in the perverted perception of those around her. Angelo himself recognizes the paradox inherent in the fact that it is Isabella's modesty that attracts him, not her 'lightness,' so that he may 'sin in loving virtue' (ii.ii.183).

At this point a curious role-exchange takes place. Although Angelo tries to retain an illusion of mastery and identification with 'soul' ('Redeem thy brother / By yielding up thy body to my will' [ii.iv.162–3]), other passages reveal that Angelo is now really identified with appetite, a lower faculty, not will:

> I have begun,
> And now I give my sensual race the rein:
> Fit thy consent to my sharp appetite.   (ii.iv.158–60)

Thus Isabella, who comes to *function* as tempting flesh, remains in essence a saint or soul and assumes control of the action, while Angelo, who begins as pure will, betrays his name and falls ignominiously victim to lust.

Problems still remain in this most difficult play, however, and Isabella herself cannot range the claims of body and soul in any firm hierarchy of value. 'I had rather give my body than my soul' (ii.iv.56), she glibly states, but when pressed further says she would rather die than 'yield / My body up to shame' (ii.iv.103–4). This, logically, makes sense only if to die is assuredly to save the soul while to live, having lost her 'chastity' (not a bodily but a spiritual thing to her) would condemn both body and soul eternally – a position that takes us back to the argument of Sonnet 146, that to kill the body is to save the soul.[18] The same logic propels her to that controversial and oft-quoted conclusion, 'More than our brother is our chastity' (ii.iv.184).

Leaving aside this logic-chopping that has been the despair of many readers of the play, no work of Shakespeare's shows more clearly the vulnerability of soul to the temptations of the flesh or the ruinous consequences of yielding. From the whore-houses of the sub-plot, through the love affair of Claudio and Juliet, to the palace of Angelo, sensual temptation works its destruction.

Yet the claims of the body are not ignored. At a very basic level, they represent life itself. Pompey, the bawd, is 'a poor fellow that would live' (ii.i.220); burgeoning life gives the doomed Juliet a reprieve; and Lucio points out the irony of Claudio's condemnation to death for creating new life. The body also asserts its claims in Claudio's instinctive cry, 'Sweet sister, let me live' (iii.i.132), that flies in the face of all logical arguments about the superiority of chastity to life, the precedence saving the soul takes over preserving the body.

In this complex play, the claims of both body and soul are given due weight. And ultimately, it is not body or soul as such that is condemned but unbridled passion and untutored 'virtue.' If marriage itself can be seen as a symbolic reconcilation of the claims of body and soul, then that is precisely what we find in the multiple pairings at the end of Measure for Measure. Even Angelo, who has moved from being a 'motion ungenerative' through a stage of being controlled by mere lust, will complete his transformations by accommodating the demands of the body to lawful wedlock. For Isabella too, marriage provides the means whereby she can reconcile 'chastity' and her role as a woman. Thus, despite its dark side, Measure for Measure ends by asserting the comic values of life and regeneration.

These plays by Shakespeare always subordinate figurative meaning to 'real' action and character on the stage. Nevertheless, the pervasive ideas of the period are present in our greatest dramatist; used with subtlety and skill they give an added resonance to the very human predicaments the plays present. Unobtrusive, their recognition helps not only to explicate individual passages but, more importantly, to enrich our understanding of the whole.

Conclusion

The early seventeenth century could quite naturally use the body/soul dichotomy to give a moral resonance to conflict in literature, superimposing medieval morality on a more sophisticated classical dualism. The survival and even renaissance of medieval habits of thought in the early seventeenth century has been amply demonstrated. Their specific manifestation in the revival of the body and soul dialogues not only sheds light on a small neglected area of seventeenth-century literature but illuminates one aspect of a much larger body of works, both lyrical and dramatic, in the period. It also suggests questions – which it is beyond the scope of this book to answer in any detail – about the origins and nature of dualism itself.

With the Restoration, the concerns of society changed completely. Man no longer believed he had been put on earth 'to live well in order that he might die well.' The movement from tragedy to comedy was just one manifestation of a refusal to look for *exempla* or universal patterns in either drama or life. At the same time, serious philosophical enquiry began to look for unity rather than duality in man himself. Eighteenth-century rationalism wished to see man as a unified being in a social context; nineteenth-century romanticism extended this to include man's harmony with nature and, by extension, with God himself.

But man's experience of the self has remained somewhat at variance with these explanations. Unity may be the desired goal, but division and conflict are more frequently what is actually felt. Perhaps the reason that 'unity' or 'oneness' is so often claimed as the goal of the mystical life is because it is so manifestly *not* what is experienced in earthly life. And in the twentieth century we have not denied the experience but simply invented new terms to describe it. Freud produced a psychological explanation for this conflict and a whole new vocabulary to replace the seventeenth-century one. The *super-ego* and *id* take over from the soul and body while 'repression' supersedes 'proper subordination.'

Similarly, modern science has produced a physiological explanation based on what we know of the brain itself, divided into two hemispheres with differing areas of control. In a recent poem, 'The Anatomy of Migraine,' Amy Clampitt exploits this perception of dualism in a way that is strikingly modern while acknowledging its descent from Hippocrates, Plato, Galen, and Descartes, among others. The double-hemisphered mind itself is seen as the seat of dualism, 'the neurobiological / dilemma of the paired, the hemispheric,' which 're-ramifies – bright, dark; left, right; / right, wrong –' that fights against the integration of the self, 'the precarious sense of I am I.' Here, interestingly, the contradictory impulses are seen as implicitly moral, though divorced from a specific frame of reference. And these opposing forces extend like a destructive force throughout the universe, 'as though / the cosmos repented of itself, of all those / promises, all those placebos.'[1]

There are manifest differences, of course, between these works and the seventeenth-century debates. A conflict between the *ego* and the *id* or a cerebral division within the skull may have moral overtones, but they are divorced from any specific frame of reference. There is no sure winner; there is no hell-mouth into which the unlucky victims are thrust. What we have is a described state rather than a conclusive struggle, and any direct seventeenth-century links are with Marvell, not Crashaw.

When the conflict is externalized on the stage, the same general observations apply. Strindberg's *Dance of Death* is psychologically as devastating as anything in Jacobean drama, but there is a curious sense of *stasis* about the play. It is descriptive, not dynamic – and even the descriptive element lacks any explanation of motivation except as one of the conditions of the individuals in particular and marriage in general. The incompatibility of the Captain and his wife is as much a 'given' as that of soul and body, but the roles are less clearly differentiated, and potential punishment after death is downplayed in relation to the actual punishment in life. Similarly, in Edward Albee's *Who's Afraid of Virginia Woolf?*, one finds conflict without the possibility of resolution, and not even a devil in sight to carry off the offending pair! The whole frame of reference is psychological, not moral.

What the seventeenth-century use of the body/soul motif offered was a device that gave meaning and pattern to man's dualistic experience of the self and his behaviour to others. Despite sophisticated attempts, we have not wholly succeeded in denying the experience. Unable to assent to the old interpretation of it, we still seek for new ones.

Appendix

Notes

Bibliography

Index

Crashaw's Translation and Later Versions of Body and Soul Ballads

There is firm textual evidence that the ballad versions of 'Saint Bernard's Vision' are all descended originally from Crashaw's translation and then from one another. The general resemblances have been outlined in the text; a more detailed examination of specific similarities and differences that evolved follows.

The content of Crashaw's dialogue and that of the earliest ballad diverges significantly only near the end of each. The second speech by body, in Crashaw's translation, ends with a reference to death and the last judgment that is equivalent to the last two lines of stanza 23 of the ballad ('But [oh] I know that at the latter houre, / Both thou and I shall find a death most soure'). Soul then responds by wishing it were a beast rather than a creature capable of and responsible for sin (a sentiment found in the medieval 'Vision'), and only after this does the body again speak to inquire about hell. In the ballad, this speech by the soul is omitted altogether, and the request to be told about hell is added to the end of the body's previous speech. The specific reference to Dives, incorporated into the soul's reply to the question about hell in the ballad (and repeated in later versions, including the nineteenth-century one), has no equivalent in any earlier debate, although Crashaw's reminder that the torments of 'great ones' are more terrible than those of others may have provided an oblique hint for this addition. The chorus of devils in the ballad comes before the author's description of them and is contained in one three-stanza section, while in Crashaw's translation the author's description precedes their speech, which is broken into two sections with an appeal by the soul to Jesus in the middle. Finally, the 'beauteous young man' who, in the ballad, bids the author awake and write, has no equivalent in Crashaw's work, and the lament on the state of the world that Crashaw takes from his medieval model is missing in the ballad.

Stylistically the two are also similar, often using the same phrases and rhymes with only minor variations. The opening lines of each are nearly identical (see appended texts), but later on the ballad's simpler rhyme scheme (aabb instead of abab) and the need to condense lead to some interesting adaptations. The ballad writer may simply omit lines 2 and 4 of a stanza, and in this way, with a few minor changes, produce a coherent couplet from lines 1 and 3. Thus stanza 37 of Crashaw's poem is in the ballad reduced to the two-line couplet:

> When I would thee (O Body) have control'd,
> Straight the worlds vanities did thee with-hold.

In other cases, where the whole of the stanza is retained, a slightly more complex adaptation changes the rhyme scheme while retaining both the sense and the same rhyme words. Compare, for example, stanza 25 in Crashaw with the equivalent stanza 12 in the ballad. The sense of each line is identical, but the end words are shifted (changed in only one instance) so as to fit in with the different rhyme schemes.

Just as surely as the original ballad derives from Crashaw, so the last surviving ballad, though printed one and a half centuries later, derives from the first. Exactly how they relate to one another and to the intermediate versions of 1683, 1730, and 1776 is more difficult to determine.

The intermediate versions all come in a direct line of descent from the 1640 ballad. All have the same stanzas in the same order, although there are some significant changes in the wording. These variants increase as one moves through the successive versions, and some of the changes in 1683 are reproduced in 1730 and 1776 as well, thus indicating that these versions derive successively from one another rather than independently from the 1640 ballad. Most of the changes are not of any great significance. Some show the influence of oral transmission as when 'sease' in stanza 20 of 1640 becomes 'cease' in the 1683 version – a change that makes no sense at all and can only be explained by the similar sound of the two words. Certain other changes can be attributed to printing errors. Thus 'Both' at the beginning of line 4, stanza 23, becomes 'But' in 1683, which simply repeats the first word of the line immediately above. This mistake, along with other similar ones, is repeated in the version of 1730, indicating its dependence on the printed version of 1683. Any real evidence of oral transmission exists only between the versions of 1640 and 1683, and between the nineteenth-century ballad and earlier versions.

There is a general tendency to simplify and modernize the language in the later ballads. 'Form'd' (1640) becomes 'fram'd' (1683), and finally 'made' (1730). More significantly, 'knowledge' in stanza 13 of the earlier versions becomes 'science' in 1776. In general, the changes cannot be said to be improvements. On the contrary, the rhythm of the verse deteriorates and, even worse, the clear-cut theological arguments of the 1640 version become obscured as they are handed down through successive adaptations. Thus in stanza 6 of the 1776 version 'thy sin' becomes 'my sin,' an explicit acknowledgement of guilt on the part of the soul that would have been impossible at a time when the fundamental principles of the debate were fully understood.

The gap between these ballads and that printed in the early nineteenth century is greater than that between any of the earlier versions. Its general indebtedness to the earlier ballads is abundantly clear, but there is a more marked deterioration in both the verse and the theology. A general carelessness is apparent in the thought and construction of the poem as a whole – a carelessness compounded by what one presumes to be the mistakes of the typesetter. The first line, for example, has lost a complete foot of the metre; in line 3 'departed' has become 'depart of,' thus causing needless ambiguity about whether the whole is taking place within a separation scene. In stanza 2, the soul awakes with tears, an action usually reserved for the author at the end of the vision. The first speech of the soul in the nineteenth-century poem begins abruptly with the *ubi sunt* formula, omitting stanza 3 of the seventeenth-century ballad, which begins with the conventional address, 'O sinfull Flesh.' In some cases lines, slightly altered to fit a new context, are transferred between body and soul in the two versions. For example, the lines 'But by thy sinne whilst we on Earth aboade, / I am made fouler than a loathsome Toade,' spoken by the soul in the seventeenth-century poem, become 'For whilst on earth in sin I have abode, / Which makes me fouler than the loathsome toad' spoken by the body in the nineteenth-century one. And in stanza 6 of the nineteenth-century work, two lines originally attributed to soul are here changed to be spoken by Body and then annexed to two lines from a separate speech originally by Body.

In general, the nineteenth-century version is shorter and omits, significantly, portions of the theological/philosophical argument, while retaining most of the passages of invective and descriptions of the terrors of hell. The result is a much cruder and less interesting work. In addition, the longer, more coherently argued statements by body and soul in the seventeenth-century work are shortened to two or three stanza sections in the later poem, thus reinforcing the emphasis on charge and countercharge rather than on precise argument. And the personal, feminine soul ('her') in the seventeenth-century version becomes a neuter 'it' in the nineteenth-century one.

What is almost certain from the nature of the changes wrought is that here, as between the versions of 1640 and 1683, one is dealing, in part at least, with an oral tradition. The change from 'departed' to 'depart of,' already noted, is the sort of error that is more easily explained through verbal transmission than written. The transformation of 'wailing' to 'waking' is a similar instance of meaning altering more than sound. There is a close correspondence between the descriptive opening and conclusion of the two versions, but the central section is full of omissions, confusion, and discrepancies. Again, this is consistent with oral transmission, since description is easier to remember and pass on in this way than complex argument. The confusion in the attribution of lines to body and soul and the changes that make a specific passage appropriate to a different speaker are also more explicable if they occurred through an oral tradition. In some cases, coherent argument in the seventeenth-century version becomes garbled nonsense in the nineteenth as, for example, when 'The Body of it selfe none ill hath knowne' becomes 'The body of itself is evil grown.' Clearly, the author or transcriber of the later work had either no knowledge or a very imperfect one of the theological assumptions underlying the debate.

One oddity is the number of end rhymes that have changed. One would expect these to survive in an oral tradition. However, they have been changed frequently, and in many cases unsatisfactorily, to fit the altered wording and sense of the lines. Possibly the writer, preparing for the printer the ballad that he knew through oral transmission, simply invented appropriate rhymes where he could not recall the original.

A final peculiarity stems from the company this ballad keeps. Published in London, it is bound with various Irish pamphlets published in Limerick and Dublin. They include other songs and ballads (one on the Battle of the Boyne) as well as 'A Paraphrase on the Explanation of the Holy Sacrifice of the Mass,' and a translation of the 'Pange Lingua.' One must ask, therefore, whether this version of the ballad is English or Irish. If it is Irish, and particularly if its transmission to or within Ireland was at least in part oral, this would go a long way to explain its greater differences from any of the earlier ballads as well as the particular nature of the differences – the omissions and changes in end rhymes.

It is also worth noting that by this date the dialogue would be most at home in a Catholic, not a Protestant tradition. Certainly, body and soul literature flourished in Catholic Spain into the nineteenth century. It is possible, of course, that the printed ballad is entirely English and merely came into the hands of an Irish collector and was thus bound with the Irish tracts. But the discrepancies between it and the earlier English versions make it seem more likely that, although printed in London, it is the work of an Irish writer.

Transcriptions of three of the body and soul dialogues – William Crashaw's translation of a manuscript version of 'Saint Bernard's Vision,' the earliest seventeenth-century ballad version of the same dialogue, and the nineteenth-century ballad – are printed below. None of these is readily available in a printed text. Numbers in brackets beside stanzas in the seventeenth and nineteenth-century ballads indicate corresponding stanzas. Stanzas marked* in the seventeenth-century ballad have no equivalent in the nineteenth-century one.

The second part. To the same tune.

The Soule answereth.

Fond flesh, remember Dives was denay'd,
When for one drop of water so he pray'd:
Thy question (senselesse Body) wanteth reason,
Redemption now is hopelesse, out of season.

Vile Body goe, and rot in bed of Clay,
Untill the great and generall Judgement day:
Then shalt thou rise and be with me condemn'd,
To Hells hot lake, for ever without end.

So fare thou well, I must no longer stay,
Harke how the fiends of Hell call mee away:
The losse of Heavenly ioyes tormenteth mee
More than all tortures that in Hell can be,

The Divells speake,

Ho, are you come, whom we expected long?
How we will make you sing another song:
Howling and yelling still shall be your note,
And molten lead be powred downe your throat.

Such horror? wee doe on our servants load,
How thou art worse than is the crawling Toad:
Ten thousand thousand torments thou shalt bide,
When thou in flaming Sulphure shalt be fride.

Thou art a souldier of our campe enrol'd,
Never henceforth shalt thou the light behold:
The paines prepar'd for thee no tongue can tell,
Welcome, O welcome to the pit of Hell.

The Writer speaketh,

At this the groaning Soule did weepe most sore,
And then the fiends with ioy did laugh and roare:
These Divells seem'd more blacke than pitch or night,
Whose horrid shapes did sorely me affright.

Sharpe steely forkes each in his hand did beare,
Tushed their teeth, like crooked mattocks were,
Fire and Brimstone then they breathed out,
And from their nostrils snakes crawl'd round about.

Foule filthy hornes on their blacke browes they wore,
Their nayles were like the tushes of a Bore:
Those fiends in chaines fast bound this wretched Soule,
And drag'd him in, who grievously did howle.

Then straight me thought appeared to my sight
A beautious young man, cloathed all in white,
His face did shine, most glorious to behold:
Wings like the Raynebow, and his hayre like Gold.

With a sweet voyce, All haile, all haste (quoth hee)
Arise and write what thou didst heare and see:
Most heavenly musicke seemed then to play,
And in a cloud he vanisht quite away.

Awaking straight, I tooke my pen in hand,
To write these lines the yong man did command,
And so into the world abroad it sent,
That each good Christian may in time repent.

Then let us feare the Lord both night and day,
Preserve our Soules and Bodies wee thee pray,
Grant that we may so run this mortall race,
That wee in Heaven may have a resting place.

Preserve the King, the Queene and Progeny,
The Clergy, Councell, and Nobility,
Preserve our soules, O Lord, we doe thee pray,
Amen, with me let all good Christians say. FINIS.

The Soule answereth.

MOst wretched Flesh, which in thy time of life
Wast foolish, idle, vaine, and full of strife;
Though of my substance thou didst speake to me,
I doe confesse I should have bridled thee.

But thou through love of pleasure soule and ill,
Still me resisted and would have thy will:
When I would thee (O Body) have control'd,
Straight the worlds vanities did thee with-hold.

So thou of me didst get the upper hand,
Inthralling mee in worldly pleasures band,
That thou and I eternall shall be drown'd
In Hell, when glorious Saints in Heaven are crown'd.

But flatt'ring fancies did thy mind so please,
Thou never thought to dye, till death did seaze:
This was thy fault, and cursed is our fate,
Which we repent, but now alas too late.

The Body speaketh.

Oh now I weepe being scourg'd with mine owne rod,
Wee both stand guilty fore the face of God:
Both are in fault, and yet not equally,
The greatest burthen (Soule) on thee doth lye.

So wit so meane, but this for truth it knowes,
That where most gifts of vertue God bestowes,
There most is due, and ought repayed bee;
And unto this there's none but will agree.

But foolishly thou yeeldedst unto mee,
And to my vaine desires didst some agree;
But (oh) I know that at the latter houre,
Both thou and I shall find a death most soure.

I greatly feare an everlasting fire,
Yet one thing more of thee I doe desire:
Hast thou beene yet amongst the fiends of Hell?
Is no hope left, that we with Christ may dwell?

Printed at London for I. Wright, dwelling in Giit-spur street.

The second part of 'Saint Bernard's Vision,' from the Roxborough Ballads
(see pages 209–14)

The / Complaint / or / *Dialogve*, / Betwixt
The *Soule* and the *Bodie* of / *a damned man.*
Each laying the fault vpon / *the other.*

Supposed to be written by S. Ber-/nard *from a nightly vision
of his;* / and now published out of an *an-/cient Manuscript
Copie.*
By William Crashaw.

The Speakers
1. *The Avthor*
2. *A Soule departed*
3. *A dead Carcasse*
4. *The Diuels*

THE AVTHOR
1 In silence of / a Winters night,
A sleeping, yet / a waking spirit:
A liuelesse body / to my sight
Methought appeared / thus addight.

2 In that my sleepe / I did descry,
A Soule departed / but lately
From that foule body / which lay by,
Wailing with sighes / and loud did cry.

3 Fast by the body / thus she mones,
And questions it / with sighes and grones.
O wretched flesh, / thus low who makes thee lye?
Whom yesterday / the world had seene so high?

4 Wast not but yesterday / the world was thine?
And all the Country / stood at thy deuotion?
Thy traine that followed thee / when thy Sunne did shine
Haue now forsaken thee: / (O dolefull alteration!)

5 Those Turrets gay / of costly Masonry,
And larger Palaces / are not now thy roome,
But in a Coffin / of small quantity,
Thou lyest interred / in a little tombe.

6 Thy Palaces, what helpe / they thee, or buildings?
Thy graue vneth's / of largenesse for thy feet:
Henceforth thou canst / hurt none with thy false iudgings,
For thy misdeeds / in hell we both must meete.

7 I, I poore soule / oh I, a noble creature,
Formed and made / in likenesse of my God,
Adorn'd with graces / of most comely feature
Am now so chang'd / as fouler then a Toad.

8 O wretched flesh / with me that art forlorne,
If thou couldst know / how sharpe our punishment?
How iustly mightest / thou wish not to be borne,
Or from the wombe / to tombe to haue beene hent.

9 This I confesse / no wonder, for in life
To one good deed / thou neuer wouldst agree;
But to each greatest sinne / didst runne with strife,
For which, for euer / we must damned be.

10 I am, and ay must be.[sic] / in bitter paine,
No tongue of liuing man / hath power to tell
One of the smallest / torments I sustaine,
Where (which is worst) / I must for euer dwell.

11 Where be those Lord-ships / thou hast laid together?
Thy lofty Palaces, / thy Castles strong?
Thy heapes of gold / which were thy chiefest treasure,
Thy Rings and Iewels / which about thee hung?

12 Where thy rich beds, / thy sumptuous Tapestry,
Thy change of rayment, / many coloured vesture?
Thy dainty Spices / (baites of luxury)
Plate, Tables, Carpets, / and rich furniture?

13 Where now thy wilde Fowle, / and thy Venison,
Thy dainty fishes, / and thy chosen wine?
In thy now Kitchin / meate is dressed none
Such plagues for sinners / God doth still assigne.

14 How lik'st thou now poore foole, / thy latter lodging,
   The roofe whereof / lyes euen with thy nose?
   Thy eyes are shut, / thy tongue cannot be iogging,
   Nothing of profite / rests at thy dispose.

15 What erst thou hast / most wretchedly beene scraping,
   By vsury, deceit, / rage and oppression,
   In all thy life, with toyle / and greedy gaping,
   Are hid by death / in earth and putrifaction.

16 Thou art not now / begirt with troopes of friends,
   The flower of all thy beauty / lies in dust:
   The bands of euery loue / doe heere take end,
   Yea, thine owne wife / now thinkes all teares vniust.

17 In thy left kindred / henceforth trust no more,
   For, for thy Vine-yards, / fields of grasse and corne:
   And (which thy plagues encrease) / thy treasured store:
   Few dayes (know foole) / thy after Heires will mourne.

18 I doe not thinke / thy Wife or Children left
   Would lose one penny, / or one patch of lands:
   For vs which are from her / and them bereft,
   Though it might quite vs, / from these horrid bands.

19 Now wretched flesh thou seest / how nought reputed
   Is the worlds glory, / false, deceitfull, fell,
   With anguish fraught, / with sinne and vice polluted,
   And clothed in the / noysome bane of hell.

20 Thy garments wretched foole, / are farre from rich,
   Thy vpper garment, / hardly worth a Scute:
   A little linnen / shrouds thee in thy ditch,
   No rents nor gifts men bring, / nor make their suite.

21 Thinke not, though yet / no torments thou endure,
   Thou neuer shalt / but sleepe for euer free:
   For all Gods Scriptures / which are true and sure,
   Witnesse, at last, / thou shalt be plagu'd with me.

22 Thee which the poore / didst rob, and not defend,
Wormes gnaw in earth / and rottennesse thy bone:
But longer stay I must not: / heere I end,
To this, I trow, / answer thou knowest none.

The Body answereth.

23 Thus said the Soule: at last / the gastly Coarse
Straines vp it selfe / as being new reuiued:
And with deep grones / as if it had beene hoarse,
Askt, who such witlesse / reasons had contriued?

24 Art thou, quoth it, my Soule / which thus dost faine?
All that thou saist / is neyther true nor stable:
For I will proue / with arguments most plaine,
If some be true / in many thou dost fable.

25 I (as thou saist) / haue led thee oft astray,
And from well-doing / haue enforst thy loue:
But if the flesh / can leade the Soule away
The fault's more thine then mine, / which thus I proue.

26 The world and power of hell / did both conspire,
And did the flesh / to them associate;
Which if the constant / soule cause not retire,
Both needs must enter / at sins wretched gate.

27 But as thou sayst, / our God did thee create,
Good, noble, vnderstanding, / he thee made;
And like himselfe, / he fashioned thy state,
And made me seruant / to what ere thou said.

28 Therefore, if thou / my Mistris ought to be,
And reason had, / by which thy office was
Vs both to gonerne [sic]: / why did'st thou suffer me
Without restraint / in wicked race to passe?

29 Is't iust to charge / the Body, as the Spirit?
Which being rightfull / Mistris, yet will serue;
To tame the flesh, / the spirit ought of right
With abstinence, and / stripes, if she'l not swerue.

30 The bodies workes / be from the soule deriued,
   By meanes thereof / in life it flourisheth:
   That flesh which by / the soule is not assisted;
   By easie baites / the world soone vanquisheth.

31 The body of it selfe / none ill hath knowne,
   All that it knowes / proceedeth from thy head:
   If I doe what thou bidst / the fault's thine owne,
   For without thee / the body resteth dead.

32 Why should poore hand-maid / (flesh) be charg'd with
                                          blame,
   In working onely / as thy instrument?
   The soule commandeth all, / hers be the shame
   Of all my frailties, / since I want judgement.

33 Therefore I weene / thy guilt exceedeth mine,
   In following my lust / so fraile, and foule:
   But oh the wormes doe / teare me in my shrine,
   I therefore say no more, / farewell, poore soule.

   The Soule Replies.
34 Nay (said the Soule) / Ile stay by thee a while,
   And if I can, / thine arguments confute:
   Why rail'st thou on me / in this bitter stile,
   Striuing to me / thy whole guilt to impute?

35 Most wretched flesh / which in thy time of life
   Wast foolish, idle, / vaine, why dost thou wreake
   Thy wrath in railing words / to make new strife?
   Though for the substance / 'tis true that thou dost speake.

36 For truth it is, / and stands with reason plaine,
   I should haue bridled thee / and rul'd thy will,
   But thou through loue / of pleasure foule and vaine,
   And sensuall appetites / me resisted still.

37 When I would thee / O body haue control'd,
   And haue subdu'd, / with watching, fast, and paine,

    Straights the worlds vanity / did thee with-hold,
    And to his vaine delights / drew thee againe.

38 So thou of me / didst get the vpper hand,
    And of my mildnesse / made so bad construction,
    That thralling me / in worldly pleasures band
    Eternally hast drown'd / me in destruction.

39 I know my guilt, / and this my trepasse was,
    That being chiefe / I did not thee restraine:
    But thou deceiuedst me / with so faire a glasse,
    That thy offence / the greater ought remaine.

40 The vaine worlds practices, / baites and delights,
    If thou hadst left / with stedfast constancy,
    And so with-stood / Sathans inchanting sleights,
    Heauen had beene ours, / with Saints and Deity.

41 But flattering fancies / of the world did please,
    And made thee hope / a lasting life to haue;
    Thou neuer thoughtst / to dye, till death did ceaze:
    And hal'd thee from / thy Court to dirty graue.

42 The world, and subtile / men, haue both one guise,
    Where most it smiles, / and most bestoweth honor,
    There soonest it / deceiues, soonest death cries,
    And changeth wealth / to wormes, to stinch and horror.

43 He which in life / did fawne and was thy friend,
    Will not now cast / a looke vpon thy graue.
    Then gan the body weepe / weighing this end,
    And lowly, in his stile, / such answer gaue.

The body answereth.
44 I In my life, / which had so great command,
    In iewels, riches, / lands did so abound:
    Built Palaces, / and iudged many a land.
    Think'st thou I thought / of Tombe in this base ground?

45 Oh, now I see, / and find it to my griefe,
    That neither gold; / nor wealth, nor larger rent,

Honour, strength, knowledge, / nor soueraigne hearbs reliefe,
Can cure deaths bitter / sting, nor it preuent.

46 Before our God / we guilty both doe stand,
And both in fault, / but not both equally,
The greatest burden / lyeth on thy hand:
And this to proue / full many reasons lye.

47 No wit so meane, / but this for truth it knowes:
Iustice it selfe / and reason both agree,
That where most gifts / of vertue God bestowes,
There most is due, / and ought repayed be.

48 Life, Memory, / and powerfull vnderstanding
God gaue to thee, / and with it sense of might,
Wherewith thou shouldst / haue curb'd at the commanding
Concupiscence, / and followed that was right.

49 Then since thy dower / of vertue stretcht so farre,
And foolishly thou / gau'st thy selfe to me,
And my entisements / neuer would'st debar,
That thy fault greatest is / all men may see.

50 Further I adde / (with anguish of my heart)
Which mind owne case / doth plainly demonstrate:
The flesh can nothing / doe, if soule depart,
It neither moues, / nor stirs, early or late.

51 It neither sees, / nor speakes: then is this proued,
The Soule giues life, / no power in flesh doth rest:
If then the Soule / rightly her God had loued,
The flesh had neuer / her great power supprest.

52 If Gods loue, liuing, / thou hadst holden deare,
And poore mens causes / rightly hadst definde,
And vnto wicked / counsels giuen no eare,
Nor me nor thee / worlds vanitie had twinde.

53 I that liu'd gay, / and gorgeous in attyre,
Loe, what of all / now vnto me remaines;

Wormes, rottennesse, / and narrow lodge of mire.
These after all / delights, are left my gaines.

54 And (oh) I know, / that at the later houre
I shall arise / and as I did offend
With thee shall finde / a second death most soure,
An euerlasting / death, death without end!

The soule confesseth.
55 With hollow fearfull voice / then howles the soule:
Oh, had I not / amongst the creature beene,
Why with his creatures, / did God me enroule?
Whom he foreknew / should perish thus for sinne?

56 Happy are you / bruit beasts, happy your state,
You wholly dye / at once, and only rot:
Once dead, all torments / cease, such is your fate.
Oh! were such end / for sinners, such their lot.

The Body askes the Soule a Question.
57 Then, quoth the Body / to his pensiue Ghost,
If thou hast beene / among the fiends in hell,
Tell me, I pray / what sawest thou in that Coast?
Is no helpe left / from thence with Christ to dwel?

58 For Kings and great men / what is their prouision,
Which liuing, / Lorded it in high degree.
For them is any / hope left of redemption,
For money, / lands, bequests, or other fee?

The Soule giues answer.
59 The question, senslesse body, / wanteth reason:
For when to hell / the wicked damned be,
Redemption then is hopelesse, / out of season:
Bootlesse are almes-deeds, / prayers and charity.

60 If all the piety / of men should pray,
If all the world / in price were offered,
If all good men should / fast both night and day,
For this not one / should be deliuered.

61 The roaring diuell, / cruell and full of rage,
   For infinite of worlds, / or any gaine,
   Would not forgoe / one soule, shut in his cage,
   Nor ease his torments, / nor make lesse his paine.

62 And to thy question, / what is there prepar'd
   For Lords and great ones, / Gods Law is expresse:
   The more that here / one is aduanc'd or fear'd,
   More fearfull is his fall, / if he transgresse.

63 A rich man therefore / dying in his sinne,
   No man shall sharper / torments feele than hee.
   How much more pleasures / that he liued in,
   So much more grieuous / shall his torment be.

The Author in vision.
64 After the Soule had said / these mournfull words,
   Behold, two fiends / more blacke then pitch or night,
   Whose shapes with pen to write / no wit affords,
   Nor any hand / of painter pourtray right.

65 Sharpe steely prickes / they did in each hand beare,
   Sulphure and fire / flaming they breathed out,
   Tusked their teeth / like crooked mattocks were,
   And from their nostrils / snakes crawld round about.

66 Their eares with running / sores, hung flapping low,
   Foule filthy hornes, in their / blacke browes they wore,
   Full of thicke poison / which from them did flow,
   Their nayles were like / the tushes of a Bore.

67 These finds [sic] in chaines / fast bound this wretched soule,
   And with them hal'd her, / howling into hell.
   To whom, on flockes, / ran other diuels more,
   And gnashing with their teeth, / to dancing fell.

68 They welcom'd her / with greetings full of woe,
   Some wrested her with cords, / senselesse of dread,
   Some snatcht and tore with hooks, / drawne to and fro;
   Some for her welcome / powr'd on scalding lead.

Diuels.

69 Such horror we / doe on our seruants load,
   Then (as halfe wearied) / the diuels cryed,
   Now art thou worse / then was the crawling Toade,
   Yet thousandfold / worse torments thee abide.

The Soule cryes out.

70 After all this, the groaning / Soule deepe sighed,
   And with what voyce / it could, low murmured:
   But when within / the gates of hell she entered,
   Shee howled out / *Iesus* the sonne of *Dauid*.

The Diuels answer.

71 Then all the diuels / together loud did cry,
   Too late, too late, / thou callest on thy God;
   Here is no roome / for *Miserere mei*:
   o [sic] hope of easement / from this bitter rod.

72 Neuer hence forth shalt thou / the light behold,
   Thou must be alter'd / to another hue:
   Thou art a Souldier / of our Campe enrol'd;
   Such is the comfort / that in hell is due.

The Author concludeth.

73 Then I awaked / full of feare,
   And much amaz'd / my selfe did reare:
   To God I said / with folded hands
   O shield me from / such grieuous bands.

74 I left the world / and it forsooke:
   Of goods and lands / no care I tooke:
   I did renounce / each worldly thing,
   And gaue my selfe / to Christ my King.

75 The world is drownd / in sinne and vice,
   All order chang'd, / not one man wise:
   Both Iustice, and / Religion lost,
   And all the world / in turmoile tost.

76 The world to ruine / runnes amaine,
   False gods are now / set vp againe:

Vnto the rich / their hands men hold,
He is the God, / that hath the gold.

77 The vertues of / Diuinity,
Are chok't, / faith, hope, and charity.
The brood of / couetise and craft,
Beare all the sway, / and sit aloft.

78 Be thou noble, / wise and faire,
Courteous, / lowly, debonaire,
And poore, thou maist / do what thou can:
But onely money, / makes the man.

79 If I be clad in rich array, / and well attended euery day,
Both wise & good I shal be thoght; / my kindred also shall
be sought.
I am (say men, / the case is cleere)
Your cousin sir / a kinsman neare.

80 But if the world / doe change and frowne,
Our kindred is / no longer knowne:
Nor I remembred / any more,
By them that honoured / me before.

81 O vanity, / vile loue of mucke!
Foule poyson, / wherefore hast thou struck
Thy selfe so deep, / to raise so high,
Things vanishing / so sodainly?

82 For if the world / could three things giue,
Lusty youth, / and long to liue,
Children strong, / and faire of feature,
Riches then were / a good treasure.

83 But know (poore foole) / these end with death,
From first till now, / all lose their breath:
Liuing to day, / to morrow gone,
All flesh must die, / death spareth none.

84 And as it's certaine all must die,
So whither they goe, none can descry,

Which made a wise-man thus to say;
I quake and tremble night and day,
First thinking of my present case,
Then of that strange & fearful place
To which I must: but specially
Of that which ther's prepar'd for me.

85 Thinking of death I sigh & weep,
For three things which / in heart I keepe:
That dye I must, / but know not when,
Nor who shall be my fellow then.
Therefore to thee (my God) I pray
That I may liue with thee for aye.

THE END.

Saint *Bernards* Vision

or,

A briefe Discourse (Dialogue-wise) betweene the Soule and the Body of
a dam-/ned man newly deceased, laying open the faults of each other:
With a speech / of the Divels in Hell. To the Tune of, *Fortune my Foe.*

The Writer speaketh.

1(1) As I lay slumbring in my Bed one Night,
A fearfull Vision did me sore affright:
Me thought I saw a Soule departed late,
By it the Body, in a poore estate.

2(2) Wailing with sighes, the Soule aloud did cry
Upon the Body, in the Coffin by:
And thus the Soule to it did make her moane,
With grievous sobs, and many a bitter groane.

The Soule speaketh.

3* O sinful Flesh, which now so low doth lye,
Whom yesterday the World esteem'd so hye;
It was but yesterday the World was thine,
Thy Sunne is set, which yesterday did shine.

4(3) Where is that Traine that did attend on thee?
Where is thy Mirth? where is thy Jollitie?
Where are thy sumptuous Buildings, and thy Treasure?
Thy pleasant Walks, in which thou took'st such pleasure?

5(4) Gone is thy Traine, thy Mirth to mourning turn'd,
Thou in a Coffin in thy Shrine art Unr'd:
For thy rich Clothes, thou hast a Winding-sheet,
Thy high-built Roofe now with thy Nose doth meet.

6(6) But I (poore Soule) was fram'd a noble creature,
In likenesse to my God, of heavenly feature:
(14) But by thy sinne, whil st [sic] we on Earth aboade,
I am made fouler than a loathsome Toade.

7(7) O wretched Flesh, with me thou art forlorne,
   That well may it wish thou never hadst bin borne;
(11) Thou never would'st to any good agree,
   For which we evermore shall damned bee.

8* I am and must for ever be in paine,
   No tongue can tell the torments I sustaine;
   Both thou and I, we must descend to Hell,
   Where we infrying [sic] flames for aye must dwell.

9* It was thy Pride, Deceit, and Luxurie,
   Hath brought these torments both on me and thee,
(7) Thy Wife, thy Children, Friends, which thou didst trust,
   Doth loath thy Carcas, lying in the Dust.

10(13) The Booke of God, which is both true and sure,
   Witnesse at large what sinners shall endure:
   Thou that within thy Bed of Earth art layd,
   Arise, and answer to these things I sayd.

The Body answereth.
11(5) I know thee well, my Soule, which from me fled,
   Which left my Body senselesse, cold, and dead:
   Cease then to say, the fault was all in mee,
   When I will prove the fault was most in thee.

12* Thou say'st that I have led thee oft astray,
   And from well-doing drawne thee quite away,
   But if the Flesh the Spirits power can move,
   The fault is thine, as I will plainly prove.

13(9) God you doe know, created thee most faire,
   And of Celestiall knowledge gave you share:
(6) I was your servant, form'd of Dust and Clay;
   You to command, and I for to obay.

14(9) 'Twas in your power for to restraine my will,
   And not to let me doe those things were ill.
 * The Bodies workes be from the Soule derived,
   And by the Soule the Body should be guided.

15(10) The Body of it selfe none ill hath knowne:
       If I did what thou didst, the guilt's thine owne:
       For without thee, the Body resteth dead;
       The Soule commands it rests upon thy head.

16* So to conclude, thy guilt exceedeth mine;
      Oh, how the wormes doe teare me in my Shrine!
      And therefore fare thou well, poore sinfull Soule,
      Whose trespasses passe mine, though they are foule.

The second part. To the same tune.

The Soule answereth.
17(11) Most wretched Flesh, which in thy time of life
       Wast foolish, idle, vaine, and full of strife;
    * Though of my substance thou didst speake to me,
       I doe confesse I should have bridled thee.

18(8) But thou through love of pleasure foule and ill,
      Still me resisted and would have thy will:
    * When I would thee (O Body) have control'd,
      Straight the worlds vanities did thee with-hold.

19(12) So thou of me didst get the upper hand,
       Inthralling mee in worldly pleasures band,
       That thou and I eternall shall be drown'd
       In Hell, when glorious Saints in Heaven are crown'd.

20(15) But flatt'ring fancies did thy mind so please,
       Thou never thought to dye, till death did seaze:
       This was thy fault, and cursed is our fate,
       Which we repent, but now alas too late.

The Body speaketh.
21(14) Oh now I weep being scourg'd with mine owne rod,
       Wee both stand guilty 'fore the face of God:
    * Both are in fault, and yet not equally,
      The greatest burthen (Soule) on thee doth lye.

22* No wit so meane, but this for truth it knowes,
      That where most gifts of vertue God bestowes,

There most is due, and ought repayed bee;
And unto this there's none but will agree.

23* But foolishly thou yeeldedst unto mee,
And to my vaine desires didst soone agree;
But (oh) I know that at the latter houre,
Both thou and I shall find a death most soure.

24(16) I greatly feare an everlasting fire,
Yet one thing more of thee I doe desire:
Hast thou been yet amongst the fiends of Hell?
Is no hope left, that we with Christ may dwell?

The Soule answereth.
25(17) Fond flesh, remember *Dives* was denay'd,
When for one drop of water so he pray'd:
Thy question (senselesse Body) wanteth reason,
Redemption now is hopelesse, out of season.

26(18) Vile Body goe, and rot in bed of Clay,
Untill the great and generall Judgement day:
Then shalt thou rise and be with me condemn'd,
To Hells hot lake, for ever without end.

27(19) So fare thou well, I must no longer stay,
Harke how the fiends of Hell call mee away:
The losse of Heavenly joyes tormenteth mee
More than all tortures that in Hell can be.

The Divells speake.
28(20) Ho, are you come, whom we expected long?
Now we will make you sing another song:
Howling and yelling still shall be your note,
And molten lead be powred downe your throat.

29(21) Such horror wee doe on our servants load,
Now thou art worse than art the crawling Toad:
Ten thousand thousand torments thou shalt bide,
When thou in flaming Sulphure shalt be fride.

30(22) Thou art a souldier of our campe enrol'd,
Never henceforth shalt thou the light behold:
The paines prepard for thee no tongue can tell,
Welcome, O welcome to the pit of Hell.

The Writer speaketh.

31(23) At this the groaning Soule did weepe most sore,
And then the fiends with joy did laugh and roare:
These Divells seem'd more blacke than pitch or night,
Whose horrid shapes did sorely me affright.

32(24) Sharpe steely forkes each in his hand did beare,
Tusked their teeth, like crooked mattocks were,
Fire and Brimstone then they breathed out,
And from their nostrils Snakes crawl'd round about.

33(25) Foule filthy hornes on their blacke browes they wore,
Their nayles were like the tuskes of a Bore:
Those fiends in chaines fast bound this wretched Soule,
And drag'd him in, who grieviously did howle.

34(26) Then straight me thought appeared to my sight
A beautious young man, cloathed all in white,
His face did shine, most glorious to behold,
Wings like the Raynebow, and his hayre like Gold.

35(27) With a sweet voyce, All haile, all haile (quoth he)
Arise and write what thou didst heare and see:
Most heavenly musicke seemed then to play,
And in a cloud he vanisht quite away.

36(28) Awaking straight, I tooke my pen in hand,
To write these lines the yong man did command,
And so into the world abroad it sent,
That each good Christian may in time repent.

37(29) Then let us feare the Lord both night and day,
Preserve our Soules and Bodies wee thee pray,
Grant that we may so run this mortall race,
That wee in Heaven may have a resting place.

38* Preserve the King, the Queene and Progeny,
   The Clergy, Councell, and Nobility,
   Preserve our soules, O Lord, we doe thee pray,
   Amen, with me let all good Christians say.   FINIS.

Printed at London for *I. Wright*, dwelling in Gilt-spur street.

A VISION OR DIALOGUE,
Between a departed Soul and the Body

London: Printed for the Author [1800?]

1(1) As I lay on my bed one night,
      A fearful vision did me sore affright,
      I thought saw [sic] a soul depart of late,
      By it a body in a foul estate.

2(2) Waking with tears the soul aloud did cry
      Unto the body in a coffin by,
      And thus the soul to it did make its moan,
      With sobs and cries and many a bitter groan [sic]

[Soul]
3(4) Where is the train that us'd to wait on thee?
      Where is thy mirth? where is thy jollity?
      Where is thy sumptuous buildings and thy treasuse, [sic]
      Thy pleasant walks in which took pleasure?

4(5) Gone is thy train, thy mirth to mourning come,
      Thou art now silent in thy coffin-tomb,
      For thy rich cloth thou hast a winding-sheet,
      Thy high-built roof now thy mouth does meet.

[Body]
5(11) I know thee well, my soul that from me fled,
      And left me here both lifeless cold and dead,
      Although you think the fault is all on me,
      But I will prove the fault does lie on thee.

6(6) You, my soul, was fram'd a noble creature,
      In likeness to the Lord in ev'ry feature,
(13) But I, thy servant, made of earth and clay,
      Thine to command, and mine for to obey [sic]

[Soul]
7(7) O wicked flesh that now art left forlorn
      Well may I wish I never had been born,
(9)   Thy wife and children whom thou loved well,
      Will take no pains to save thee now from hell,

8(18) My command you never did fulfil,
   But still resisted and done what was ill.
 (9) It is thy pride, thy sloth and lechery.
   I greatly fear will damn both you and me [sic]

[Body]
9(14) It was in thy power tó restrain thy will,
   And not let me do those things that are ill,
 (13) For God you know created you most fare,
   And of celestial knowledge gave you share.

10(15) The body of itself is evil grown,
   Since you misguided me, the faults your own,
   without [sic] the soul, the body lies desert,
   Therefore the fault does rest upon thy heart.

[Soul]
11(17) O wretched body, who in the time of life,
   Was idle, vain, foolish, and full of strife,
 (7) With me in reason you would not agree,
   For which you evermore will damned be.

12(19) You still of me kept the upper hand,
   Inthraling me in sinful pleasures, and
   Both you and I for ever shall be drown
   In hell, when glorious saints in heaven are around.

13(10) The word of God that is both true and sure,
   Witness at large what sinners must endure,
   Thou wricked [sic] carrin who in the grave is laid,
   Arise and answer to these words I say,

[Body]
14(21) I weep severe being scourged with my own rod
   Being now convicted before the face of God,
 (6) For whilst on earth in sin I have abode,
   Which makes me fouler than the loathsome toad.

15(20) False flattering fancy did my mind so please,
   I never thought to die till life did cease,
   This was my fall and cursed was my fate,
   Of which I now repent alas too late!

16(24) I greatly fear an everlasting fire,
    One thing more I wish for to enquire,
    Have you been yet amongst the flames of hell,
    Is there no hopes that we with Christ may dwell.

[Soul]
17(25) Remember flesh how Dives was deny'd
    When for one drop of water he so pray'd,
    Your question senseless body want reason,
    Redemption now is hopeless now quite out of season.

18(26) Vile body rot now in thy bed of clay,
    Until the great and general judgment day
    Then shall you and I justly be condemn'd,
    To hell's hot flames forever without end,

19(27) So fare you well I can no longer stay,
    Hark how the Fiends of hell call me away,
    The loss of heavenly joys doe grieve me more,
    Than all the torments that I can endure.

[Devils]
20(28) O art thou come whom I expected long
    I have your place prepared a dungeon strong,
    In scalding flames you must for ever float,
    And melted lead pour down your throat.

21(29) Such horrors we do on our Servants load,
    This lake of fire must be your abode,
    Ten thousand torments now thou must abide,
    When thou in flaming fire shall be fried.

22(30) Thou art a soldier in our camp enrol'd,
    Never more shall thou the light behold,
    The pains prepared for you no tongue can tell,
    Welcome O welcome to the flames of hell.

[Author]
23(31) At this the frighted soul did weep full sore
    The Fins [sic] at him did loudly scoff and roar
    Those Devils seemed more black than night,
    Whose horrid shapes did sorely me affright [sic]

24(32) Sharp steely forks each in their hands did bear,
There [sic] tusky teeth like cruel tygar's were,
Fire and flames each spirit foamed out,
And from their nostrils snakes did crawl about,

25(33) Black branchy horns on their brows they wore,
Their nails were lik the tusks of any boar,
Those Fiends with chains of fire bound the soul,
And drag'd him off who grievously did howl.

26(34) Straightway appeared in my sight. [sic]
A beauteous young man, cloath'd all in white,
Whose face did shine most glorious to behold,
Wings like the rainbow, and his hair like gold.

27(35) With his sweet voice all hail, all hail,
Quoth he arise, and write what thou dost see,
Heavenly music then did seem to play,
And in clouds he vanished quite away.

28(36) Waken then, I took my pen in hand,
To write these things to this young man did name, [sic]
And so abroad into the world I sent,
That each poor christian may repent.

29(37) Dear christians fear the Lord both night and day
Let us humbly fast give alms and pray,
Lord give us strength to run this mortal race,
That we in heaven may find a resting plac [sic]

Notes

1 G.S. Kirk, *Heraclitus: The Cosmic Fragments*, Fr. 10, p 168. See also
  A.H. Armstrong, *An Introduction to Ancient Philosophy* 3rd ed., to
  whose work I am in general indebted for this overview of early
  philosophers.
2 See C.J. de Vogel, *Pythagoras and Early Pythagorianism* 181.
3 The precise relationship of these Forms to the world of sensible things
  has been a matter of philosophical dispute for centuries. The Forms
  are 'real' and 'independent' of the world of sensible objects, yet the latter
  must be related to them in some manner, as Socrates insists in the
  Parmenides. They are thus said to 'participate' in the Forms or to
  'imitate' them as patterns, but neither of these explanations is wholly
  satisfactory from either the scientific or commonsense points of view,
  as Aristotle discerns in his *Metaphysics*. (See *The Parmenides* 128E–
  133, in Francis Cornford, *Plato and Parmenides* 69–93.)
    Neither is the identification of fixity with the deity consistent. While
  it exists in the *Phaedo*, *Republic*, and *Parmenides*, in the *Phaedrus*
  and *Laws* God is the supreme instance of mobility, and the *Timaeus*
  contrasts God and the World-Soul as the principles of fixity and self-
  motion respectively. (See Charles Hartshorne and William L. Reese,
  Philosophers Speak of God 54.) For the history of the debate as to
  whether the forms are within the Good or outside it, see H.A. Wolfson,
  'Interpretations of Platonic Ideas,' *Religious Philosophy* 27–68.
4 See C.A. Van Peursen, *Body, Soul, Spirit* 39.
5 'And in fact we perceive that, if we are ever to know anything absolutely,
  we must be free from the body and must behold the actual realities
  with the eye of the soul alone. And then ... when we are dead we are
  likely to possess the wisdom which we desire and claim to be

anamoured of, but not while we live' (Plato, *Phaedo*, trans. Harold N. Fowler 66 d, e).

For a discussion of Plato's use of the prison analogy, see C.J. de Vogel, 'The Soma-Sema Formula: Its Function in Plato and Plotinus Compared to Christian Writers,' in *Neoplatonism and Early Christian Thought: Essays in Honour of A.H. Armstrong*, ed. H.J. Blumenthal and R.A. Markus 79–95. He argues that the passages in the *Phaedo* (62b) and *Cratylus* (400c) show the body to be more a 'fence' than a tomb which, by keeping the soul within its bonds, allows it to pay its penalties.

6 Plato, *Timaeus*, trans. Rev. R.G. Bury 69e. 'Wherefore, since they scrupled to pollute the divine, unless through absolute necessity, they planted the mortal kind apart therefrom in another chamber of the body, building an isthmus and boundary for the head and chest by setting between them the neck, to the end that they might remain apart.'

7 Plato, *Phaedrus*, trans. Harold N. Fowler 246 a, b; 253 d

8 See P. Merban, 'Greek Philosophy from Plato to Plotinus,' *The Cambridge History of Later Greek and Early Medieval Philosophy*, ed. A.H. Armstrong 28: 'Plato's statements concerning the nature of the soul are inconsistent (why modern interpreters devote so much effort to proving the opposite is incomprehensible) ...'

9 Plato, *Phaedo*, 66b: 'So long as we have the body, and the soul is contaminated by such an evil, we shall never attain completely what we desire, that is, the truth ... And the body fills us with passions and desires and fears and all sorts of fancies and foolishness, so that, as they say, it really and truly makes it impossible for us to think at all. The body and its desires are the only cause of wars and factions and battles ...'

Also, 94b: 'Does it [the soul] yield to the feelings of the body or oppose them? I mean, when the body is hot and thirsty, does not the soul oppose it and draw it away from drinking, and from eating when it is hungry, and do we not see the soul opposing the body in countless other ways?'

10 Frederick Copleston, *A History of Philosophy* 1 301ff

11 Aristotle, *De Anima*, version of William of Moerbeke and Commentary of St Thomas Aquinas, trans. K. Foster and S. Humphries 403a, 17ff.: 'Now all the soul's modifications do seem to involve the body – anger, meekness, fear, compassion, and joy and love and hate. For along with these the body also is to some degree affected.'

12 'It is necessary then, that the soul be a substance in the sense of the specifying principle of a physical body potentially alive. Now substance [in this sense] is act; it will therefore be the act of a body of this sort ...

If, then, there is any one generalisation to be made for any and every soul, the soul will be the primary act of a physical bodily organism' (Aristotle, *De Anima*, 412a, 20–8).

13 Aristotle, *De Anima*, 413a, 1–5 See J.L. Ackrill, 'Aristotle's Definition of Psyche,' *Articles on Aristotle*, ed. Jonathan Barnes, Malcolm Schofield, and Richard Sorabji IV 65–75. See also in the same volume the article by Charles Kahn, 'Sensation and Consciousness in Aristotle's Psychology.' He discusses the ways in which Aristotle avoids the dualism of Descartes. 'The great difference in Aristotle's view is the total lack of the Cartesian sense of a radical and necessary incompatibility between "thought" or awareness on the one hand, and physical extension, on the other. The soul is defined for Aristotle not by those properties in which no body can share, but precisely by those capacities which only a body can provide' 26–7.

14 Aristotle, *Generation of Animals*, trans. Arthur Peck 737a, 7ff.: 'Consider now the physical part of the semen. (This it is which, when it is emitted by the male, is accompanied by the portion of soul-principle and acts as its vehicle.) Partly this soul-principle is separable from physical matter – this applies to those animals where some divine element is included, and what we call Reason is of this character – partly it is inseparable.'

15 See Richard Sorabji, 'Body and Soul in Aristotle,' *Articles on Aristotle* 44–5.

16 See Jonathan Barnes, 'Aristotle's Concept of Mind,' *Articles on Aristotle* 40.

17 Aristotle, *De Anima*: 'But as regards intellect and the speculative faculty, nothing has so far been demonstrated; but it would seem to be another kind of soul, and alone capable of being separated, as the eternal from the perishable' (413b, 25ff.). 'Only separated, however, is it what it really is. And this alone is immortal and perpetual' (430a, 22ff.).

18 This may have its origins in Aristotle's *De Anima*, 412b, 6ff., but its application becomes literal, not merely an analogy, in Aristotle's followers. 'So one can no more ask if the body and the soul are one than if the wax and the impression it receives are one.'

19 Plotinus, *Enneads* 5.3.11, trans. S. MacKenna, 3rd ed. 392

20 R.A. Norris, *Manhood and Christ* 14

21 See A.H. Armstrong, 'Plotinus,' *The Cambridge History of Later Greek and Early Medieval Philosophy*' 225.

22 'As the Soul is evil by being interfused with the body and by coming to share the body's states and to think the body's thoughts, so it would be good, it would be possessed of virtue, if it threw off the body's moods

and devoted itself to its own Act – the state of Intellection and Wisdom – never allowed the passions of the body to affect it ...' (Plotinus, *Enneads* 1.2.3, p 32).

23 Plotinus, *Enneads* 4.4.18, p 301

24 Ibid. 4.8.6, p 362

25 Armstrong, *Cambridge History* 255

26 Plotinus distinguishes clearly between body and matter. 'For body is a later production, a compound made by Matter in conjunction with some other entity.' This body is 'something that is neither Real-Being nor Matter' (*Enneads*, 3.6.7, p 208).

27 Ibid. 3.6.13, pp 215–16

28 See Norris, *Manhood and Christ* 15: 'If the dualistic strain in Platonism proceeds on the assumption of a fundamental opposition between soul and its material container, the optimistic and monistic strain assumes, on the contrary, that embodiment is the natural and inevitable condition of the soul, and one to which, therefore, it is naturally adapted.'

29 H.W. Robinson, 'Hebrew Psychology,' in *The People and the Book*, ed. A.S. Peake 362.

30 'While *sarx* stands for man, in the solidarity of creation, in his distance from God, *soma* stands for man, in the solidarity of creation, as made for God' (J.A.T. Robinson, *The Body* 31). 'Flesh' alone can also refer to man's transitory nature. (See Van Peursen, *Body, Soul, Spirit* 96–7.)

31 *The Epistle to Diognetus* vi.5,7, ed. L.B. Radford 66–7

32 *Dictionnaire de théologie catholique*, ed. A. Vacant, E. Mangenot, and E. Almann, I, col. 983 (hereafter *DTC*)

33 *DTC*, I. 984

34 Ibid. 985

35 'De Anima,' *The Writings of Tertullian*, trans. P. Holmes, II 419

36 See Tertullian, 'De Anima' 429

37 See Paul O. Kristeller, *Renaissance Thought* 51.

38 'Those rational beings who sinned and on that account fell from the state in which they were, in proportion to their particular sins were enveloped in bodies as a punishment; and when they are purified they rise again to the state in which they formerly were, completely putting away their evil and their bodies. Then again a second or a third or many more times they are enveloped in different bodies for punishment' (G.W. Butterworth, *Origen on First Principles* 126).

39 *DTC* I 999

40 Irenaeus and Eastern writers such as Methodius of Olympus and Athanasius believed Original Righteousness to have been merely a superadded quality, and hence took a much less serious view of the Fall. But

it was the Western tradition that, through Augustine, was dominant in seventeenth-century England.

41 N.P. Williams, *The Ideas of the Fall and of Original Sin* 218

42 Ibid. 235–6. The function of the mother is purely passive (see n14 above). This is taken up by Aquinas and is seen to have implications for the conception and birth of Christ which remain as late as the seventeenth century.

43 A.H. Armstrong (*Saint Augustine and Christian Platonism* 8) questions whether Plato believed souls to be immortal by nature or simply by the unchanging good will of the Demiurge creator.

44 'But if our creation (albeit mortal) be the work of God; how is punishment then to enter into God's benefits, that is, our bodies? ... Wherefore our true religion rightly affirms Him the Maker both of the world and all creatures therein, bodies and souls, of which man the chief piece in earth was alone made after His image ...' (Augustine, *The City of God* Book 12, Ch. 26, trans. John Healey, ed. R.V.G. Tasker i, 370).

45 'For the soul, being now delighted with perverse liberty and scorning to serve God, could not have the body as formerly at its command: and having willingly forsaken God as its superior, it could not have its inferior so serviceable as it desired, nor could it have the flesh subject as it might have had always, had it remained itself God's subject' (*City of God* Book 13, Ch. 13, ii.10).

46 *City of God* Book 14, Ch. 3, ii.29

47 Ibid. Ch. 16, ii.47

48 See Aquinas, *Summa Theologica*, (hereafter *ST*), Part I, Question 90, trans. The Fathers of the English Dominican Province, Part I, Third Number 249–56.

49 Copleston, *A History of Philosophy* II 404–5

50 'Ancient philosophers made no distinction between sense and intellect, and referred both to a corporeal principle. Plato, however, drew a distinction between intellect and sense; yet he referred both to an incorporeal principle, maintaining that feeling, just as understanding, belongs to the soul as such. From this it follows that even the souls of brute animals are subsistent. But Aristotle held that of the operations of the soul, understanding alone is performed without a corporeal organ' (*ST* I. 75.3, pp 7–8).

51 *ST* I. 77.8, p 70.

52 'For the sensitive appetite is naturally moved, not only by the estimative power in other animals, and in man by the cogitative power which the universal reason guides, but also by the imagination and sense' (*ST*, I. 81.3, p 130).

53 *ST*, I. 81.3, p 129

54 'Sin consists chiefly in an act of the will, which is not hindered by weakness of the body: for he that is weak in body may have a ready will for action, and yet be hindered by a passion ... Hence when we speak of sins of weakness, we refer to weakness of soul rather than of body. And yet even weakness of soul is called weakness of the flesh, in so far as it is owing to a condition of the flesh that the passions of the soul arise in us, through the sensitive appetite being a power using a corporeal organ' (*ST*, I-II.77.3, p 362). Concerning the transmission of sin, Aquinas says that a Catholic must hold that it is passed on to one's descendants by way of origin. But it is *not* passed on by traducianism. He sees Adam as a kind of first mover who inclines all his seed to sin, and this sin is passed on from the father only. See *ST*, I-II.81.5, p 410: 'For it has been stated that original sin is transmitted by the first parent in so far as he is the mover in the begetting of his children: wherefore it has been said that if anyone were begotten materially only, of human flesh, they would not contract original sin. Now it is evident that in the opinion of philosophers, the active principle of generation is from the father, while the mother provides the matter. Therefore original sin is contracted, not from the mother, but from the father: so that, accordingly, if Eve, and not Adam, had sinned, their children would not contract original sin.'

55 Duns Scotus, for example, reacted against Aquinas' close association of body and soul, insisting that in its own nature the soul is a purely spiritual substance, and only in its earthly life is it connected to the body (Z. Kuksewicz, 'Criticisms of Aristotelian Psychology and the Augustinian-Aristotelian Synthesis,' *The Cambridge History of Later Medieval Philosophy* ed. Norman Kretzmann, Anthony Kenny, and Jan Pinborg 627).

56 'Lectures on Genesis I-V,' *Luther's Works*, ed. Jaroslav Pelikan, I 185

57 Ibid. 60–1

58 Ibid. 84

59 Ibid. 100

60 'The scholastics argue that original righteousness was not a quality superadded to man's nature but, like some adornment, was added to man as a gift ... But this idea must be shunned like poison, for it minimizes original sin' ('Lectures on Genesis,' 164–5).

61 Ibid. 114

62 Luther, *A Commentary on St Paul's Epistle to the Galatians*, trans. based on the 'Middleton' edition of the English version of 1575 505

63 Ibid. 504

64 Luther, *Works*, 1 62
65 'Those who have said that original sin is 'concupiscence' have used an appropriate word, if only it be added ... that whatever is in man, from the understanding to the will, from the soul even to the flesh, has been defiled and crammed with this concupiscence. Or, to put it more briefly, the whole man is of himself nothing but concupiscence' (Calvin, *Institutes of the Christian Religion*, ed. J.T. McNeill 252).
66 Ibid. 193
67 Ibid. 192

CHAPTER TWO

1 See, for example, Nemesius, *The Nature of Man*, trans. G. Wither 125. 'The *body* being an *instrument* which the *soule* useth, if it bee well fitted for the same, is a helper unto the *soule*; and she the better useth it to her own contentment. But, if it be not every way framed and tempered for the *soule's* use, it becommeth her hindrance, and much adoe hath she to strive against the unfitnesse of her *instrument*.'
2 *Complaynt of the Soule* sig. Avii^r
3 Richard Carpenter, *The Sovles Sentinel ... A Sermon Preached at the Funerall ... of Sir Arthur Ackland Knight* 30
4 Thomas Adams, *Workes* 230
5 J. Guillemand, *A Combat betwixt Man and Death*, trans. E. Grimeston 552
6 John Donne consolidates the arguments for the body in an eloquent passage in a sermon preached on Easter Day, 1625: 'That God, all Spirit, served with Spirits, associated to Spirits, should have such an affection, such a love to this body, this earthly body, this deserves this wonder. The Father was pleased to breathe into this body, at first, in the Creation; The Son was pleased to assume this Body himself, after, in the Redemption; The Holy Ghost is pleased to consecrate this body, and make it his Temple, by his sanctification; In that *Faciamus hominem, Let us*, all us, *make man*, that consultation of the whole Trinity in making man, is exercised even upon this lower part of man, the dignifying of his body' (John Donne, *Sermons*, ed. G.R. Potter and E.M. Simpson vi, 265–6).
7 Aristotle, *De Anima* 425
8 Edmund Porter, *God Incarnate* 23
9 These treatises provide an interesting small survey of the change from an almost complete dependence on authority to the increased use of logic and physical observation. The Huguenot Philippe de Mornay,

whose *The Soules own evidence for its own Immortality* was translated into English by Sir Philip Sidney, rests his case on that most popular of all authorities, Plato. John Jackson, in *The Soule Is Immortall*, still refers to a wide and rather incongruous variety of authors to support his views – Hermes, Josephus, Ovid, Porphyry, and particularly Aristotle. But by 1652 Seth Ward, writing *A Philosophicall Essay Towards an Eviction of ... the Immortality of the Soule of men ...* ignores authority and demonstrates his position by a logic that owes something to Descartes. Whatever is incorporeal is immortal; the soul is an incorporeal substance; therefore the soul is immortal. And in 1655 Edmund Porter, while occasionally quoting such ancient writers as Chrysostom, is more impressed by the contemporary observations of Sir Thomas Browne. He cites as prime evidence the passage in *Religio Medici* stating that the soul must be inorganical since 'in the dissecting of a man no Organ is found proper to the Reasonable Soule ...' (*God Incarnate* 24).

10 See Donne, *Sermons* II 358: 'For ... at our inanimation in our Mothers womb, our immortall soule when it comes swallowes up the other soules of vegetation, and of sense, which were in us before.'

11 See Nicholas Mosley, Ψυχοσοφια: *or Natural and Divine Contemplations of the Passions and Faculties of the Soul of Man* 34, 90ff.

12 See Simon Harward, *A Discovrse Concerning the Soule and Spirit of Man* 14^v.

13 This is the division of both Augustine and Luther (see Ch. 1,). When will is not seen as a faculty of the rational soul its place is taken by imagination, and the trio then becomes understanding, imagination, and memory.

14 Richard Hooker, 'Ecclesiastical Polity,' I.vii.3, *Works*, ed. John Keble, 7th ed. I 221

15 Ibid. I 223

16 Donne, *Sermons* VI 321. The conflict between the two points of view may originate in the contrast between the anthropomorphic God of Genesis, whose will is absolute but arbitrary, and the Greek demiurge who brings to reality only what reason shows is possible and must choose from these possibilities the best. (See Albrecht Dihle, *The Theory of Will in Classical Antiquity* 144ff.) Dihle shows how Augustine, drawing on both traditions, reinterprets the Greek hermeneutical term 'will' as an anthropological one and from this develops a philosophical description of the biblical teachings concerning man's fall, salvation, and moral conduct.

17 Even they tried to save the freedom of the will, verbally at least, in the

eighth of the Lambeth Articles, though the general tone of the articles is opposed to such a freedom. See H.R. McAdoo, *The Spirit of Anglicanism* 31.

18 Joseph Hall, *The Great Imposter* 17–18

19 Edward Reynolds, *A Treatise of the Passions and Facvlties of the Soule of Man* 541–2

20 William Perkins, 'A Salve for a Sicke Man,' *Works* I 486

21 Adams, *Workes* 669

22 Donne, *Sermons* I 290. In a letter to Sir Henry Goodyere, he describes the mind as 'those thoughts and affections, and passions, which neither soul nor body hath alone, but have been begotten by their communication, as music results out of our breath and a cornet' (Edmund Gosse, *Life and Letters of John Donne* I 184).

23 See Nemesius, *The Nature of Man* 6. Nemesius, in fact, attributes the analogy to Plato, which makes sense of the fact that he uses it to disparage the body and assert the soul's superiority.

24 Mosley, Ψυχοσοφια 23. This is a rather extraordinary argument, since it implies that form can be conceived of as separate from matter. Unlike Platonic 'forms,' Aristotelian form cannot really be thought of in isolation in this way. An even more extreme view of their mutual dependency is found in a treatise by Samuel Haworth ('Ανθρωπωλογια or *A Philosophic Discourse Concerning Man being the Anatomy both of his Soul and Body* 15) in which he insists that not the soul alone but the union between body and soul is the form of man.

25 See A.C. Pegis, *St Thomas and the Problem of the Soul in the Thirteenth Century* 196.

26 Pierre Du Moulin, *The Christian Combate, or a Treatise of Afflictions ...* , trans. John Bulteel 3–4. See also Henry Hills, *A Short Treatise Concerning the Propagation of the Soul* 97. 'For the soul is not more imprisoned in regard of her Union with the body, than the body in regard of its Union with the soul ...'

27 See Donne, *Sermons* VI 297. 'But God hath not onely given man such an immortall soule, but as body that shall put on Incorruption and Immortality too, which he hath given to none of the Angels. In so much, that howsoever it be, whether an Angel may wish it selfe an Archangel ... yet man cannot deliberately wish himself an Angel, because he should lose by that wish, and lacke that glory, which he shall have in his body.'

28 Donne, *Sermons* II 63

29 Ibid. VI 75

30 Adams, *Works* 913

31 See Mosley, Ψυχοσοφια 31–2

32 This depravity, as Perkins specifies (*Works* I 20), is in the quality, not the substance of the faculties. Cf. Luther's views, Ch. 1, 17–18.

33 'Death brought in by sin, was nothing *superinduced* to man; man onely was *reduced* to his natural condition, from which before Adams fall he stood exempted by supernatural favour ...' (Jeremy Taylor, Ἐνιαυτοσ: *A Course of Sermons for All the Sundays of the Year* 'Sermons ... for the Summer half-year' 32)

34 *Deus Justicatus* 16

35 Richard Baxter, *Two Disputations of Original Sin* 67–8. See also Richard Sibbes, *The Complete Works* I 172.

36 Donne, *Sermons* VII 218

37 Baxter, *Two Disputations* 218

38 Donne, *Sermons* V 155. Contrast Hooker, 'Eccl. Pol.,' v.lvi.7, *Works* II 250.

39 Adams, *Workes* 479

40 Donne, *Sermons* V 172. See also Reynolds, *A Treatise* 398: 'It is improbable that any staine should be transfused from the Body to the Soul, as from the foule vessell to the cleane water put into it ... Nothing is the seat of sin which cannot be the seat of Death the wages of sin.'
   'Originall sinne therefore most probably seemeth to arise by *Emanation*, partiall in the parts, totall in the whole from Mans *Nature* as *guilty, forsaken*, and *accursed* by God for the sinne of *Adam*. And from the parts not considered absolutely in themselves, but by virtue of their concurrence and *Vnion*, whereby both make up one compounded Nature.'

41 See Ch. 1, 9–10.

42 See Baxter, *Two Disputations* 105. Baxter's concept of the soul is more material than Perkins' 'spiritual and invisible substance,' which comes into the body by infusion, but it cannot be understood as crudely physical. It can exist out of the body; it is not divisible or partible. His opposition to Henry More's theories of the soul (see p 50) are further evidence that, in his own terms, he considered it to be wholly 'spiritual.'

43 Taylor, *Unum Necessarium* 391

44 Ibid. 372

45 Taylor, *An Answer to a Letter Written by R.R., the Ld. Bp. of Rochester* 5

46 See Sibbes, *Works* V *146, 144*.

47 Hooker, 'Eccl. Pol.,' I.vii.3, *Works* I 221

48 Taylor, *Deus Justicatus* 21–2

49 John Downame, *The Conflict betweene the Flesh and the Spirit* 50

50 Adams, *Workes* 161. See also ibid. 914: 'The body is the instrument of the soule: it acts, what the other directs: so it is the externall, actuall, and instrumentall offender: Satan will come with a *Habeas corpus* for it. But I am perswaded, if he take the Body, he will not leave the Soule behind him.'

51 See Donne, 'Why are wee by all creatures waited on,' *Divine Poems*, ed. Helen Gardner 10, and also *Sermons* II 152.

52 Donne, *Sermons* VIII 106–7

53 Perkins, 'An Exposition of the Creed,' *Works* 321

54 William Bates, *The Four Last Things*, 2nd ed. 53

55 Lancelot Andrewes, *Ninety-Six Sermons* I 439. 'It is true in sin the sense, and so the soul, is first in fault. In at that gate it first comes, and out at that it must first go.'

56 See Samuel Hoard, *The Soules Miserie and Recoverie* 377–8. 'The body is the souls servant, by which her commands are put in execution, it is her *instrument*, by which she doth either good or evill: nor is it a meere *passive* instrument, which the soule may command at her pleasure, and make use of to what purposes shee listeth; but *active*, such an instrument as hath some power over, and influence upon the soule ...' Hoard traces this influence specifically to the humours of the body and the way in which they influence the disposition.

57 Henry Smith, *Sermons* II 298

58 See Donne, *Sermons* IV 194 ('Every man is a little *Church* ... ; and in every man there are two sides, two armies; the flesh fights against the Spirit'), and Adams, *Workes* 124, where he argues the Galatians passage has been 'prefigured' by the strife of Esau and Jacob in the womb, with Rebecca representing the state of a regenerate soul 'wherein, till *this mortall shall put on immortalitie*, and glory swallow up corruption, there must be a perpetuall conflict.' While Donne sets the struggle within the whole man, Adams, drawing on Origen's interpretation and imagery, sets the conflict specifically within the soul, thus making the purely figurative significance of the two combatants clear.

59 Perkins, 'Two Treatises ... II. Of the combat of the flesh and spirit,' *Works* I, 467

60 Downame, *The Conflict ...* 10

61 See Donne, *Sermons* IV 61.

62 Sibbes, *Works* I 338

63 Donne quotes Gregory of Nyssa, who 'takes the Body to be spoken *De nutribili*, The flesh and bloud of man, And the soule *De sensibili*, The operation of the senses, and the Spirit *De Intellectuali*, The Intellectuall, the reasonable faculties of man; That in the body, Man is conformed

to Plants that have no sense, In the soule, to Beasts, that have no reason, In the spirit, to Angels' (Donne, *Sermons*, v 65).

64 Adams, *Workes* 679

65 Baxter, *Of the Immortality of Mans Soul*, 'Of the Nature of Spirits' 4.

66 Adams, *Workes* 361

67 Sir Francis Bacon, 'The Great Instauration,' *Works*, ed. James Spedding, R.L. Ellis, and D.D. Heath IV 26

68 Bacon, 'Novum Organum,' *Works* IV 57

69 Ibid. 59

70 Bacon, 'De Augmentis,' *Works* IV 401

71 Bacon, 'Of the Advancement of Learning,' *Works* III 379

72 Bacon, 'De Augmentis,' *Works* IV 405-6

73 Ibid. 406

74 René Descartes, 'Meditations,' *Philosophical Works*, trans. E.S. Haldane and G.R.T. Ross I 157

75 Descartes, 'Principles of Philosophy,' *Works* I 221

76 Descartes, 'Meditations,' *Works* I 190

77 Descartes, 'Rules for the Direction of the Mind,' *Works* I 38

78 Descartes, 'The Passions of the Soul,' *Works* I 345-6

79 'For what I here name spirits are nothing but material bodies and their one peculiarity is that they are bodies of extreme minuteness and that they move very quickly like the particles of the flame which issues from a torch' (Descartes, 'The Passions of the Soul,' *Works* I 336).

80 Descartes, 'The Passions of the Soul,' *Works* I 347

81 Ibid., 350

82 Ibid., 352-3

83 Ibid., 353

84 Ibid. 354

85 See Frederick Copleston, *A History of Philosophy* IV 121: 'Descartes appears to be in a difficult position. On the one hand, his application of the criterion of clarity and distinctness leads him to emphasize the real distinction between soul and body and even to represent each of them as being a complete substance. On the other hand, he does not want to accept the conclusion which appears to follow, namely, that the soul is simply lodged in a body which it uses as a kind of extrinsic vehicle or instrument.'

86 His influence is also evident in the works of other seventeenth-century writers such as William Ramesey (*Mans Dignity and Perfection Vindicated*) and William Brent (*Discourse upon the Nature of Eternitie*).

87 Digby comments thus on Descartes' explanation of sense impressions: 'He is ... the first that I have ever mett with, who hath published any

conceptions of this nature, whereby to make the operations of sense intelligible' (Sir Kenelm Digby, *Two Treatises ... The Nature of Bodies; the Nature of Mans Soule* 276).

88 Digby, *Two Treatises* 284-5
89 Ibid. 276-7
90 Ibid. 392
91 Ibid. 444
92 'The Third Set of Objections [by Hobbes] with the Author's Reply,' Descartes, *Philosophical Works* II 62
93 Thomas Hobbes, 'Human Nature,' *English Works*, ed. Sir William Molesworth IV 2-15
94 Hobbes, 'Leviathan,' Pt 1, 'Of Man,' *Works* III 29
95 Hobbes, 'Human Nature,' *Works* IV 31
96 Hobbes, 'Leviathan,' Pt 1, *Works* III 48
97 'But the opinion that such spirits were incorporeal, or immaterial, could never enter into the mind of any man by nature; because, though men may put together words of contradictory signification, as *spirit* and *incorporeal*; yet they can never have the imagination of any thing answering to them ...' (Hobbes, 'Leviathan,' Pt 1, *Works* III 96). (See also 'Human Nature,' *Works* IV 60-1.)
98 Hobbes, 'Leviathan,' Pt 4, 'Of the Kingdom of Darkness,' *Works* III 640
99 Hobbes, 'Leviathan,' Pt 4, *Works* III 616
100 This is the passage that so impressed Edmund Porter (see n9). Browne claims the soul must be immaterial because there is no organ or instrument in the body for this soul that he can discover, 'for in the braine, which we tearme the seate of reason, there is not any thing of moment more than I can discover in the cranie of a beast: and this is a sensible and no inconsiderable argument of the inorganity of the soule, at least in that sense we usually so receive it' (Sir Thomas Browne, 'Religio Medici,' *Works*, ed. Geoffrey Keynes, rev. ed. 1 47).
101 Browne, 'Urne-Burial,' *Works* I 158
102 Browne, 'Religio Medici,' *Works* I 16
103 Ibid. 29
104 Browne, 'Pseudodoxia Epidemica,' Bk I, *Works* II 19
105 Ibid. 26
106 See Jeffrey Barnoux, 'The Separation of Reason and Faith in Bacon and Hobbes, and Leibniz's *Theodicy*,' *Journal of the History of Ideas* XVII 4 (Oct.–Dec. 1981) 615. It was the Cambridge Platonists, he argues, who broke with the notion 'of the separation of religion and philosophy ... From the Cambridge Platonists this new or revived attitude spread through the Latitudinarians and gave a generally underesti-

mated or neglected unBaconian aspect to the approach to relations of reason and faith characteristic of the Royal Society.'

107 A similar optimism about human nature has already been noted in the works of Jeremy Taylor, but among the Cambridge Platonists it became the basis of a system of thought that went far beyond anything anticipated by Taylor.

108 John Smith, 'Attaining to Divine Knowledge,' *The Cambridge Platonists*, ed. E.T. Campagnac 93–6

109 Smith, 'The Immortality of the Soul,' *Cambridge Platonists* 150–1

110 Ibid. 152

111 See F.I. MacKinnon, ed. *Philosophical Writings of Henry More* xx: 'More's way out of the dualistic dilemma was not that of denying the reality either of matter or of spirit, but consisted in bringing them closer together, denying the fissure between them by asserting that their likeness and their connection are far more fundamental than their differences. The exact line between soul and body in man, between spirit and matter in the universe, becomes in More's hands a wavy, misty boundary, so that it is impossible to trace just where, for him, the one passes over into the other.'

112 More, 'An Antidote Against Atheism,' *Philosophical Writings* 24

113 More, 'The Immortality of the Soul,' ibid. 118

114 More, 'The Easie, True, and Genuine Notion and Consistent Explication of the Nature of a Spirit,' ibid. 207, and 'The Immortality of the Soul' 65

115 More, 'The ... Nature of a Spirit,' ibid. 216

116 See More, 'The Immortality of the Soul,' ibid. 163: 'The *Soul* separate from this *Terrestial* Body is not released from all *Vital Union* with *Matter*. There are four kinds of souls – seminal forms, souls of brutes, the human soul, and the souls of Angels.'

117 Cf. Origen, Ch. 1, 12. For the biblical source of this idea, see 1 Cor. 15.39, 40.

118 MacKinnon, *Philosophical Writings of Henry More* 307

119 More, 'The Immortality of the Soul,' ibid. 155

120 Ralph Cudworth, *The True Intellectual System of the Universe* 862: 'There is a *Scale* or *Ladder* of *Entities* and *Perfections* in the Universe, one above another, and the Production of things cannot possibly be in Way of *Ascent* from *Lower* to *Higher*, but must of necessity be in way of *Descent* from *Higher* to *Lower*.'

121 See J.A. Passmore, *Ralph Cudworth: An Interpretation* 23: 'The field of the incorporeal is so extended that Cudworth's dualism loses a great

deal of its theological significance. His is a dualism of force and matter, activity and passivity, not a dualism of spirit and body.'

122 Cudworth, *True Intellectual System* 172
123 Ibid. 344
124 See ibid. 784–92.
125 Ibid. 818
126 Baxter, *Of the Immortality of Mans Soul,* 'Of the Nature of Spirits' 43
127 Ibid. 4. The pamphleteer M.S., probably also a nonconformist, takes a similar stand against More and Cudworth, insisting, like Baxter, that souls can exist free from all body. He also attacks Cudworth's treatment of soul which, to him, seems to make no distinction between animal life and the rational soul of man, and hence to make brute souls immortal. The material and the immaterial, body and soul, must be preserved as two quite distinct though interacting entities within man. (See *A Philosophical Discourse of the Nature of Rational and Irrational Souls,* by M.S. It seems probable that M.S. is Matthew Sylvester [1636–1708], a nonconformist divine who, by 1667, had become pastor of a congregation at Rutland House, London. Here, in 1687, Richard Baxter became his unpaid assistant. Sylvester was Baxter's literary executor and edited the *Reliquae Baxterianae.* There is evidence that he knew both Whichcote and Tillotson.)

CHAPTER THREE

1 See Rosemary Woolf, *The English Religious Lyric in the Middle Ages* 89. She mentions, briefly, the three chief aspects of the debate but, as her inclusion of it in the chapter 'Lyrics on Death' would indicate, places prime emphasis on the *ubi sunt* and *contemptus mundi* elements.
2 For an early sixteenth-century example, see pp 71 and the frontispiece.
3 For much of the above account I am indebted to the study by Louise Dudley, *The Egyptian Elements in the Legend of the Body and the Soul.*
4 Quoted by Dudley, *Egyptian Elements* 104
5 The most detailed study of the development of the debate remains that of Th. Batiouchkof, 'Le Débat de l'Ame et du Corps,' although his work has been supplemented by more recent studies, notably those of Louise Dudley and Rosemary Woolf, cited above; E.K. Heningham (*An Early Latin Debate of the Body and the Soul*); H. Walther ('Das Streitgedicht in der lateinischen Literatur des Mittelalters,' *Quellen und Untersuchungen zur lateinischen Philologie des Mittelalters*); Rudolf Willard ('The Address of the Soul to the Body').

6 Batiouchkof, 'Le Débat' 9–10. The 'tour of the universe' is a common element in many legends dealing with the fate of the soul after death. Angels or demons come to show the soul the fate of both the blessed and the damned to make their suffering more acute if they are to be consigned to hell or to make their relief greater if they are to be saved. In the 'Irish Homily,' for example, the devils allow the evil soul to ascend part of the way toward heaven in order that they may mock it.

7 This manuscript was found by Batiouchkof himself in the National Library of Rome.

8 For a detailed account of variations in the *time* of the address of the soul to the body, see the article by R. Willard, cited above.

9 For a comparison of four such passages in both Latin and the vernacular, see Louise Dudley, 'An Early Homily on the "Body and Soul" Theme.' See also a comprehensive list of treatments of this theme in Old English homilies in the article by Eleanor K. Heningham, 'Old English Precursors of *The Worcester Fragments*,' 295–6 n18.

10 'The Departed Soul's Address to the Body,' found in *Codex Exoniensis*, ed. Benjamin Thorpe 367–77, and in *The Poetry of the Codex Vercellensis*, trans. J.M. Kemble 100–10. All references are to this latter edition and line numbers are given in brackets in the text.

11 The manuscript dates from the fourteenth century, but Robert Atkinson, its editor, believes that in origin it goes back to the twelfth century. See Atkinson, *The Passions and Homilies from Leabhar Breac* 507–14.

12 Woolf, *The English Religious Lyric in the Middle Ages* 90

13 See Walther, 'Das Streitgedicht ...' 13ff.

14 Batiouchkof, 'Le Débat de l'Ame et du Corps' 541

15 Walther, 'Das Streitgedicht ...' 28

16 See E.K. Heningham, *An Early Latin Debate of the Body and Soul*. This work was published privately, and is not to be found in the catalogues of the chief British copyright libraries. A copy is, however, available in the Manuscript Room of the British Museum Library (Pamphlet 437, vol. XXXI, BM MS room).

17 There are many variant versions of 'Saint Bernard's Vision,' or the 'Visio Philiberti' (also Filibert, Fulbert) both printed and in manuscript. See E. du Méril, *Poésies Populaires Latines* 217ff.; Th. G. von Karajan, *Frühlingsgabe für Freunde älterer Literatur* 95–106. There is also a manuscript version that I have consulted in the Cambridge University Library (Add. MS 3093). All quotations are from the version printed in Thomas Wright (ed.), *The Latin Poems Commonly Attributed to Walter Mapes* and titled 'Dialogus inter Corpus et Animam.'

18 'Als I Lay in a Winteris Nyt,' printed in the appendix of Wright's *Latin*

Poems 334–46. Wright prints two versions of this poem, one from the thirteenth century and one from the fourteenth. All quotations are from the thirteenth-century version.

19 E.K. Heningham argues this convincingly in her work cited above (*An Early Latin Debate* 17–18).

20 'Un samedi par nuit,' printed in the appendix of Wright's *Latin Poems* 321–33. Because of a misplaced leaf in the manuscript, Wright has printed 'Un samedi par nuit' with two speeches each by body and soul. This is incorrect, as Batiouchkof (515n1) points out.

21 Heningham, *An Early Latin Debate* 50

22 'In a thestri stude,' Wright, *Latin Poems* 346–9

23 'The Departed Soul's Address to the Body,' lines 78–81, 113–23. For a discussion of meditative elements concerning death in these poems, see Woolf, *The English Religious Lyric in the Middle Ages* 90ff. See also an example of a prose text on the same theme from the *Summa Predicantium*, quoted in G.R. Owst, *Preaching in Medieval England* 343: 'If we would but consider well how quickly we shall be placed beneath the feet not only of men, friend and foe alike, but of dogs, and the beasts of the field – where he who now rears and possesses mighty palaces shall have a hall whose roof touches his nose – he who now can hardly decide which robe he wishes to wear, shall have a garment of earth and worms ... we should find little reason for pride.'

24 See Ch 2, pp 31–2.

25 Guiseppe Levi, *Parabeln, Legenden und Gedanken aus Thalmud und Midrasch*, trans. Ludwig Seligmann 354

26 For a discussion of Plutarch's debate, see H. Gaidon, 'Echos de la littérature antique au Moyen-Age.'

27 'Death,' 23–4, *An Old English Miscellany*, ed. Richard Morris 169

28 Guillaume de Deguileville, *The Pilgrimage of the Life of Man*, trans. John Lydgate, ed. F.J. Furnivall

29 Guillaume de Deguileville, *The Booke of the Pylgremage of the Sowle*, trans. from the French and printed by William Caxton, 1483, ed. K.I. Cust 57

30 It is difficult to understand how a critic such as H.R. Swardson (*Poetry and the Fountain of Light* 93) concludes that the body plays 'a part that can only be described as that of the straight man.'

31 Wright, *Latin Poems* 335

32 Ibid.

33 For a detailed study of the horse and rider analogy in body and soul dialogues, see Sr Mary Ursula Vogel, *Some Aspects of the Horse and Rider Analogy in 'The Debate between the Body and the Soul'*. Oddly

enough, she does not discuss or even mention the fact that in the *Phaedrus* myth the horses are faculties of the soul, while here they are faculties of the body.

34 Wright, *Latin Poems* 331. A parallel to these accusations is found in the twelfth-century work attributed to Hildebert of Lavardin, 'De Querimonia et Conflictu Carnis et Spiritus'. Here body notes that the soul claims to have been conquered by proximity to the flesh in the way that Hercules' life was threatened by the poisoned shirt his stepmother sent him. But, the body claims, the soul's death is really quite different from his, for Hercules did not poison the garment himself. The soul, however, has used the body as its servant in all the purposes it now abhors, and thus it poisoned the shirt that has destroyed it.

35 The intimate connection between the heart and eye and body and soul debates has been pointed out by many critics and is even demonstrated, in one case, by the inclusion of a heart and eye debate within the general framework of a body and soul debate. (See the debate by Bonvesin da Riva, which also includes a dialogue of the members, printed in Batiouchkof's article, 'Le Débât de l'Ame et du Corps' 541.)

36 Wright, *Latin Poems* 93–5.

37 See J.H. Hanford, 'The Debate of the Heart and Eye'

38 This is printed by Carleton Brown, 'A Homiletical Debate between Heart and Eye,' *Modern Language Notes* 198

39 Ibid. A rather different tradition of heart and eye debates, linked to the courtly love tradition, also exists. (See Wright, 'Le Débât du Cuer et de l'Oeil,' *Latin Poems* 310–21, and a fifteenth-century English version edited by Eleanor Hammond, 'The Eye and the Heart.' The latter was printed by Wynken de Worde, which shows its popularity.) Here it is a question of responsibility for the sufferings of love rather than for sin and, after an abortive attempt at combat, the disputants are brought before Venus' court of love. Venus, who knows her court cannot be maintained without both, postpones judgment and writes to her true lovers promising a chaplet of roses to him who can resolve the matter. J.H. Hanford (see n37), who discusses the relationship between this love dispute and other heart and eye debates, concludes that the love dispute is probably the original. This seems unlikely in view of the close links the scholastic and homiletic disputes have with ancient debate literature. It appears more probable that this is a later embellishment of that tradition in which most of the serious elements have been lost.

40 Printed in Walther, 'Das Streitgedicht ...' 215–16

41 'Streit des fleischlischen und des geistigen Menschen,' ibid., 216–18

CHAPTER FOUR

1 See n1, Chap. 2, p 223.

2 See John Chrysostom, *Exposition upon the Epistle to the Ephesians,* 'truly and faithfully translated out of Greeke' 63: 'For, this is the vertue of the flesh, to be made subiect to the soule: but it is wickednesse to reigne ouer the soule. For, even as an horse is faire, and well underlaid, but that appeareth not without a rider: so (fareth it with) the flesh also, when we cut off the wanton praunsing thereof.'

3 'The Droomme of Doomesday,' trans. George Gascoigne sig. Dv^v. In the dedication, Gascoigne claims he found the volume in his library and does not know its author.

4 'And thy body shall be punysshed with ye for it sunned with the and thou in it ... and it shall haue no payn but for the / for it myght not synne but by the' (*Complaynt of the Soule* sig. B1^r).

5 The 'Dance of Death,' usually in the form of a ballad, continues to exist throughout the sixteenth century and enjoys a marked rise in popularity in the decade between 1625 and 1635. The later versions tend to place greater emphasis on repentance and preparation for death ('Death's loud Allarum,' 1635, begins 'Lament you sinnes, good people all lament') and may include topical references (Walter Colman in 'La danse machabre,' 1633, cites Buckingham as an example of the vanity of human life cut short), while the earlier ones stick closer to the traditional motif of death, the reaper, coming for all stations of men (see 'The Daunce and Song of Death,' 1569, and 'Dance of Death,' 1580). In 'The doleful Dance, and Song of Death' (1625?), the first line, 'Can you dance the shaking of the sheets,' sounds a typically seventeenth-century emphasis on the physical horrors of death. Most of these works are accompanied by woodcut illustrations. Indeed, it may be the traditional visual element of the genre that enabled it to have a continuous history when the body and soul dialogues temporarily disappeared.

6 See Chap. 2, p 34.

7 J.P. [John Phillip, described as a student at Cambridge], 'A Sommon to repentance Given vnto Christians' sig. Avii^v–Aviii^r

8 John Hagthorpe, *Divine Meditations and Elegies* 4

9 A sample of the titles alone show the universality of the preoccupation: *A Dialogue of Dying Wel* by Don Peeter of Luca, 'translated first into French and now into English' [by R.V.]; George Strode, *The Anatomie of Mortalitie; A Monument of Mortalitie;* Edmund Layfield, *The Mappe of Mans Mortality and Vanity;* Alice Sutcliffe, *Meditations of Man's*

Mortalitie. For a comparatively recent discussion of the seventeenth-century preoccupation with death and dreams of death, see Elisabeth Bourcier, 'Mort, rêves et surnaturel chez les Anglais au xvie siècle,' published by the University of Lille as part of 'Actes du Colloque' on the general subject *La Mort, le fantastique, le surnaturel du xvie siècle à l'époque romantique*.

10 Edmund Porter, Θεὸς'ΑνΘρωποφόρος *God Incarnate* 47. '*When a guilty soul departeth, troops of evil, and unhappy angels drag it to their own quarters.* These are the Messengers which are sent for mens soules, some terrible, and feared; others of pleasant appearance, and desired ...'

11 Guillemand, *Combat betwixt Man and Death* 749–50

12 John Donne, 'Of the Progresse of the Soule' ll 93–106, *Poems*, ed. H.J.C. Grierson I 254

13 'Therefore seeing the diuels appeare before her with moste foule and vglie shapes, like fiers lyons watching to deuour her, she then more vnhappie than any other creature, in that instant feeleth such bitter grief and sorrow, that she is forced for vehemencie of her vnspeakable passions, to forsake for euer her miserable and contemptible bodie. And so suddaynlie taken by those cruel fiendes of hel, she is with such grief as cannot bee vttered bound and brought against her wil, to that vnhappie and sorrowful countrie, where being cast in burning fire she their [sic] remayneth in euerlasting wo and payne: and the dead carkas now become carrion, and all foule and stinking, with a little sound of belles, and with weeping teares of kinsfolkes is brought vnto the graue, whereafter it is put in the ground, it is soone deuoured of wormes, & turned into earth and ashes (Don Peeter of Luca, 'A Dialogue of Dying Wel,' 19ʳ–19ᵛ).

14 John Welles, *The Soules Progresse to the Celestiall Canaan, or Heavenly Jervsalem*. Page numbers are given in brackets in the text.

15 'Cursed be the day that I was first united to so leud a body: oh, that I had but so much favour as that I might never see thee more! our parting is bitter and dolefull, but our meeting againe to receive at that dreadfull day, the fulnesse of our deserved vengeance will be farre more terrible and intollerable ... Thou filthy carcase, with fare ill, farre well, I leave thee (Welles, *The Soules Progresse* ... 115).

16 'Yea, this deformity of will is so violent, that oftentimes in the regenerate soule, the appetite will not obey the government of reason, and the will wandreth after, and yeelds consent to sinfull motions. How great then is the violence of the appetite and will in the Reprobate soule, which still remaines in her naturall corruption?' (ibid. 109–10).

17 This does not mean that all those who wrote such treatises were non-

conformists in the strict sense of the term. The prevalence of essentially 'Puritan' theology was much more widespread than that. I am using the term to indicate certain theological views and preoccupations rather than a formal position.

18 See Chap. 2, pp 32–3. See also 'A Wakening of Worldlings,' in *A Monument of Mortalitie* 66

19 William Foster, *The Means to Keepe Sinne from Reigning in Our Mortall Body* 18–19 (a sermon preached at Paul's Cross, 26 May 1629)

20 See Roger Deakins, 'The Tudor Prose Dialogue: Genre and Anti-Genre.' He distinguishes between those few sixteenth-century dialogues that follow the rules for dialogue set down by such a humanist as Carlo Sigonio, which he categorizes as 'genre' dialogues, and the vast body of Tudor dialogues, which 'fly in the face of the conventions of the dialogue genre.' All the dialogues discussed here are, according to his division, 'anti-genre' dialogues.

21 Michael Wodde, 'A Dialogve, or Familiar Talke betwene Two Neighbours ...' sig. Eiiiᵛ. See also Robert Legate, 'A Briefe Catechisme and Dialogue betwene the Husbande and his Wyfe ... ,' where the purely instructive nature of the dialogue is even more obvious.

22 'A Short Dialogve, wherein is proved, that no man can be saved without good workes' (Oxford 1604)

23 Compare, for example, W. Hall's 'A Dialogue about Justification by Faith,' which merely rehearses the extreme Protestant position in its simplest form.

24 See the 'Advertisement to the Reader' of Walter Charlton's *The Immortality of the Human Soul demonstrated by the Light of Nature, in two Dialogues*: 'Among the Ancient Philosophers ... nothing was more frequent, than to deliver their opinions and documents, as wel Physical as Moral, in the plain and familiar way of *Dialogue* ...'

25 John Deacon and John Walker, *Dialogicall Discourses of Spirits and Divils*, 'To the Reader'

26 Francis Thynne, 'The debate betweene *Pride and Lowlines.*' The attribution to Thynne is doubtful. See J. C. Jordan, *Robert Greene* 122 n65.

27 *A new dialoge called the endightment agaynste mother Messe*, attributed to 'W.P.' The STC gives the author as William Punt.

28 R.M., *A Profitable Dialogue for a peruerted Papist*

29 George Gifford, *A Dialogve concerning Witches and Witchcraftes*

30 Barnaby Rych, *A Right Exelent and pleasaunt Dialogue, betwene Mercvry and an English Souldier ...*

31 Robert Vaughan, *A Dyalogue defensyve for Women ...*

32 *A Pleasant Dialogue or Disputation betwene the Cap, and the Head*

33 Francis Davison, *A Poetical Rhapsody 1602–1621*, ed. H.E. Rollins I 279–80

34 'A Dialog betweene the auctour and his eye,' *The Paradise of Dainty Devices 1576–1606*, ed. H.E. Rollins 106

35 Bartholomew Robertson, *The Crowne of Life*

36 'The cunning Age,' *A Pepysian Garland*, ed. H.E. Rollins 239–43

37 'The Hower is come,' BL MS Add 29396, pp 86ᵛ–89ʳ. I am indebted to Mary Chan for drawing my attention to this dialogue. For a discussion of its probable date, see her article 'Drolls, Drolleries and Mid-Seventeenth-Century Dramatic Music in England' 126 n13.

38 B.H. Bronson ('The Dialogue Song; or, Proteus Observed') argues this point – that the great increase in dialogues in the 1650s is due to the dearth of any other outlet for drama. His remarks are applied specifically to the musical song, which he sees as a rudimentary kind of drama, but they may be relevant to other forms of dialogue as well. Mary Chan, in the article cited in n37 carries the same line of argument farther to show how these musical dialogues (frequently performed, she believes) prepared the way for the rapid development of opera after the Restoration.

39 Thomas Lupton, *A Dreame of the Diuell and Diues* sig. G6ᵛ–G7ʳ

40 'As I lay slombrynge in manner of a trans,' *Songs and Ballads*, ed. Thomas Wright 89–93

41 Richard Niccols, *Sir Thomas Overbvries Vision* 3–4

42 Richard Niccols, 'A Winter Nights Vision,' in *A Mirror for Magistrates*. Page numbers are given in brackets in the text after quotations.

43 John Wharton, *Wharton's dreame* sig. A1ᵛ

44 W.D., *A Midnights Trance, Wherein is discoursed of Death, the nature of Sovles, and estate of Immortalitie* 4

45 For example, 'Greenes Vision' (by Robert Greene), while ostensibly a repentance for his misspent life, is largely taken up with the telling of tales by Chaucer and Gower. And the elaborate setting of 'A Winter Nights Vision' (see p 8) leads anticlimactically to what is, in effect, an addition to *A Mirror for Magistrates*. Some are obviously political, such as *The Vision and Discovrse of Henry the seuenth* (1610) [by Thomas Gainsford], which praises the union of Great Britain and the architect of that union, King James.

46 Richard Barnfield, *The Combat, betweene Conscience and Couetnesse in the Minde of Man*, appended to *The Encomion of Lady Pecunia*

47 Harry Morris, *Richard Barnfield, Colin's Child* 110

48 Ibid. 108

49   Now had the cole-blacke steedes, of pitchie Night,

> (Breathing out Darknesse) banisht cheerfull Light,
> And sleepe (the shaddowe of eternall rest)
> My seuerall senses, wholy had possest.
> When loe, there was presented to my view,
> A vision strange, yet not so strange, as true.
>
> ('The Combat,' D^r)

50 See above, n44.
51 The term is J.B. Leishman's. See *The Art of Marvell's Poetry* 210.

CHAPTER FIVE

1 William Crashaw, *The Complaint or Dialogve, betwixt the Soule and the Bodie of a damned man*. STC 1909.3 is the edition quoted.
2 See P.J. Wallis, 'The Library of William Crashawe,' *Transactions of the Cambridge Bibliographical Society*. Which manuscript version Crashaw used to make his translation is uncertain. William Yates, who owned the manuscript of the *Visio* now in the Cambridge University Library (Add MS3093) bound up with a copy of Crashaw's translation, assumes the Cambridge MS to have been that which Crashaw used. However, there are significant discrepancies between this MS and the Latin version Crashaw prints opposite his translation.
3 What is assumed to be the 1613 edition entered to L. Becket in that year exists only in two copies, both with the date cropped. The transcription in the appendix is of the 1662 edition.
4 'Saint Bernards Vision or, A briefe Discourse (Dialogue-wise) betweene the Soule and the Body of a damned man newly deceased ... ,' collected in *The Roxborough Ballads* 1.376–7. The date 1640 is tentatively assigned in the British Museum catalogue. It was only entered in the Stationer's Register on 13 Mar. 1656. (See H.E. Rollins, *An Analytical Index to the Ballad-Entries [1557–1709] in the Registers of the Company of Stationers of London*.) Ballads, however, often were not entered promptly, and Rollins particularly notes the large number of entries in 1656 compared with earlier years, which makes it likely that the ballad was written well before that date of entry.
5 For a more detailed examination of the differences between Crashaw's poem and the ballads, see the appendix note, 'Crashaw's Translation and Later Versions of Body and Soul Ballads.'
6 Rollins lists another edition of the ballad entered in the Stationers Register on 1 Mar. 1675, which is probably identical with the version found in the Roxborough collection to which the BM catalogue assigns the tentative date of 1683. A final version in the Roxborough collection

is similarly tentatively dated 1730. In addition, an adaptation was published, probably in Edinburgh, in 1776, and in 1800(?) we have an anonymous version that survives bound in a BM collection of Irish tracts (BM 11622.de.15.[45]). For a discussion of these later ballads and their relationship to their seventeenth-century prototype, see the appendix.

7 William Prynne, 'The Soules Complaint against the Body,' *Mount-Orgueil*. Page numbers of references are given in brackets in the text.

8 A medieval precedent for this can be found in Hildebert's *De Querimonia et Conflictu Carnis et Spiritus* (see n34, Ch. 3, p 234) where Soul addresses the author, who is strongly identified with 'body.' A similar confusion between the use of 'body' in the strict sense of the material part of man's nature and the use of 'body' to represent the whole man will be found in James Howell's dialogue, discussed below.

9 Humphrey Mill, 'A divine speech of the Soule to the bodie,' *Poems Occasioned by a Melancholy Vision*

10 Richard Brathwait, *The Last Trumpet: or a Six-Fold Christian Dialogue*. Page numbers are given in brackets in the text.

11 James Howell, *The Vision: or a Dialog between the Soul and the Bodie*. All further references are given in the text.

12 A medieval precedent for a debate that is primarily a discussion dialogue is the 'Debate between Body and Soul' found in a Bordeaux MS and printed by Walther ('Streit zwischen Korper und Seele' 218–21). In this debate the body begins by asking for supremacy over the soul, and the soul responds by becoming a catechist and giving the body godly instruction.

A seventeenth-century example of the tendency of the 'morality' dialogue to become a 'discussion' dialogue, with the consequent dissociation of content from speaker, has already been briefly noted in *The Crowne of Life* (see p 79). While this work is set in the form of a dialogue between the flesh and the spirit, it is really an 'art of living and dying well' combined with an exposition of such matters as justification by faith, the fate of the soul after death, and the resurrection of the body. Flesh interrogates spirit, but the interrogation could just as well be attributed to a dying man and a priest. This work is by no means a Platonic dialogue since there is no genuine discussion of the issues involved, but it is an example of the way in which a potentially dramatic theme has been turned to the use of exposition.

13 'O Me! how much reason have I to rue the time that ever I was cloistered up among those walls of clay; What cause have I to repent that ever I was thrown into that dungeon, that corrupt mass of flesh? For when I entered, I bore the image of my Creatour in some lustre, but since

that time, 'tis scarce discernible on me, in regard of those leprous spots and taintures which I have contracted from those frail corporeal organs, which have so pitifully disfigured and transformed me, that I cannot be called the same Thing I was at first, the Character of my Creatour being almost quite lost in me' (Howell, *The Vision* 1–2).

14 See Ch. 3, p 66.

15 See Ch. 2, p 42.

16 Henry Nicholson, *A Conference between the Soul and Body Concerning the Present and Future State*

17 This is Nicholson's argument for a locality for hell: 'They that would have Hell no local Place, say it will not be so confined by local Circum-scriptions, but it will be every where, wherever the Damn'd do rove, they carry their Hell with them: and in like manner, that to the blessed Heaven will be every where also. Now if Hell must be every where, and Heaven every where, it will follow, that Hell and Heaven will be mixt through one another, which is so monstrous absurd, that it is not to be thought of' (p 168).

18 'A Dialogue betweene the Soule and the Body,' in *A Poetical Rhapsody 1602–1621* I 197

19 Andrew Marvell, 'A Dialogue between the Soul and the Body,' in *Poems and Letters*, ed. H.M. Margoliouth I 20–1

20 For a discussion of the identity of A.W., see *A Poetical Rhapsody* II 53–71.

21 See Ch. 3, p 67.

22 See Ch. 1, pp 9–10.

23 See Richard Baxter, *Dying Thoughts upon Philippians 1.23* 19: 'Sondius de Orig. Animae (though an heretical Writer) hath said much to prove that the Body is a hinderance, and not a help to the Soul's Intuition. And if Ratiocination be a compound act, yet Intuition may be done for ever by the Soul alone.'

24 See Henry Vaughan, 'Man,' in *Works* ed. L.C. Martin 427. See also 'The Tempest' 461, and 'Distraction' 413. All further references to Vaughan's works are to this edition.

25 Pierre Legouis, in his book on Marvell (*Andrew Marvell* 39) rightly notes the lack of any conclusion: 'In this *estrif* or *disputoison*, scholastic in its subtlety, where Soul and Body both seem to be in the right when railing at each other, Marvell seeks rather to parade his ingenuity than to persuade or move; if he at all gives the impression of sincerity he owes it to the confession of his perplexity when confronted with one of the most abstruse problems of divinity and philosophy.'

26 Kitty Scoular Datta, in 'New Light on Marvell's "A Dialogue between

the Soul and Body",' points out certain similarities to Plutarch. However, she also sees the dialogue as heavily indebted to such contemporary
sources as Hermann Hugo's *Pia Desideria* and Samuel Purchas's *Purchas
his Pilgrim*. Since the examples she cites from these sources are primarily
instances of ideas so conventional as to be unassignable to a 'source'
(such as Hugo's elaboration of the prison analogy), I remain uncon-
vinced about the influence of these Christian precedents. Her perception of the implicit elements of urbane Platonism in the stand of the
soul and the rural hedonism in that of the body (pp 253–4) is, in contrast,
most illuminating and reveals a new dimension to the traditional intel-
lect/passive matter stance of each.

27 Francis Quarles, *Emblemes* Bk 3. xiv.181–2

28 Richard Baxter, *Poetical Fragments* 65–74. The poem in question is
dated 29 Oct. 1659. All further references are given in the text. See
also Baxter's *Two Disputations*, where he paraphrases the Galatians
passage: 'This flesh as the principle that prevaileth in some, is opposed
to the spirit which prevaileth in others, and their fruits opposed' (p 127).

29 See 'Self-Denial,' sig. F^r:

>   Flesh: *What! become Nothing! ne're perswade me to it.*
>   *God made me Something: and I'le not undo it.*

30 See Walter Scott (trans.), *Hermetica* 1 235: 'Birth is not a beginning of
life, but only a beginning of consciousness; and the change to another
state is not death, but oblivion. And this being so, all the things of which
every living creature is composed, – gross matter, and vital spirit, and
soul, – are immortal; and so, by reason of their immortality, every living
creature is immortal.' See also Ch. 6 n20.

31   But thou
>   Shalt in thy mothers bosome sleepe
>   Whilst I each minute grone to know
>   How near Redemption creepes.   ('Death,' ll 27–30)

This seems to imply that, in contrast to the soul, the body will not
have any *conscious* knowledge of the passing of time.

32 See L.C. Martin, 'Henry Vaughan and "Hermes Trismegestus".'

33 See John Milton, 'De Doctrina Christiana,' *The Works of John Milton*
217, 219: 'The death of the body is the loss or extinction of life. The
common definition, which supposes it to consist in the separation of
soul and body, is inadmissible. For what part of man is it that dies
when this separation takes place? Is it the soul? This will not be admitted
by the supporters of the above definition. Is it then the body? But how
can that be said to die, which never had any life of itself? Therefore the
separation of soul and body cannot be called the death of man.'

CHAPTER SIX

1 N.J.C. Andreasen (*John Donne: Conservative Revolutionary* 19) explains the same contradictory phenomena by categorizing both Ovidian love with its excessive emphasis on the senses and Petrachan love with its excessive idealism as negative *exempla* (both *cupiditas*) in contrast to the 'positive idealism' of what he calls 'Christian Platonism' (*caritas*) in which the body is not rejected but accepted as a means of ascent to heavenly love.

2 See, for example, the contrasting attitudes of Jeremy Taylor and Baxter to man's 'natural' state (Ch. 2, p 28). See also Douglas Bush, *Prefaces to Renaissance Literature* 47: 'The theology of Luther and Calvin ... set a gulf between the absolute and inscrutable sovereignty of God and the depravity of man, who was impotent without the gift, the arbitrary gift, of grace.'

3 J. McKevlin, *A Lecture in Love's Philosophy* 36ff. Also, Douglas Peterson (*The English Lyric from Wyatt to Donne* 290) argues that there is in the 'Songs and Sonnets' 'a kind of extended comparison that reaffirms and elaborates correspondences between modes of being and action which in the neo-Platonic view are construed as irreconcilably antithetical.'

4 John Donne, 'The Relique,' ll 6, 10, 11, *The Elegies and the Songs and Sonnets*, ed. Helen Gardner 89. All other references to the 'Songs and Sonnets' are to this edition and are given in brackets in the text.

5 Andreasen, *John Donne* 213

6 George Williamson, 'The Convention of The Extasie/Seventeenth-Century Contexts,' 63–77

7 Wilbur Sanders (*John Donne's Poetry* 92) insists that the similarity between the two poems is merely superficial; I disagree.

8 The incorporation of this Aristotelian point of view into certain aspects of Neoplatonic thought has its precedents, as Donald L. Guss points out in a passage he quotes from Equicola: 'The entire philosophy of Aristotle, prince of philosophers, shows the actions of the soul to be joined to those of the body, and those of the body to those of the soul, mingled and united: like wax imprinted on a seal, like sight in the eye's pupil, like matter and form, thus making one thing alone do body and soul combine to form man ...' (*John Donne, Petrarchist* 143). See Ch. 1, n18.

9 Many critics would disagree. Andreasen, for example, claims the poem uses 'Ovidian irony to portray an idolatrous relationship which masquerades as Platonic idealism' (p 76). Examples of Donne writing within

a more exclusively Platonic context, in which earthly love and beauty lead to heavenly, are to be found not in his secular love poems but in the divine poems. The sonnet, 'Since she whome I lovd, hath payd her last debt,' written after the death of his wife, is the classic example of this: 'Here the admyring her my mind did whett / To seeke thee God; so streames do shew the head' (John Donne, *Divine Poems*, ed. Helen Gardner 14–15. All other references are to this edition and are given in brackets in the text). Earthly love, in this context, is by no means base, but its chief value lies in its ability to lead to heavenly love. We are dealing with two types of love here, existing at different points on a scale of value, rather than with a distinction between love conceived in the mind and love executed by the body.

10 Mary Ellen Rickey makes this point in her book *Utmost Art: Complexity in the Verse of George Herbert* 21, when she says that Herbert 'adapts the materials of the *carpe diem* tradition so that they constitute an argument for purity of soul, rather than for enjoyment of immediate physical pleasure.'

11 See Ch. 2, p 50.

12 See Harold E. Toliver, 'Pastoral Form and Idea in Marvell,' *Seventeenth Century English Poetry*, ed. William R. Keast 357: 'The soul in "The Garden," singing and waving in its plumes the various lights, combines the creative power of the mind and the vegetative functions of the body reveling in melons and curious peaches.'

13 George Herbert, 'Home' ll 61–4, *Works* ed. F.E. Hutchinson 109. All other references are to this edition and are given in brackets in the text.

14 See Patrick Cruttwell, *The Shakespearean Moment* 86.

15 John Donne, 'To the Countesse of Salisbury,' ll 52–54, *Poems* ed. H.J.C. Grierson I 289. All references to poems by Donne not included in the two editions by Gardner are to this edition. Further references are given in brackets in the text.

16 See *Sermons* VI 357: 'Their first-born is dead; the body was made before the soul, and that body is dead.' This is radically opposed to the line of thought springing from Origen, who believed in the pre-existence of souls (Ch. 1, pp 12–13). It is compatible with the matter-form analogy, since matter is always prior to form in time. But Aquinas, though an Aristotelian in most respects, believed both body and soul to have been formed simultaneously.

17 See William Cartwright, 'On the Death of ... Mrs. *Ashford*,' *Comedies, Tragi-Comedies, with Other Poems* 301:
    If Souls from Souls be kindled as some sing,

> That to be born and Light'ned is one Thing;
> And that our life is but a tender Ray
> Snatch'd by the Infant from the Mothers Day;
> And if the Soul thus kindled must have been
> The framer of the Body, the Souls Inn ...

18 It is noteworthy that this passage follows that quoted above in which 'soul' is the rational soul, and the souls of growth and sense are closely linked with the body.

19 See Elizabeth Holmes, *Henry Vaughan and the Hermetic Philosophy.* See also B.F. Steward 'The Meaning of "Silex Scintillans" '; L.C. Martin, 'Henry Vaughan and "Hermes Trismegistus" '; W.O. Clough, 'Henry Vaughan and the Hermetic Philosophy.'

20 The sydereal spirit 'lives and moves in all elementary creatures, and in the indissoluble bond of body and soul, the purest and most noble essence in which lie hid all mysteries in their inexhaustible fulness of marvellous virtue and efficacy' (*The Hermetic Museum*, trans. A.E. Waite I 78, quoted by Holmes, *Henry Vaughan and the Hermetic Philosophy* 34.) This sydereal spirit bears a similarity to Henry More's 'vital congruity' and Cudworth's 'plastic nature,' though these latter are basically attempts to find a philosophical solution to the dichotomy between body and soul, while Vaughn's is spiritual and mystical in nature.

21 If, as Wood's *Fasti Oxoniensis* indicates, Burton was still a chaplain of Sir Orlando's in 1669, Traherne doubtless came under his influence (K.W. Salter, *Thomas Traherne* 19). See also Carol L. Marks, 'Thomas Traherne and Cambridge Platonism.'

22   Ye Thoughts and Apprehensions are
>   The Heavenly Streams which fill the Soul with rare
>   Transcendent Perfect Pleasures.
> (Thomas Traherne, 'Thoughts. I,' ll 25–7, *Centuries, Poems, and*
>   *Thanksgivings* II 169)

23 Richard Crashaw, 'To the Name Above Every Name, the Name of Jesus,' *Poems* 239–45. For a discussion of the concrete elements in Crashaw's poetry with special reference to the emblem books, see E. Austin Warren, *Richard Crashaw* 74–5.

24 Christ, the Word, must be served with the best words the preacher could offer. See Joan Webber, *Contrary Music: The Prose Style of John Donne* 123ff. See also Ch. 7, pp 143–4.

25 Donne, *Sermons* VIII 83

26 Thomas Jenner, *The Soules Solace*

27 Lord Herbert of Cherbury, 'Epitaph, *Caecil. Boulstr.,*' *Poems* 20

28 This new vitality disappears in the latter half of the century with the rediscovery of allegory by poets such as More, but it is now a more artificial allegory, a construct no longer based on traditional systems of correspondence (see also chapter 5, p 107).

29 John Milton, 'Paradise Lost,' v, ll 571–74, *Poetical Works*, ed. Helen Darbishire I 114. All further references are to this edition and are given in brackets in the text.

30 See Augustine, *The City of God*, trans. Marcus Dods 97–8, quoted in Leland Ryken, *The Apocalyptic Vision in Paradise Lost* 8. I am indebted to Ryken's book for much of the following discussion of accommodation.

31 'De Doctrina Christiana,' *The Works of Milton* xiv 31

32 See Ryken, *The Apocalyptic Vision* 12.

33 See R.A. Shoaf, *Milton, Poet of Duality* 7ff.

34 See Ch. 1, p 11.

35 *De Doctrina Christiana* xv 41

36 Leland Ryken, in his article '*Paradise Lost* and Its Biblical Epic Models' (*Milton and Scriptural Tradition*, ed. J.H. Sims and L. Ryken 43–81), shows how Milton transforms the very values of epic, basing them on biblical models. Thus military values are replaced by pastoral and domestic ones; the tradition theme of human greatness becomes one of divine greatness and human smallness, and even warfare, kingship, and heroism are spiritualized.

37 For a cogent summary of this, see Barbara Lewalski, *Protestant Poetics and the Seventeenth-Century Religious Lyric* 114ff.

38 See William A. Madsen, *From Shadowy Types to Truth* 57.

39 The extent to which Milton accepts the Genesis account of the Fall as literally true has been disputed, though here I incline to the view of Isabel MacCaffrey that 'the claim for the truth of events is absolute: these things happened; for the truth of images – the poem's places and personages – less absolute, but still insistent that the qualities and potencies bodied forth in them are real' (*Paradise Lost as 'Myth'* 21).

40 *De Doctrina Christiana* xiv 35

41 This is reminiscent of Aquinas's explanation of how the sensitive appetite can move the will 'by a kind of distraction.' It is also rather similar in theory to the 'distraction' explanations of sin by Digby and Descartes, though they are more interested in the mechanics of the operation than Milton is.

42 See *De Doctrina Christiana* xv 181, 183: 'If the circumstances of this crime are duly considered, it will be acknowledged to have been a most heinous offence, and a transgression of the whole law. For what sin can

be named, which was not included in this one act? It comprehended at once distrust in the divine veracity, and a proportionate credulity in the assurances of Satan; unbelief; ingratitude; disobedience; gluttony; in the man excessive uxoriousness, in the woman a want of proper regard for her husband, in both an insensibility to the welfare of their offspring, and that offspring the whole human race; parricide, theft, invasion of the rights of others, sacrilege, deceit, presumption in aspiring to divine attributes, fraud in the means employed to attain the object, pride, and arrogance.'

43 See Ch. 5 n33.

44 A.B. Chambers, who discusses the precise significance of the 'deceived' Eve and the 'undeceived' Adam in his article, 'The Falls of Adam and Eve in *Paradise Lost*' (*New Essays on Paradise Lost*, ed. Thomas Kranidas 118–30), also considers that Milton uses the common allegory of Adam as soul and Eve as body (p 128).

45 Against this dramatic representation of Adam and Eve as soul and body, we have Milton's explicit statement in *Colasterion* that husband and wife *cannot* be seen, literally, in this light. He says 'that to divorce a relative and metaphorical union of two bodies into one flesh cannot be likened in all things to the dividing of that natural union of soul and body into one person, is apparent of itself' (*Students' Milton* 716, quoted by Madsen, *From Shadowy Types to Truth* 68).

46 This combination of literal and allegorical truth is in the best tradition of Christian exegesis and contrasts, for example, with Henry More's interpretation of the Fall, which is solely allegorical, and greatly influenced by his own Neoplatonic ideas (see Madsen, ibid, 46–8).

47 See Charles A. Huttar, 'The Christian Basis of Shakespeare's Sonnet 146,' *Shakespeare Quarterly* xix 362. A subsequent article in the same journal (xxv 109–22) by Michael West attempts to link the sonnet to the genre of body and soul dialogues, but the author distinguishes the two Pauline attitudes towards body without, apparently, perceiving that they are intimately bound up with literal and figurative usage. Similarly, he fails to distinguish between those dialogues that take place between body and soul and those between flesh and spirit. Thus he misses the true historical origins of the two attitudes towards body that he observes in the sonnet.

CHAPTER SEVEN

1 For a discussion of the 'true' analogy and its role in imaginative literature, see William F. Lynch, sj, *Christ and Apollo*.

2 See Ch. 3, p 65.
3 'Complaynt of the Soule' sig. Avii[r]
4 Migne, *Patrologia Latina* CLXXI, col. 998
5 John Welles, *The Soules Progresse* 53
6 J. Guillemand, 'A Combat ...' 554
7 J. Woolton, 'A Treatise of the Immortalitie of the Soule,' 'The Epistle Dedicatorie' fol. iii[r]
8 Guillemand, 'A Combat ...' 553
9 Donne, *Sermons* VI 356
10 Adams, *Workes* 202: 'We are all housholders; our bodies are our houses; our soules our goods; our senses are the Doores and Windowes, the Lockes are *Faith* and *Prayer*.'
11 Adams, *Workes* 40
12 Donne, *Sermons* VI 273
13 Ibid. 87
14 W.D., *A Midnights Trance* 65, and Donne, *Sermons* III 160
15 Thomas Beverley, *The Great Soul of Man* 264
16 Adams, *Workes* 834
17 Ibid. 230
18 Du Moulin, *The Christian Combate ...* 157
19 Donne, *Sermons* II 338
20 J. Woolton, 'A Treatise ...' fol. 52[r]
21 Edward Reynolds, *A Treatise of the Passions and Faculties of the Soule of Man* 7
22 Nathaniel Culverwel, 'An Elegant and Learned Discourse of the Light of Nature,' *The Cambridge Platonists*, ed. E.T. Campagnac 225
23 Adams, *Workes* 342
24 Quoted by G. Bullough (ed.) in *Philosophical Poems of Henry More* 202
25 Donne, *Sermons* III 239
26 Ibid. 259–60
27 See Lynch, *Christ and Apollo* 146. He describes this essentially Platonic theory of participation according to which 'only oneness, the principle of unity, truly *is*, while the many members of this unity derive themselves from this principle. Thus, in a reality of the sensible order ... there is an absolute fact called the one and a fact called the many which has everything it has by participating in "the one".'
28 Andrewes, *Ninety-Six Sermons* I 90
29 Donne, *Sermons* X 112: 'Language must waite upon matter, and *words* upon *things*. In this case ... the matter, that is, the doctrine that we preach, is the forme, that is, the Soule, the *Essence*; the language and words wee preach in, is but the Body, but the *existence*.'

30 Ibid, VI 102: 'As the soul is infused by God, but diffused over the whole body, and so there is a *Man*, so *Faith* is infused from God, but diffused into our *works*, and so there is a *Saint* ... Faith is incorporated and manifested in a body, by works ...'

31 Ibid. IX 334

32 Ibid. VIII 268

33 Ibid. X 116

34 Ibid. IV 368

35 Ibid. IX 257

36 Reynolds, *A Treatise* ... 4–5

37 Pierre Du Moulin, *The Christian Combate* ... 56. See also Adam's use of this analogy, Ch. 2 n58.

38 Adams, *Workes* 124

39 Simon Harward, *A Discovrse Concerning the Soule and Spirit of Man* 69ʳ

40 Du Moulin *The Christian Combate* ... 3–4. See Ch. 2, p 26.

41 Lynn Thorndike, *The 'Sphere' of Sacrobosco and Its Commentators* 123

42 Guillaume de Deguileville, *The Pilgrimage of the Life of Man*, ll 12257–70. See Ch. 3, p 62.

43 James Howell, *Familiar Letters*, ed. J. Jacobs 1 336

44 For a more detailed account of the transition from Sacrobosco's moralization of the heavenly system to Donne's, see my note 'A Precedent for Donne's Imagery in "Goodfriday, 1613. Riding Westward".'

45 Reynolds, *A Treatise* 529. See also Joseph Hall, *The Great Imposter* 18, and Nicholas Mosley, *Natural and Divine Contemplations* ... 134–5: 'The Soul of Man ... is divided into the Intellectual faculty answering in analogy to the *primum mobile* or Eighth Sphaer; and the Irrational faculty answering in similitude to the Sphaer of the Planets; for this faculty is opposite, and contrary to the Intellectual, and moves contrary to it, as the Planets do in a Counter-motion to the Eighth Sphaer ...' It is probably significant that neither Reynolds nor Mosley specifies that the motion of the under planets is eastward. Reynolds simply calls it 'another motion,' and Mosley a 'contrary' one, thus avoiding eliciting the Christian connotations of the East in the minds of his readers.

46 Donne, *Sermons* X 43. See also IX 50–1: 'There this world beganne; the Creation was in the east. And there our next world beganne too. There the gates of heaven opened to us; and opened to us in the gates of death; for, our heaven is the death of our Saviour, and there he lived, and dyed there, and there he looked into our west, from the east, from his Terasse, from his Pinacle, from his exaltation ... the Crosse.'

47 Ibid. IX 50. This passage closely precedes that quoted in n46 above. Matter and image, body and soul are thus further enriched by being associated with north and south, mortality and eternity respectively.

48 Ibid. VI 75

49 See n29. This particular example is verbally confused by Donne's use of 'matter' in the sense of 'subject-matter,' which hence is itself 'form' in the Aristotelian sense in relation to the words that go to make it up. Paradox is achieved at the expense of clarity.

50 Samuel Haworth, Ἀνθροπωλογια or, A Philosophic Discourse Concerning Man 16

51 Donne, Sermons V, 355. See also Nemesius, The Nature of Man 266 and Ch. 2 n1

52 Baxter, Dying Thoughts, 163–4.

53 Adams, Workes 662

54 Beverley, The Great Soul of Man 220

55 W.D., 'A Midnights Trance' 8

56 J. Guillemand, A Combat ... 120

57 Phillip Mornay, The Soules Own Evidence for Its Own Immortality 2: 'The outward man is that which we see with our eys which forgoeth not his shape when it is dead, no more than a Lute forgoeth his shape when the Luteplayer ceaseth from making it to sound ...'

58 William Bates, Considerations of the Existence of God, and of the Immortality of the Soul 215

59 Ibid. 166

60 John Davies of Hereford, Mirum in Modum sig. D2

61 Adams, Workes 636. See also another analogy by Adams in which the soul is the housewife, the body the house. 'She is a careful house-wife, disposing all well at home; conseruing all formes, and mustring them to her owne seruicable vse. The senses discerne the out-side, the circumstance, the huske of things: she the inside, the vertue, the marrow ...' (p 679)

62 See Ch. 5, pp 89–90.

63 Adams, Workes 196. Cf. Adam's similar identification of their two children, Ishmael and Isaac, Ch. 7, p 146

64 Rycharde of saynt Vyctor, 'A Verray deuote treatyse,' sig. A1ᵛ

65 William Sclater, Deaths Summons, and the Saints Duty 74–5

66 Adams, Workes 431

67 Woolton, 'A Treatise ...' fol. 32ʳ

68 J. Welles, The Soules Progresse 92

69 Donne, Sermons VIII 117

70 Ibid. I 220–1: 'As Plato says of a particular body, he that will cure an ill

Eye, must cure the *Head*; he that will cure the *Head*, must cure the *Body*; and he that will cure the *Body*, must cure the *Soul* ... so in Civil Bodies, in States, Head, and Eye, and Body; Prince, and Council, and People, do all receive their health and welfare from the pureness of *Religion* ...'

71 Ibid. 227. See also 'Elegie on Mrs Boulstred,' l 39, I 283: 'Her Soule and body was a King and Court.'

72 Andrewes, *Ninety-Six Sermons* I 91. Hooker denies the validity of this particular analogy, however, in a passage in which the emphasis on the preservation of the two natures in Christ is key. See Hooker, 'Eccl. Pol.,' v.lii.4, *Works* II 226: 'The words of Cyril were in process of time so taken as though it had been his drift to teach, that even as in us the body and the soul, so in Christ God and man make but *one nature*. Of which error, six hundred and thirty fathers in the council of Chalcedon condemned Eutyches. For as Nestorius teaching rightly that God and man are distinct natures, did thereupon misinfer that in Christ those natures can by no conjunction make one person; so Eutyches, of sound belief as touching their true personal copulation, became unsound by denying the difference which still continueth between the one and the other Nature.'

73 Nemesius, *The Nature of Man* 205–6

74 Donne, *Sermons* VI 155

75 Ibid. VII 231–2

76 Baxter, *Dying Thoughts* 135; Donne, *Sermons* II 216

77 Simon Harward, *A Discovrse Concerning the Soule and Spirit of Man* 13ʳ (misprinted 31ʳ). See also Edward Popham, *A Looking-Glasse for the Sovle* 8: 'What is the body without the *Soule*, but a corrupt carkasse? And what is the *Soule* without God, but a Sepulchre of sinne?' For an older example of the same analogy, see *Complaynt of the Soule* sig. A6ʳ.

78 Donne, *Sermons* VIII 260: 'And this soul of the world is the Holy Ghost, who doth that office to the soule of every Christian, which the soul it self doth to every naturall man, informs him, directs him, instructs him, makes him be that he is, and do that he doth.'

79 Ibid. VI 129

80 Ibid. 128. See also an analogy between body, soul, and the spirits and the three steps of redemption – the covenant (birth, the body), grace (baptism, the soul), and works (spirits 'that unite and confirm all'), ibid. II 261–2.

81 Ibid. VII 448

82 Dennis R. Klinck, '*Vestigia Trinitatis* in Man and His Works in the English Renaissance,' *Journal of the History of Ideas* 14. For a detailed

discussion of the uses of the trinity analogy in the Renaissance and its application on a much wider basis than to man himself, see the whole of this article.

83 Adams, *Workes* 679

84 See Donne, *Sermons* II 72–3

85 Ibid. III 328. See also John Woolton, *A Newe Anatomie of whole man ...* fol. 11ʳ: 'The eternall Father signifieth the Minde begetting in Cogitation the eternall word, the second person in the Trinitie. The Image formed in cogitation, signifieth the sonne of God: And the Will shadoweth the holye Ghoste.'

86 Donne, *Sermons* III 264

87 Ibid. 145

88 Ibid. 144

89 Ibid. II 340. See also Adams, *Workes* 66, and Donne, *Sermons* VIII 104: 'But Mariage amongst Christians, is herein *Magnum mysterium,* A Sacrament in such a sense; a mysterious signification of the *union of the soule* with Christ ...'

90 Cudworth, *The Union of Christ and the Church in a Shadow* 3

91 John Randall, *The Description of Fleshly Lvsts* 12–13

92 Ibid. 19

93 Jeremy Taylor, 'Sermons Preached at Golden-Grove Being for the Winter Half-Year,' *A Course of Sermons for All the Sundays of the Year* 98

94 Sir Thomas Browne, 'Pseudodoxia Epidemica,' *Works*, ed. Keynes II 20

95 Sir John Hayward, *The Second Part of The Sanctuary of a troubled Soul* 'To the Reader': 'The sensuall powers did tumult, and break loose from their obedience, and have ever since runne to their objects with so violent a course, that commonly they draw the will after them. [sic] which also flattereth feeble reason (as Eve entised Adam) to taste of the forbidden fruit; even to submit it selfe to the service of sensualitie ...'

96 Edward Reynolds, *A Treatise* 64

97 Wright, *Latin Poems* 328

98 For a more detailed account of the history of this analogy, see my article 'Body, Soul, and the Marriage Relationship: The History of an Analogy.'

99 Taylor, 'Sermons Preached at Golden-Grove Being for the Winter Half-Year' 172

100 Ibid. 177. See also Donne, *Sermons* V 208. Here the flesh/spirit analogy emphasizes chiefly the antagonistic side of their relationship. '*Caro conjux,* our flesh is the wife, and the spirit is the husband, and they two will never agree. But *si dominetur uxor, perversa pax,* says he [Augustine], and that's a more ordinary case, then we are aware of, that the wife

hath got the Mastery, that the weaker vessell, the flesh, hath got the victory; and they, there is a show of peace, but it is a stupidity, a security, it is not peace.'

101 Donne, *Sermons* IV 245
102 'Sir Kenelm Digby to Sir Edward Stradling,' *Cabala* London 1663, 226
103 Mosley, *Natural and Divine Contemplations* ... 226–7. See also Donne's reference to the flesh after the Resurrection, when the soul will 'no longer call her prison, nor her tempter, but her friend, her companion, her wife ...' (*Sermons* III 112)

CHAPTER EIGHT

1 All quotations are from the Revels editions of the plays with the following exceptions: *Antonio and Mellida, Antonio's Revenge, The Dutch Courtesan* by Marston and *The Broken Heart* by Ford are Regents Drama Series editions, and *The Revenge of Bussy d'Ambois* is from T.M. Parrot's edition of the collected plays of Chapman. Act, scene, and line references are given in the text.
2 See Robert Ornstein's discussion of this lack of a moral norm with particular reference to *The White Devil*, in *The Moral Vision of Jacobean Tragedy* 130–3.
3 See George L. Geckle, 'Fortune in Marston's *The Malcontent*' and Ronald J. Palumbo, 'Emblematic Characters in Marston's *Antonio* Plays.'
4 See Millar MacLure, *George Chapman* 112.
5 A.L. and M.K. Kistner ('Thomas Middleton's Symbolic Action,' 15) argue that Middleton 'uses symbolic action, in general, to make concrete the abstract, to make physical the spiritual and literal the metaphorical.' I would claim rather that these dramatists, Middleton included, use symbolic action to add a spiritual and metaphorical element to the physical and literal.
6 See Irving Ribner, *Jacobean Tragedy: The Quest for Moral Order* 7: 'It [the drive of Jacobean dramatists] is a drive to find a basis for morality in a world in which the traditional bases no longer seem to have validity.' Ribner sees the career of Bussy d'Ambois in the corrupt court as a specific example of this quest. See also Ornstein, *The Moral Vision of Jacobean Tragedy* 31: 'They cling to a traditional moral view of politics even though they sense that medieval ideals are no longer meaningful to their society.'
7 For a similar analogy between two types of women and the higher and lower faculties of the soul in a non-dramatic work, see John Downame, *The Conflict betweene the Flesh and the Spirit* 26. He cites Lewis

Grenada's comparison of the higher faculties of the soul to a wife of great beauty, and the lower to a witch and sorceress, for whom the husband puts away his wife.

8 See Ch. 7, p 159.

9 The distinction between virtuous and wanton love is sometimes equated not with two kinds of love between men and women but with the difference between the love of friends and sexual love. Malheureux in *The Dutch Courtesan*, contemplating his promise to kill Freevill to please his mistress, speaks thus:

> ... Think more, to kill a friend
> To gain a woman, to lose a virtuous self
> For appetite and sensual end, whose very having
> Loseth all appetite and gives satiety –
> That corporal end, remorse and inward blushings
> Forcing us loathe the steam of our own heats,
> Whilst friendship clos'd in virtue, being spiritual,
> Tastes no such languishings and moments' pleasure
> With more repentance ... (ii.ii.206–14)

Thus the corporal appetite involved in gaining a woman is contrasted with the spirituality of friendship.

10 Cf. Donne's presentation of the opposite side of the case:

> But we by'a love, so much refin'd,
> That our selves know not what it is,
> Inter-assured of the mind,
> Care lesse, eyes, lips, and hands to misse.
>
> ('A Valediction: forbidding Mourning,' ll 17–20, p 63)

11 The homiletic nature of the play has been widely recognized. Anne Lancashire, in her introduction to the Revels edition, cites the generic names, unlocalized scene, moral counterpointing of main plot and sub-plot, and general moral criticism (pp 38–9). She concludes, 'The play is indeed a part of the general resurgence of what has been termed 'medievalism' in Jacobean England, in its homiletic characteristics, abstract meanings, emphasis on worldly pleasures as vanities, and pre-occupation with the contemplative life and with death' (p 48).

12 The opposition between Govianus and the Tyrant is itself characterized as a flesh/spirit one by Anne Lancashire: 'Structured upon the traditional opposition of good king and tyrant ... it presents above all the clash between worldly greatness and moral goodness, flesh and spirit' (*The Second Maiden's Tragedy* 39).

13 See ibid. 47.

14 See p 169.

15 Critical opinion on both Chapman's intention and achievement in the creation of Bussy is sharply divided. For both Ribner and Ornstein, he represents the virtuous man inevitably caught and destroyed in a corrupt world, although Ornstein recognizes the inherent contradition between Bussy's words and actions and the consequent failure of the play to portray coherently a single moral design (p 54ff.). Ennis Rees (*The Tragedies of George Chapman: Renaissance Ethics in Action*), on the other hand, sees the same contradiction as deliberate irony (p 39ff.), and concludes that Chapman condemns Bussy for being an 'active man.'

16 See Ribner, *Jacobean Tragedy* 29: 'She [Tamyra] is an embodiment of the animal passion which is a part of the nature with which Bussy must live.'

17 William Shakespeare, *Othello*, ed. M.R. Ridley and *Measure for Measure*, ed. J.W. Lever. All further references are to these Arden editions and are given in the text.

18 See Ch. 6, p 137.

CONCLUSION

1 Amy Clampitt, 'An Anatomy of Migraine,' *The New Yorker* (11 Aug. 1986) 24–5

Bibliography

Manuscripts

'The Hower is come' BL MS Add 29396, pp 86^v–89^r
Visio Lamentabilis or Visio Fulbert. Add MS.3093, Cambridge University
  Library. This is bound with translations of it by William Crashaw and
  William Yates, and The Vision by James Howell.

Printed Books

Primary Sources

Abernathy, John, Bishop of Caithness A Christian and Heavenly Treatise,
  Containing Physicke for the Soule London 1622
Adams, Thomas Workes London 1629
Andrewes, Lancelot Ninety-Six Sermons Oxford 1841–3
Aquinas, Saint Thomas Summa Theologica trans. The Fathers of the English
  Dominican Province. 22 vols. London 1911–22
Aristotle De Anima Version of William of Moerbeke and Commentary of St
  Thomas Aquinas, trans. K. Foster and S. Humphries. London 1951
– Generation of Animals trans. Arthur Peck. London 1943
Augustine The City of God trans. J. Healey, ed. R.V.G. Tasker. London 1945
– 'On the Soul and Its Origin' in The Anti-Pelagian Works of St Augustine,
  trans. P. Holmes, II (Edinburgh 1874), 203–339 (vol. 12 of Works ed. M.
  Dods)
Bacon, Sir Francis Works, ed. J. Spedding, R.L. Ellis, and D.D. Heath. London
  1857–74
Bankes, Lawrence The Safegard of the Soule London 1619

Barnfield, Richard *The Combat, betweene Conscience and Couetnesse in the Minde of Man* London 1598

Bates, William *Considerations of the Existence of God, and of the Immortality of the Soul* London 1676

– *The Four Last Things* 2nd ed. London 1691

Baxter, Richard *Dying Thoughts upon Philippians 1.23* London 1683

– *Of the Immortality of Mans Soul* London 1682

– *Poetical Fragments* London 1681; rept 1971

– *Two Disputations of Original Sin* London 1675

Beesley, Henry *The Soules Conflict* London 1656

Beverley, Thomas *The Great Soul of Man* London 1676

Boyd, Zacherie *The Last Battell of the Soule in Death* Edinburgh 1629

Brathwait, Richard *The Last Trumpet: or a Six-Fold Christian Dialogue* trans. John Vicars. London 1635

Brent, William *A Discourse upon the Nature of Eternitie* London 1655

Browne, Sir Thomas *Works* ed. Geoffrey Keynes, rev. ed. London 1964

Calvin, John *Institutes of the Christian Religion* trans. F.L. Battles, ed. J.T. McNeill. 2 vols. London 1961 (Vols. xx and xxi of the Library of Christian Classics)

– *Theological Treatises* ed. J.K.S. Reid. London 1954 (Vol. xxii of the Library of Christian Classics)

Campagnac, E.T. (ed.) *The Cambridge Platonists* Oxford 1901

Carpenter, Richard *The Sovles Sentinel ... A Sermon Preached at the Funerall ... of Sir Arthur Ackland Knight* London 1612

Cartwright, William *Comedies, Tragi-Comedies, with Other Poems* London 1651

'The Castle of Perseverance' *Chief Pre-Shakespearean Dramas* ed. J.Q. Adams (London 1924) 265–87

Chapman, George *Bussy d'Ambois* ed. N. Brooke (Revels Plays) London 1964

– *The Revenge of Bussy d'Ambois, Collected Plays* ed. T.M. Parrot 1 (London 1910)

Charlton, Walter *The Immortality of the Human Soul demonstrated by the Light of Nature, in two Dialogues* London 1657

Chrysostom, John *Exposition upon the Epistle to the Ephesians* (trans.) London 1581

Complaynt of the Soule London [1519?]

Crashaw, Richard *Poems* ed. L.C. Martin. Oxford 1957

Crashaw, William *The Complaint or Dialogve, betwixt the Soule and the Bodie of a damned man* London 1622

Cudworth, Ralph *The True Intellectual System of the Universe* London 1678

– *The Union of Christ and the Church in a Shadow* London 1642
D., W. *A Midnights Trance, Wherein is discoursed of Death, the nature of Sovles, and estate of Immortalitie* London 1619
Davies, John, of Hereford *Mirum in Modum: A Glimpse of Gods Glorie and the Soules Shape* London 1602
Davison, Francis *A Poetical Rhapsody 1602–21* ed. H.E. Rollins. Cambridge, MA 1931–2
Deacon, John and Walker, John *Dialogicall Discourses of Spirits and Divils* London 1601
Deguileville, Guillaume de *The Pilgrimage of the Life of Man* trans. John Lydgate, ed. F.J. Furnivall. London 1899–1904
– *The Booke of the Pylgremage of the Sowle*, printed by William Caxton, 1483, ed. K.I. Cust. London 1859
Dekker, Thomas *Dekker his Dreame* London 1620
'A Departed Soul's Address to the Body' *Codex Exoniensis* ed. Benjamin Thorpe. London 1842 367–77
'A Departed Soul's Address to the Body' *The Poetry of the Codex Vercellensis* trans. J.M. Kemble. London 1843; rpt 1971
Descartes, René *Philosophical Works* trans. E.S. Haldane and G.R.T. Ross. Cambridge 1911
'A Dialog betweene the auctour and his eye' *The Paradise of Dainty Devices 1576–1606* ed. H.E. Rollins. Cambridge, MA 1927
A Dialogue betwixt the Devil and the Ignoramus Doctor [London 1679?]
Digby, Sir Kenelm *Two Treatises ... The Nature of Bodies: The Nature of Mans Soule* Paris 1644
Donne, John *The Divine Poems* ed. Helen Gardner. Oxford 1952
– *The Elegies and the Songs and Sonnets* ed. Helen Gardner. Oxford 1965
– *Poems* ed. H.J.C. Grierson. Oxford 1912
– *Sermons* ed. G.R. Potter and E.M. Simpson. Berkeley, CA 1953–62
Downame, John *The Conflict betweene the Flesh and the Spirit* London 1618
'The Droomme of Doomesday' trans. George Gascoigne. London 1576
Du Moulin, Pierre *The Christian Combate, or a Treatise of Afflictions ...* trans. John Bulteel. London 1623
Edwards, M. (compiler) *The Paradise of Dainty Devices (1576–1606)* ed. H.E. Rollins. Cambridge, MA, 1927
Epistle to Diognetus, The ed. L.B. Radford. London 1908
Ford, John *The Broken Heart* ed. Donald K. Anderson (Regents Renaissance Drama Series) Lincoln, NB, 1968
Foster, William *The Means to Keepe Sinne from Reigning in Our Mortall Body* London 1629

Gainsford, Thomas *The Vision and Discovrse of Henry the seuenth* London 1610

Gifford, George *A Dialogve Concerning Witches and Witchcraftes* London 1593

Glanvill, Joseph *Lux Orientalis, or, An Enquiry into the Opinions of the Eastern Sages Concerning the Prae-Existence of Souls* [London] 1662

Greene, Robert *Greenes Vision* London 1592

Guillemand, J. *A Combat betwixt Man and Death*, trans. E. Grimeston. London 1621

Hagthorpe, John *Divine Meditations and Elegies* London 1622

Hall, Joseph *The Great Imposter* London 1623

Hall, W. *A Dialogue about Justification by Faith* London 1610

Halliwell, J.O. (ed.) *Early English Miscellanies* London 1855

Hammond, Eleanor 'The Eye and the Heart' *Anglia* XXXIV (1911) 235–65

Harward, Simon *A Discovrse Concerning the Soule and Spirit of Man* London 1604

Haworth, Samuel *ΑνΘροπωλογια or A Philosophic Discourse Concerning Man being the Anatomy both of his Soul and Body* London 1680

Hayward, Sir John *The Second Part of The Sanctuary of a troubled Soul* London 1636

Lord Herbert of Cherbury *Poems* ed. G.C. Moore-Smith. Oxford 1923

Herbert, George *Works*, ed. F.E. Hutchinson Oxford 1941

Heywood, Thomas. *Pleasant Dialogues and Drammas* London 1637

Hildebert of Lavardin 'De Querimonia et Conflictu Carnis et Spiritus' *Patrologia Latina* CLXXI 989–1004

Hill, William. *The Infancie of the Soul* London 1605

Hills, Henry *A Short Treatise Concerning the Propagation of the Soul* London 1667

Hoard, Samuel *The Soules Miserie and Recoverie* London 1636

Hobbes, Thomas *The English Works* ed. Sir William Molesworth. London 1839–45

Hooker, Richard *Works* ed. John Keble. 7th ed. Oxford 1888

Howell, James *Familiar Letters* ed. J. Jacobs. London 1890–2

– *The Vision: or a Dialog between the Soul and the Bodie* London 1651

– *A Winter Dreame* London 1649

'The Irish Homily' Robert Atkinson *The Passions and the Homilies from Leabbar Breac* (Dublin 1867) 507–14

Jackson, John *The Soul Is Immortal* London 1611

Jenner, Thomas (collector) *The Soules Solace* London 1626

Layfield, Edmund *The Mappe of Mans Mortality and Vanity* London 1630

Legate, Robert *A Briefe Catechisme and Dialogue betwene the Husbande and his Wyfe ...* London 1554

Lupton, Thomas *A Dreame of the Diuell and Diues* London 1589

Luther, Martin *A Commentary on St Paul's Epistle to the Galatians* trans. based on the 'Middleton' edition of the English version of 1575. London 1953

– 'Lectures on Genesis i–v,' *Works*, ed. Jaroslav Pelikan. i. St Louis, MO 1958

– *Lectures on Romans*, trans. W. Pauck. London 1961 (Vol. 15 of the Library of Christian Classics)

M., R. *A Profitable Dialogue for a peruerted Papist* London 1609

Marston, John *Antonio and Mellida* and *Antonio's Revenge* ed. G.K. Hunter (Regents Renaissance Drama Series) 2 vols. London 1965, 1966

– *The Dutch Courtesan* ed. M.L. Wine (Regents Renaissance Drama Series) London 1965

– *The Malcontent* ed. G.K. Hunter (Revels Plays) London 1975

Marvell, Andrew *Poems and Letters* ed. H.M. Margoliouth. Oxford 1927

Middleton, Thomas *Women Beware Women* ed. J.R. Mulryne (Revels Plays) London 1975

Mill, Humphrey 'A divine speech of the Soule to the bodie' *Poems Occasioned by a Melancholy Vision* London 1639, sig. I 4^v–I 5^r

Milton, John *Poetical Works* ed. Helen Darbishire. Oxford, 1952–5

– 'De Doctrina Christiana' *The Works of John Milton* xv ed. Frank A. Patterson. New York 1933

More, Henry *Philosophical Poems*, ed. G. Bullough. Manchester 1931

– *Philosophical Writings*, ed. F.I. Mackinnon. New York 1925

– *Poems*, ed. A.B. Grosart. Chester Worthies Library 1878

Mornay, Phillip *The Soules own evidence for its own Immortality*, trans. Sir Philip Sydney. London 1646

Morris, Richard (ed.) *An Old English Miscellany* London 1872

Mosley, Nicholas. Ψυχοσοφια: or *Natural and Divine Contemplations of the Passions and Faculties of the Soul of Man* London 1653

Nemesius *The Nature of Man* trans. G. Wither. London 1636

Niccols, Richard 'A Winter Nights Vision' in *A Mirror for Magistrates* London 1610

– *Sir Thomas Overbvries Vision* London 1616

Nicholson, Henry *A Conference between the Soul and Body Concerning the Present and Future State* 2nd ed. London 1705

Origen on First Principles ed. J.W. Butterworth. London 1936

P., J. [Phillip, John] *A Sommon to repentance Given vnto Christians* London 1584

Patrick, Simon *A Friendly Debate between a Conformist and a Non-Conformist* 4th ed. London 1669

Peeter of Luca, Don *A Dialogue of Dying Wel* trans. R.V. Antwerp 1603

Pepysian Garland, A ed. H.E. Rollins. Cambridge, MA 1922

Perkins, William. *Works* 3 vols. Cambridge, 1608–9

P.[hillip], J.[ohn] 'A Sommon to repentance Given vnto Christiane' London 1584

Plato *Phaedo*, trans. Harold N. Fowler. London 1926

– *Phaedrus*, trans. Harold N. Fowler. London 1926

– *Timaeus*, trans. Rev. R.G. Bury. London 1929

A Pleasant Dialogue or Disputation betwene the Cap, and the Head London 1564

Plotinus *Enneads*, trans. S. MacKenna. 3rd ed. London 1962

Popham, Edward *A Looking-Glasse for the Sovle* London 1619

Porter, Edmund Θεὸς'Ανθρωποφόρος *God Incarnate* London 1655

Prynne, William 'The Soules Complaint against the Body' *Mount-Orgueil* (London 1641) 173–84

P.[unt], W.[illiam] *A new dialoge called the endightment agaynste mother Messe* London 1548

Quarles, Francis *The Complete Works in Prose and Verse* ed. A.B. Grosart. Edinburgh 1880

– *Emblemes* Cambridge 1643

Ramesey, William *Mans Dignity and Perfection Vindicated* London 1661

Randall, Giles (ed.) *Theologica Germanica: or, Mysticall Divinitie; with a Treatise of the Soul* London 1648

Randall, John *The Description of Fleshly Lvsts* London 1622

Reynolds, Edward *A Treatise of the Passions and Facvlties of the Soule of Man* London 1640

Robertson, Bartholomew *The Crowne of Life* London 1618

Rych, Barnaby *A Right Exelent and pleasaunt Dialogue, betwene Mercvry and an English Souldier ...* London 1574

Rycharde of saynt Vyctor 'A verray deuote treatyse' H. Pepwell 1521

'Saint Bernards Vision or, A briefe Discourse (Dialogue-wise) betweene the Soule and the Body of a damned man newly deceased ...' [1640?] *The Roxborough Ballads* 1 London 1774

Sclater, William *Deaths Summons, and the Saints Duty* London 1640

Scott, Walter (trans.) *Hermetica* Oxford 1924

Second Maiden's Tragedy, The ed. Anne Lancashire (Revels Plays) Manchester 1978

Shakespeare, William *Measure for Measure* ed. J.W. Lever. London 1967

– *Othello* ed. M.R. Ridley. London 1965

Short Dialogve, wherein is proved, that no man can be saved without good workes, A Oxford 1604

Sibbes, Richard *The Complete Works*, ed. A.B. Grosart. 7 vols. Edinburgh 1862–4

Smith, Henry *Sermons* London 1866

Standfast, Richard *A Dialogue between a Blind Man and Death* London 1686

Strode, George *The Anatomie of Mortalitie* London 1618

Sutcliffe, Alice *Meditations of Man's Mortalitie* 2nd ed. London 1634

S[ylvester], M[atthew] *A Philosophical Discourse of the Nature of ... Souls* London 1695

Taylor, Jeremy *An Answer to a Letter Written by R.R. the Ld. Bp. of Rochester* London 1656

– *Deus Justicatus* London 1656

– *'Ενιαυτος: A Course of Sermons for All the Sundays of the Year* London 1653. Some additions in later ed. London 1668

– *Unum Necessarium* London 1655

Tertullian 'De Anima,' *The Writings of Tertullian* trans. P. Holmes II (Edinburgh 1870) 410–541 (Vol. 15 of the Ante-Nicene Christian Library)

Thynne, Francis 'A debate betweene *Pride and Lowlines*' London [1570]

Tourneur, Cyril *The Atheist's Tragedy* ed. Irving Ribner (Revels Plays) London 1964

– *The Revenger's Tragedy* ed. R.A. Foakes (Revels Plays) London 1975

Traherne, Thomas *Centuries, Poems and Thanksgivings* ed. H.M. Margoliouth Oxford 1958

Vaughan, Henry *Works* ed. L.C. Martin. Oxford 1957

Vaughan, Robert *A Dyalogue Defensyve for Women ...* London 1542

Vaughan, Thomas *Works* ed. A.E. Waite. London 1919

'A Wakening of Worldings' *A Monument of Mortalitie* London 1621

Ward, Seth *A Philosophical Essay Towards an Eviction of ... the Immortality of the Soule of men ...* Oxford 1652

Wates, Richard *A Dialogue between Life and Death* London 1657

Webster, John *The White Devil* ed. J.R. Brown (Revels Plays) London 1960

Welles, John *The Soules Progresse to the Celestiall Canaan, or Heavenly Jervsalem* London 1639

Wharton, John *Wharton's dreame* London 1578

Whichcote, Benjamin *Works* Aberdeen 1751

White, Thomas *The Middle State of Souls* London 1659

Wodde, Michael *A Dialogve, or Familiar Talke betwene Two Neighbours ...* Roane 1554

Woolton, John *A Newe Anatomie of whole man ...* London 1576

– 'A Treatise of the Immortalitie of the Soule' London 1576

Wright, Thomas (ed.) *The Latin Poems Commonly Attributed to Walter Mapes* Camden Society, Vol. 16. London 1841

– *Songs and Ballads* London 1860

Secondary Sources

Works marked with an asterisk also contain some primary source material.

Ackerman, R. W. ' "The Debate of the Body and the Soul" and Parochial Christianity,' *Speculum* XXXVII (1962) 541–65
Allison, T.E. 'On the Body and Soul Legend' *Modern Language Notes* XLII (1927), 102–6
Andreasen, N.J.C. *John Donne: Conservative Revolutionary* Princeton 1967
Armstrong, A.H. *An Introduction to Ancient Philosophy* 3rd ed. London 1957
– *Saint Augustine and Christian Platonism* Villanova 1967
– ed. *The Cambridge History of Later Greek and Early Medieval Philosophy* Cambridge 1967
Atkinson, Robert *The Passions and Homilies from Leabhar Breac* Dublin 1887
Barnes, Jonathan, Malcolm Schofield, and Richard Sorabji, eds. *Articles on Aristotle* IV. London 1979
Barnoux, Jeffrey 'The Separation of Reason and Faith in Bacon and Hobbes, and Leibniz's *Theodicy*' *Journal of the History of Ideas* XLII 4 (1981) 607–28
Batiouchkof, Th. 'Le Débat de l'Ame et du Corps' *Romania* XX (1891) 1–55, 513–78
Blumenthal, H.J. and R.A. Markus, eds. *Neoplatonism and Early Christian Thought: Essays in Honour of A. H. Armstrong* London 1981
Bourcier, Elisabeth 'Mort, reves et surnaturel chez les Anglais au xvie siècle,' *La mort, le fantastique, le surnaturel du xvie siècle à l'epoque romantique* Lille 1979, 17–22
Bradbrook, M. C. and Lloyd Thomas, M. G. *Andrew Marvell* Cambridge 1940
Bronson, B.H. 'The Dialogue Song; or, Proteus Observed' *Philogical Quarterly* LIV 1 (Winter 1975) 117–36
*Brown, Carleton 'A Homiletical Debate between Heart and Eye' *Modern Language Notes* XXX (1915) 197–8
Bruce, J.D. 'A Contribution to the Study of "The Body and the Soul": Poems in English' *Modern Language Notes* V (1890) 385–401
Bush, Douglas *Prefaces to Renaissance Literature* New York 1965
Cassirer, Ernst *The Platonic Renaissance in England* trans. J.P. Pettegrove. Edinburgh 1953

Chan, Mary 'Drolls, Drolleries and Mid-Seventeenth-Century Dramatic Music in England' *Research Chronicle of the Royal Musical Association* XV (1979) 117–73

Clough, W.O. 'Henry Vaughan and the Hermetic Philosophy' *PMLA* XLVIII (1933) 1108–30

Copleston, Frederick *A History of Philosophy* vols I, II, IV. London 1946, 1950, 1958

*Cornford, Francis *Plato and Parmenides* London 1939

Cruttwell, Patrick *The Shakespearean Moment* London 1954

Datta, Kitty Scoular 'New Light on Marvell's "A Dialogue between the Soul and Body"' *Renaissance Quarterly* XXII (1969) 242–55

Deakins, Roger 'The Tudor Prose Dialogue: Genre and Anti-Genre' *Studies in English Literature* XX (Winter 1980) 5–23

de Vogel, C.J. *Pythagoras and Early Pythagorianism* Assen 1966

Dictionnaire de théologie catholique, ed. A. Vacant, E. Mangenot, and E. Almann. 15 vols. Paris 1903–50

Dihle, Albrecht *The Theory of Will in Classical Antiquity* Berkeley and Los Angeles 1982

Dowden, Edward *Puritan and Anglican* London 1900

Dudley, Louise *The Egyptian Elements in the Legend of the Body and the Soul* Bryn Mawr Monographs, Baltimore 1911

– 'An Early Homily on the "Body and Soul" Theme' *JEPG* VIII (1909) 225–53

du Méril, E. *Poésies Populaires Latines* Paris 1843

Durr, R.A. *On the Mystical Poetry of Henry Vaughan* Cambridge, MA 1962

Eisenring, Albert *Milton's 'De Doctrina Christiana'* Fribourg 1946

Freeman, Rosemary *English Emblem Books* London 1948

Gaidon, H. 'Echos de la littérature antique au Moyen-Age' *Mélusine* V (1890) 107–9

Garner, Ross *Henry Vaughan: Experience and the Tradition* Chicago 1959

Geckle, George L. 'Fortune in Marston's *The Malcontent*' *PMLA* LXXXVI (Mar. 1971) 202–9

Gilson, E.H. *The Christian Philosophy of St Thomas Aquinas* London 1957

– *History of Christian Philosophy in the Middle Ages* London 1955

Gosse, Edmund *Life and Letters of John Donne* 2 vols. London 1899

Guss, Donald L. *John Donne, Petrarchist* Detroit 1966

Gysi, Lydia *Platonism and Cartesianism in the Philosophy of Ralph Cudworth* Bern 1962

Haller, W. *The Rise of Puritanism* New York 1938

Hanford, J.H. 'The Debate of the Heart and Eye' *Modern Language Notes* XXVI (1911) 161–5

- 'The Mediaeval Debate between Wine and Water' *PMLA*, xxviii (1913) 315–67
Harris, R. Blaine, ed. *The Significance of Neoplatonism* Norfolk, va 1976
Hartshorne, Charles and William L. Reese *Philosophers Speak of God* Chicago 1953
*Heningham, E.K. *An Early Latin Debate of the Body and Soul* New York 1939
- 'Old English Precursors of *The Worcester Fragments*' *PMLA* lv (June 1940) 291–307
Holmes, Elizabeth *Henry Vaughan and the Hermetic Philosophy* Oxford 1932
Husain, Itrat *The Dogmatic and Mystical Theology of John Donne* London 1938
Huttar, Charles A. 'The Christian Basis of Shakespeare's Sonnet 146' *Shakespeare Quarterly* xix (Autumn 1968) 355–65
Hymen, L.N. 'Marvell's "Garden"' *ELH* xxv (1958) 13–22
Jordan, J.C. *Robert Greene* New York 1915; rpt 1965
von Karajan, Th.G. *Frühlingsgabe für Freunde älterer Literatur* Vienna 1839
Kelley, Maurice *This Great Argument* Princeton 1941
Kirk, G.S. *Heraclitus: The Cosmic Fragments* Cambridge 1970
Kistner, A.L. and M.K. 'Thomas Middleton's Symbolic Action' *Ariel* xi (Jan. 1980) 15–19
Kleinert, F.W.G. *Uber den Streit zwischen Leib und Seele.* Halle 1880. Review of this by Gaston Paris *Romania* ix (1880) 311–14
Klinck, Dennis R. '*Vestigia Trinitatis* in Man and His Works in the English Renaissance' *Journal of the History of Ideas* xlii (Jan.–Mar. 1981) 13–27
Kranidas, Thomas (ed.) *New Essays on Paradise Lost* Berkeley, ca 1969
Kretzman, Norman, Anthony Kenny, and Jan Pinborg, eds *The Cambridge History of Later Medieval Philosophy* Cambridge 1982
Kristeller, Paul O. *Renaissance Thought* New York 1961
Lamprecht, S.P. 'Innate Ideas in the Cambridge Platonists' *Philosophical Review* xxxv (1926) 553–73
Legouis, Pierre *Andrew Marvell* Rev. ed. Oxford 1968
Leishman, J.B. *The Art of Marvell's Poetry* London 1966
Levi, Giuseppe *Parabeln, Legenden und Gedanken aus Thalmud und Midrasch*, trans. Ludwig Seligmann. Leipzig 1863
Lewalski, Barbara *Protestant Poetics and the Seventeenth-Century Religious Lyric* Princeton 1979
Lynch, William F., sj *Christ and Apollo* Toronto 1963
McAdoo, H.R. *The Spirit of Anglicanism* London 1965

- *The Structure of Caroline Moral Theology* London 1949
MacCaffrey, Isabel *Paradise Lost as 'Myth'* Cambridge, MA 1959
McKevlin J. *A Lecture in Love's Philosophy* London 1984
MacLure, Millar *George Chapman* Toronto 1966
Madsen, William A. *From Shadowy Types to Truth* New Haven, CN 1968
Marks, Carol L. 'Thomas Traherne and Cambridge Platonism' *PMLA* LXXXI (1966) 521–34
Martin, L.C. 'Henry Vaughan and "Hermes Trismegistus"' *Review of English Studies* XVIII (1942) 301–7
Merrill, Elizabeth *The Dialogue in English Literature* New Haven 1911
Merton, E.S. *Science and Imagination in Sir Thomas Browne* New York 1949
Moloney, M.F. *John Donne: His Flight from Mediaevalism* Urbana, IL 1944
Morris, Harry *Richard Barnfield, Colin's Child* Tampa, FL 1963
Norris, R.A. *Manhood and Christ* Oxford 1963
Ornstein, Robert *The Moral Vision of Jacobean Tragedy* Madison and Milwaukee 1965
Osmond, Rosalie E. 'Body, Soul, and the Marriage Relationship: The History of an Analogy' *Journal of the History of Ideas* (April–June 1973) 283–90
- 'A Precedent for Donne's Imagery in "Goodfriday, 1613. Riding Westward"' *Review of English Studies* XIX (May 1968) 166–9
Owst, G.R. *Preaching in Medieval England* Cambridge 1926
Palumbo, Ronald J. 'Emblematic Characters in Marston's *Antonio* Plays' *American Notes and Queries* XVIII (Nov. 1979) 35–7
de Pauley, W.C. *The Candle of the Lord* London 1937
Passmore, J.A. *Ralph Cudworth: An Interpretation* Cambridge 1951
Pawson, G.P.H. *The Cambridge Platonists* London 1930
Pegis, A.C. *St Thomas and the Problem of the Soul in the Thirteenth Century* Toronto 1934
Peterson, Douglas *The English Lyric from Wyatt to Donne* Princeton 1967
Portalié, E. *A Guide to the Thought of Saint Augustine* London 1960
Powicke, F.J. *The Cambridge Platonists* London 1926
Raby, F.J.E. *A History of Christian-Latin Poetry from the beginnings to the close of the Middle Ages* 2nd ed. Oxford 1953
- *A History of Secular Latin Poetry in the Middle Ages* II, 2nd ed. Oxford 1957
Rees, Ennis *The Tragedies of George Chapman: Renaissance Ethics in Action* Cambridge 1954
Ribner, Irving *Jacobean Tragedy: The Quest for Moral Order* London 1962
Rickey, Mary Ellen *Utmost Art: Complexity in the Verse of George Herbert* University of Kentucky Press 1966
Robinson. J.A.T. *The Body* London 1952

Robinson, H.W. 'Hebrew Psychology' *The People and the Book* ed. A.S. Peake. Oxford 1925

Rollins, H.E. *An Analytical Index to the Ballad-Entries (1557–1709) in the Registers of the Company of Stationers of London* Durham, NC 1924; rept Hatboro, PA 1967

Rostwig, M.S. 'Andrew Marvell's "The Garden" ' *English Studies* XL (1959) 65–76

Ryken, Leland *The Apocalyptic Vision in Paradise Lost* Ithaca, NY 1970

Salter, K.W. *Thomas Traherne, Mystic and Poet* London 1964

Sanders, Wilbur *John Donne's Poetry* Cambridge 1971

Sewell, W.A. *A Study in Milton's Christian Doctrine* Oxford, 1939

Shoaf, R.A. *Milton, Poet of Duality* New Haven, CN 1985

Sims, James H. and Leland Ryken *Milton and Scriptural Tradition* Columbia 1985

Stempel, Daniel. ' "The Garden": Marvell's Cartesian Ecstasy' *Journal of the History of Ideas* XXVIII (1967) 99–114

Steward, B.F. 'The Meaning of "Silex Scintillans" ' *Philological Quarterly* XXII (1943) 79–80

Swardson, H.R. *Poetry and the Fountain of Light* London 1962

Thorndike, Lynn *The 'Sphere' of Sacrobosco and Its Commentators* Chicago 1949

Toliver, Harold E. 'Pastoral Form and Idea in ... Marvell' *Texan Studies in Literature and Language* V (1963) 83–97 Reprinted in *Seventeenth Century English Poetry* ed. William R. Keast, rev. ed. Oxford 1971, pp 356–71

Torrance, T.F. *Calvin's Doctrine of Man* London 1949

Van Peursen, C.A. *Body, Soul, Spirit* London 1966

Verbeke, Gerard *L'Évolution de la doctrine du pneuma* Louvain 1945

Vogel, Sister Mary Ursula *Some Aspects of the Horse and Rider Analogy in 'The Debate Between the Body and the Soul'* Washington, DC 1948

Wallerstein, Ruth *Studies in Seventeenth Century Poetic* Wisconsin 1950

Wallis, P.J. 'The Library of William Crashaw' *Transactions of the Cambridge Bibliographical Society* II 3 (London 1956) 223–4

*Walther, H. 'Das Streitgedicht in der lateinischen Literatur des Mittelalters,' *Quellen und Untersuchungen zur lateinischen Philologie des Mittelalters* V 2 (Munich 1920) 63–80

Warren, E. Austin *Richard Crashaw* Louisiana 1939

Webber, Joan *Contrary Music: The Prose Style of John Donne* Madison, WI 1963

Willard, Rudolph 'The Address of the Soul to the Body' *PMLA* L (1935)
   957–83
Williams, N.P. *The Ideas of the Fall and of Original Sin* London 1927
Williamson, George 'The Convention of *The Extasie*,' *Seventeenth Century*
   Contexts London 1960
Wolfson, Henry Austryn *Religious Philosophy* Cambridge, MA 1961
Woolf, Rosemary *The English Religious Lyric in the Middle Ages* Oxford 1968

Index